BLACK CINEMA & VISUAL CULTURE

This culturally and politically timely collection examines new Black films and moving images that have, once again, excited and possibly shifted the global media landscape.

At a moment some scholars have described as post-post-racial, *Black Cinema & Visual Culture* provides new, urgent definitions and theories for Black cinema and furthers the development of its critical discourses. Gathering some of the leading scholars and critics in the field, this book enriches and advances the study of Black film and media and its social and political implications at a breakthrough period of expansion in the 21st century. This anthology tackles a wide range of topics from social justice, new media, and Afrofuturism, to race, gender, sexuality, mass incarceration, cultural memory, and Afrosurrealism, exploring the current climate of Black cinematic art that has proven wildly popular with domestic and global audiences, including hit films like *Get Out* and *Marvel's Black Panther*. Together, these essays deepen understandings of Black visual culture, its creative image-makers, the political economy of Hollywood, and the cultural politics at the intersection of modern cinema, streaming platforms, and digital technologies.

Black Cinema & Visual Culture will serve as an important learning tool for university courses spanning topics in film studies, American film and television, cultural studies, American studies, African Diaspora studies, media activism, social analysis, and African-American studies. This volume will also provide a benchmark in popular and intellectual circles for anyone interested in popular culture, Black-American cinema, media, issues of race in Hollywood, or Black culture and the conditions that shape both its art and politics.

Artel Great is the George and Judy Marcus Endowed Chair in African American Cinema Studies and Assistant Professor of Critical Studies at San Francisco State University. He is an Independent Spirit Award–nominated filmmaker, cultural critic, and Black cinema scholar. Dr. Great has written on film, race, and popular culture in both academic and popular publications.

Ed Guerrero is a film historian and Black cinema scholar. He has written extensively on Black movies and his influential books explore Black cinema, its critical discourse, and political economy. Dr. Guerrero has served on numerous editorial and professional boards including the National Film Preservation Board of the Library of Congress. He has also taught Cinema Studies and Africana Studies at New York University.

BLACK CINEMA & VISUAL CULTURE

Art and Politics in the 21st Century

Edited by Artel Great & Ed Guerrero

Routledge
Taylor & Francis Group

LONDON AND NEW YORK

Designed cover image: Illustration by Dr Artel Great

First published 2023
by Routledge
4 Park Square, Milton Park, Abingdon, Oxon OX14 4RN

and by Routledge
605 Third Avenue, New York, NY 10158

Routledge is an imprint of the Taylor & Francis Group, an informa business

British Library Cataloguing-in-Publication Data
A catalogue record for this book is available from the British Library

ISBN: 978-0-367-52873-7 (hbk)
ISBN: 978-0-367-52875-1 (pbk)
ISBN: 978-1-003-07968-2 (ebk)

DOI: 10.4324/9781003079682

Typeset in Bembo
by Newgen Publishing UK

CONTENTS

CONTRIBUTORS

Terri Francis is Associate Professor of Cinematic Arts and Associate Dean for Inclusive and Critical Publics at the University of Miami. She is a scholar of African Diaspora cinemas, particularly nontheatrical and experimental film. Her book on Josephine Baker examines the artist's influence and cinematic life. Dr. Francis' work also draws on Afrosurrealism, avant-garde expression, archival research, cultural history, and visual analysis, as she examines the vicissitudes—less media reflections and more refractions—of Black performance, film feeling, and Black representation.

Herman Gray is Emeritus Professor of Sociology at UC Santa Cruz and has published widely in the areas of Black cultural theory, politics, and media. He is the author of influential books on race, television, and culture. Dr. Gray is a current member of the Board of Jurors for the Peabody Awards.

Artel Great is the George and Judy Marcus Endowed Chair in African American Cinema Studies and Assistant Professor of Critical Studies at San Francisco State University. He is an Independent Spirit Award–nominated filmmaker, social impact artist, and Black cinema scholar. Dr. Great has written on film, race, and popular culture in both academic and popular publications.

Ed Guerrero is a film historian and Black cinema scholar. He has written extensively on Black movies and his influential books explore Black cinema, its critical discourse, and political economy. Dr. Guerrero has served on numerous editorial and professional boards including the National Film Preservation Board of the Library of Congress. He has also taught Cinema Studies and Africana Studies at New York University.

Maya Iverson-Davis is an artist, scholar, and cultural curator who specializes in television, media archives/repositories, and race. Her art practice challenges ideas of time and space as abstract and constructed by our desires to be anywhere but where we currently rest. Dr. Iverson-Davis earned her PhD in Sociology at UC Santa Cruz. Her research and writing focuses on television and media as portals to alternative ways of knowing how to live.

Brandeise Monk-Payton is a media and Black cultural studies scholar and Assistant Professor of Communication and Media Studies at Fordham University. Her research specializes in the history and theory of African-American media representation and cultural production. Dr. Monk-Payton's work engages questions of race as they relate to topics in television, film, and digital media studies, as well as U.S. public and popular culture.

Fred Moten is a cultural theorist, poet, MacArthur "Genius" Fellow, and Professor of Performance Studies and Comparative Literature at New York University. He is the author of several influential books on topics spanning Black radical traditions and aesthetics. Dr. Moten's research centers Black studies, performance, poetics, and critical theory.

Michele Prettyman is a scholar of African-American cinema, visual and popular culture, media consultant, and Assistant Professor of Communication and Media Studies at Fordham University. Dr. Prettyman has published on a range of topics spanning Black film, media, and culture. Her interests also include spirituality and the ways in which spiritual and cultural practices facilitate healing from personal and racial trauma, build community, and enable creativity and well-being.

Adrien Sebro is Assistant Professor of Media Studies at the University of Texas, Austin. His research in critical media studies explores the intersections of television, film, comedy, gender, and African Diaspora studies. Dr. Sebro's scholarly interests also include U.S. Black television sitcoms, television history, and the media's role in initiating social change and activism.

Ytasha L. Womack is a critically acclaimed author, filmmaker, dancer, and independent scholar. Her creative and intellectual work distinguishes her as a champion of humanity and the imagination. Her book on Afrofuturism is a leading primer on the exciting subject which bridges science fiction, futurisms, and culture.

ACKNOWLEDGMENTS

During the development of this project, we benefited from enlightened conversations and support from many of our dear colleagues. We offer thanks to our editorial team at Routledge. Also, we are especially grateful to every one of our contributing authors. Thank you for taking the time out of your busy schedules and navigating through unprecedented challenges to produce such thoughtful and compelling work. Ed Guerrero would like to thank Bob Stam, Anna McCarthy, Zhang Zhen, and Alvina Quintana. Likewise, Artel Great extends many thanks to Gerome Walker, Benjamin and Belinda Starks, Ed Guerrero, Bambi Haggins, Berretta Smith-Shomade, Mariana Johnson, John Jeremiah Sullivan, Celine Parreñas Shimizu, Aaron Kerner, and Daniel Bernardi. Without the encouragement and support of all these wonderful people, this project would not be possible.

INTRODUCTION

Artel Great and Ed Guerrero

Black participation in American cinema is marked by a long and complicated history, one of innovation and isolation. Technological advancements in film have, to some degree, always advocated for the social position of Black people in a nation where seeing is believing or, perhaps, believing is seeing. However, as James Baldwin astutely points out, "the isolation that menaces all American artists is multiplied a thousand times, and becomes absolutely crucial and dangerous, for Black artists."[1] This fact is especially true in the world of contemporary American cinema, where the rules of the game are configured in opposition to Black film artists, some of whom inherently understand the tenuous nature of their participation in a system that undermines Black self-determination—a system that must be changed. That is to say, within the commercial film industry, white Americans freely operate, as Baldwin so aptly describes, "under the compulsion to dream, whereas Black-Americans are under the compulsion to awaken."[2] Understanding these two separate and competing impulses and obligations, which trigger contradictory goals, is an essential foundation for anyone seeking to fully grasp the sense of unease and resistance proliferating in Black America or the social urgency that permeates many of today's Black moving-image practices.

Our inspiration for this collection emerges from the central idea to generate a project that focuses on the art and politics of contemporary Black-American cinema and Black visual culture after the turn of the millennium. There have, indeed, been many notable films and cultural milestones since then. From Denzel Washington and Halle Berry's complicated and historic Oscar wins for *Training Day* (2001) and *Monster's Ball* (2001), to the emergence of significant figures like director Ava DuVernay, writer/producer Shonda Rhimes, actor Chadwick Boseman, and the multi-hyphenate Tyler Perry, as well as the resurgence of director Spike Lee with *BlacKkKlansman* (2018), are but a few prime examples. Not to mention the energetic burst of smaller Black independent films like *A Good Day to be Black*

DOI: 10.4324/9781003079682-1

and Sexy (2008), *Mississippi Damned* (2009), *Night Catches Us* (2010), *Pariah* (2010), *Restless City* (2011), *Dear White People* (2014), *Moonlight* (2016), *Sorry to Bother You* (2018), *The Forty-Year-Old Version* (2020), and *Neptune Frost* (2022), each pointing to the promise of new voices and unapologetic visions of the cinematic Black world. In the 21st century, cinema and visual culture, without question, have morphed and converged and come to stand in for, and address, the concerns of a growing demographic of American citizens, scholars, and audiences, a heterogeneous mix, that includes an expanding Black populace eager to hear their views and voices and see their narratives and images projected, broadcast, and streamed across multiple platforms and multiple screens, large and small.

Black cinema from silent-era films to the Civil Rights Movement, the L.A. Rebellion, Blaxploitation, and beyond has, in fact, always held a crucial and revered position among a large core and crossover audiences. Today, those audiences are composed of highly diverse multi-ethnic groups. Over the past two decades, a new assortment of Black film and television has again shifted the media landscape with mega-hits like *Fences* (2016), *Girls Trip* (2017), *Get Out* (2017), *Marvel's Black Panther* (2018), *Us* (2019), *One Night in Miami* (2020), *Ma Rainey's Black Bottom* (2020), *Candyman* (2021), *Nope* (2022), and *Wakanda Forever* (2022), as well as brilliant explorations of the Black world and its points of view, on TV series like HBO's *Insecure* (2016–2021), and FX's *Atlanta* (2016–2022), *Pose* (2018–2021), or *Snowfall* (2017–present). In response to this pivotal moment, our book expands and enriches the critical study of Black cinema and media, its politics, discourses, and aesthetics covering a variety of issues including racial capitalism, new technology, Afrofuturism, the carceral state, gender, and sexuality. In an ever-fluid media environment, our approach to this anthology is not intended to be exhaustive or comprehensive but rather to offer complex analyses and wide-ranging insights into an array of key contemporary Black cultural productions, from commercial smash-hit films and breakout indies, to experimental arthouse pictures, pioneering television shows, and the creative image-makers that bring these projects to life. To that extent, this collection of essays engages the shifting discourses of Black visual culture, while charting new interventions, territories, and styles that explore and challenge the status quo of the American film and media industries and its critical scholarship. This anthology focuses on the complexities, nuances, and the phenomenology of Blackness, particularly driven by a fundamental curiosity regarding the interplay between social justice, political economy, and the rising aspirations of Black cultural producers, Black cultural production, and Black production cultures.

As of this writing, our planet is in peril: deadly viruses, wars, climate change. One could almost divide our collective anxieties and travails into "B.C." and "A.C.," that is, Before Covid and After Covid. When we initially began this project, many Black-Americans found themselves mired in a recurring backlash and its attendant "culture wars" instigated by the 45th President. Black people remain forced to confront a nation divided, where truth is under fire, where science is challenged, and facts are suspiciously rendered "alternative." One fascinating unintended consequence of our political climate is the smoldering public dissatisfaction unfolding, birthing a culture of resistance that has witnessed calls for police reform and gun safety laws, while pushing back against direct attacks on basic civil and human rights, from restrictive voting laws to the denial of reproductive rights. Ironically, this tense social moment has also, to a degree, sparked a creative and robust eruption of Black visual culture that expresses resistant viewpoints. In this sense, our anthology takes a deep look at Black film and media that has, over the past 20-plus years, risen to the forefront of cultural, political, and social significance. To be certain, the cutting-edge of Black cinema and visual culture is now imbued with a renewed sense of social energy that draws and builds upon so-called Black film "waves" and "troughs" and "booms" and "busts" of the past. Moreover, this collection approaches film, television, and digital media as a catalyst to examine the cultural politics of the Black world and to address the new markets and circumstances that have come to define the rise and consumption of Black cinema and media.

As we enthusiastically committed to editing this collection, we had no idea what was to come, but of course that was "B.C."—and the world done changed. As we gained creative momentum on this project, the pandemic pushed the pause button on the world's enterprises and business. Not long after the nation went into quarantine, the world watched, in collective horror, the nine-minute cellphone video courageously filmed by Darnella Frazier who captured the public murder of George Floyd by a white Minneapolis police officer, asphyxiating George Floyd before the nation and the world, on social media and the 6 o'clock news. The brutality and nonchalant nature of this horrendous act sent tidal waves of outrage and anger across the nation. Social uprisings and protests spread from coast to coast and ultimately compelled massive protests and demonstrations around the planet. Now, perhaps, the world could finally see the nightmarish gargoyles of American racism that have haunted and terrorized Black people for far too long. Needless to say, these are, indeed, unprecedented and turbulent times. And shepherding this collection to print during what can only be described as a two-fold pandemic, one medical, the other social, has, in fact, been no easy task.

Consequently, the journey to completing this publication has not been a simple one. Nor has it been without persistent challenges. The years we've spent developing this project have given us both critical space for reflection and so much to discuss. And yet, if the three years (and counting) of living through pandemic conditions have brought anything into clearer focus, it is, perhaps, that many of the rules of the B.C. world are no longer sufficient for our survival. The fierce urgency of our times compelled us to write these essays, to save our own lives, and to, hopefully, illuminate and inspire the lives of others. Afterall, in the modern A.C. world the rulebook is up for serious revision, as we rediscover what work actually means to us, and what actually works *for* us, in the ongoing process of defining ourselves anew.

This anthology begins with Ed Guerrero's sharp analysis of Black horror films and American racial politics as refracted through Jordan Peele's breakout social horror flick *Get Out* (2017) and Mariama Diallo's indie sleeper *The Master* (2022) (Chapter 1). Herman Gray and Maya Iverson-Davis (Chapter 2) contribute with a critical examination of what it means to care for Black people in a time of widespread suffering. Their essay unpacks how television gathers audiences around cultural disputes and non-normative identities, using *Random Acts of Flyness* (HBO) as a case study on how Black creatives call us to take care of Black life. In Chapter 3, Artel Great provides us with a reflective space for a complicated reading of the mega-blockbuster film *Marvel's Black Panther* (2018), the first Black movie to gross over $1 billion at the box-office. Great proposes a critical counternarrative of the film that demonstrates the myriad ways the Hollywood industry commodifies, appropriates, and redistributes Black culture back to Black audiences. In a compelling and insightful essay (Chapter 4), Terri Francis reconsiders ideas on Afrosurrealism as a method of personal reflection and re-imagining ways of reading, teaching, viewing, and exhibition in a time when, "either questioning everything matters more than ever before, or questioning everything won't matter at all." While MacArthur Fellow Fred Moten (Chapter 5) offers a penetrating 21st century philosophical treatise theorizing the ways rhythm and sound create, amplify, and illuminate Black cinema through complex systems of interpersonal, international, economic, and spatial relationships. Moten explores the sign of gender and the politics of form across the Diaspora as a type of aesthetic organization that employs music and rhythm to enrich the invisible in Black cinema.

Turning to the ever-expanding media empire of Tyler Perry, Brandeise Monk-Payton (Chapter 6) addresses Perry's influence on Black cinema and media through the vernacular of faith, as a form of resistance to the white gaze in Hollywood. And considering the impact of new media, Adrien Sebro (Chapter 7) examines the industrial significance of digital technologies and web-based platforms on Black film production, distribution, the cinematic market, audience engagement, and the struggle for social justice and empowerment. While Michele Prettyman (Chapter 8) invites us to explore a metaphysical framework in the study of contemporary film and moving-image art, focusing on a subset of works made by Black women artists and filmmakers. In Chapter 9, Artel Great puts forth a rich and expansive essay surveying contemporary Black independent cinema's newest movements and contours, detailing both popular and under-recognized films, while exploring Black cultural production and creative expression as a medium of protest, resistance, and cultural affirmation. With an eye trained on the injustices of mass incarceration, Ed Guerrero (Chapter 10) explores cinematic depictions of the carceral state, offering a critical historiography of prison films while questioning how the color of one's skin and one's racial, economic, and sociological circumstances, along with questionable criminal laws, come together to form brutal material and psychic forces that have confined so many Black lives into "the house of many slams." Ytasha L. Womack (Chapter 11) concludes the collection looking toward the Afrofuture, examining concepts of Afrofuturism in film as a way of looking at future and alternate realities through Black cultural lenses that intersect with social imagination, technology, and freedom as an aesthetic, method, and practice.

Black Cinema & Visual Culture: Art and Politics in the 21st Century is a vital collection of expansive essays that fill a significant lacuna in critical knowledge, while providing a valuable contribution to public and scholarly media discourses and to the rich Black intellectual tradition. As we look ahead, in this twilight of late America, the future of Black participation in cinema, at all levels, pivots on the axis of freedom and (re)defining what freedom actually means for Black artists, producers, executives, audiences, and citizens. Furthermore, the future of Black cinema and media, for all intents and purposes, will be as bold or bogus, as bright or dark, as daring or docile as the thoughts and visualizations of its creators. That is to say, central issues like ownership, access to capital, and distribution, moving forward must become just as integral and important in Black film and media as authorial voice, cultural affirmation, and public (re)education that helps recalibrate and repair the fractured connections between Black audiences and Black storytellers. Sadly, the relationship between Black audiences and storytellers has been damaged over time by economics, ignorance, ego, spiritual traps, psychic abuse, the industry's emotional contagion, malicious hypnotism, or racial capitalism, false competition, cultural exploitation, or the so-called metaphoric "crabs in a barrel," or some complex combination of these. Yet, if there is a way forward it is because there are, in fact, new generations of Black filmmakers, Black creatives and executives, Black film critics and scholars on the horizon emerging, many of whom we write about extensively in the pages that follow. And these Black people understand, ontologically and epistemically, that crabs don't belong in the barrel of constricted social circumstances but rather floating free in the poetic imaginary of a liberated people.

Equally suggestive, new generations are also aligning in awareness regarding the crucial value of technology and data, community-building, critical knowledge, support and collaboration, and re-imagining the politics of Black film with an eye toward decolonization. For these reasons, critical engagement with rising Black cinema and visual culture remains an important and complex endeavor, which makes this anthology both timely and socially relevant, interrogating recent trends, while contextualizing historical foundations, and guiding us into the *Afrofuture*. It is our aim that this collection, from leading film and media scholars and critics, will provide a benchmark in popular and intellectual circles for anyone interested in Black-American cinema, media, and popular culture, issues of race in Hollywood film and television, or Black culture and the conditions that shape both its art and politics. After all, it has become urgent, in our brave new A.C. world, to provide fresh definitions and theories for Black cinema and Black expressive cultural production, and contribute to the further development of its critical vocabulary and discourses. And so we say, "sleep deep, but keep top eye open," as the double-vision of Black consciousness teaches us. Indeed, we are aware and alerted to the necessity for Black people, not simply, to awaken from the ambivalence of the American dream/nightmare but to, at all costs—*stay woke.*

Notes

1 James Baldwin, "Sidney Poitier," ed. Randall Kenan, *The Cross of Redemption: Uncollected Writings* (New York: Vintage Books, 2010), p. 217.
2 Ibid., 218.

1

THE AFROFUTURE AND BLACK HORROR IN THREE ACTS

Ed Guerrero

Act I

The Cultural Turn: In "Get Out," or "Guess Who's Coming to Dinner" … Now

As one thinks of Black horror, a few things come to mind, getting stopped by the cops, coming up short on the rent, constantly living under the rubric of suspicion, and the relentless desire to overcome and escape the chains of one's overdetermined fate under white cultural and economic hegemony. As the late rapper and poet DMX might complain, "how can I maintain with that shit on my brain." For instance, when considering dinner guests, and marking the political/social distance from 1967 to 2017, and into the near *Afrofuture*, historical, political/social circumstances have turned themselves inside out, like a glove. Dr. John Prentice (Sidney Poitier) of *Guess Who's Coming to Dinner* (1967), the original dinner guest, invited to the table of privileged wealth and whiteness via his ingénue, fiancée, was well qualified and eager for the match. The fiancée (Katharine Houghton) amounts to practically *nothing*: young, white, and fabulously rich and not much more: *nothing*. Conversely, the celebrated Doctor is *something*, or almost *something*: an accomplished physician, head of World Health Organization (WHO), a man who has risen by the bootstraps of petty bourgeois circumstance (his father is a postman), to finally arrive at the table of plenty, and with that table set on Nob Hill with a sunset view of San Francisco's back Bay to boot. One could say this is a great rise for the ambitious Doctor, but for one problem: he's *Black* and intensely so, phenotypically so, a *Black-Black* man of accomplishment. In translation, Dr. Prentice has got all the right moves: qualifications, education, travel, an antiseptic "well spoken" demeanor—all of the credits, except for that one ontological thing: he not *white*. So, in terms of the social value of Black men, and white women, one is confronted with the perfect binary match: a white girl amounting

DOI: 10.4324/9781003079682-2

to a socially questionable *nothing* paired with a Black-Black man amounting to a socially challenged "*something*." And all of this is set against the political/cultural mise-en-scene raging around them, down on the streets of Nob Hill, the culmin- ating jouissance of the Civil Rights Movement, and the resulting social mess of racial integration.

So, in the historical cinematic circumstance of the *now*, that is, in *the cultural turn*, one can analogize history as a glove turned inside out in almost every, uncanny, disturbing detail as refracted through Jordan Peele's *Get Out* (2017). Again, a phenotypically *Black-Black* man, Chris Washington (Daniel Kaluuya) younger than Dr. John Prentice, not so mature or "accomplished," this time, a rising artist, coming from "inner city" circumstances, arrives for dinner not knowing that his- torical circumstances have inverted: broadly now, it's not *guess who's coming to dinner*, but rather, guess *what's on the menu?* But also, the "rich white girl" Rose Armitage (Allison Williams) and the patina of innocence have corroded and doubled down (as in "double consciousness"). Rose Armitage is not a naive *nothing,* but conversely, a potent venomous, *something*: … the vamp of *film noir* and sci-fi horror, the white/ black widow looking for a mark, a fine athletic Black body to fetishize and steal. Accordingly, the scene/scenery and music have shifted. *Guess Who's Coming to Dinner* opens with Frank DeVol's corny but popular "The Glory of Love" as a trans- Pacific jet flies from Hawaii to San Francisco, two of the most liberal and integrated destinations in the United States. On the contrary, *Get Out* opens with a kidnapping, a brutal disappearance, and then cuts to the horrific and creepy theme "Sikiliza Kwa Wahenga" played against the traveling panorama of haunted woods that reference the ghostly, dark wilderness of the *Blair Witch Project* (1999). The mise-en-scene has definitely shifted. Now, it's not so much the social ethos hurtling toward integra- tion, but rather a stalemate, or even a shrinking away from interraciality as a uto- pian possibility. So, the expression/title "get out" finds some coincidence with the political/social backdrop of "make America great (white) again." Of course, this is a demographic impossibility but nonetheless a 19th-century dream, this time revived in the story world by scientific, medical racism and realized in *Get Out's* dream of the Coagula procedure and the transplantation of old white brains and desires into young, athletic Black bodies.

Get Out's allegory is arguably, superficially plain: a slave narrative with at least two tangled meanings, one literal and one buried, and both marinated in the rubrics of suspicion and guilt, the psychic undercurrent of "*blackpain*," the ongoing, hege- monic process of medical and scientific racism, and the experimentation with Black bodies.[1] In contrast to the esteemed Dr. John Prentice in *Guess Who's Coming to Dinner* who rushes to the table of plenty with the ambition and eagerness of a man determined to *overcome*, to shed his double consciousness and to *integrate*, Chris, in *Get Out* proceeds cautiously, with a congenial manner thinly masking his weary prudence. For Chris, as with all Black people, the rubric of suspicion is doubled: he is both *suspicious* and *"the usual suspect."* With paused ambivalence, he questions his girlfriend about the invitation to a weekend at her parents' isolated country estate, allegorically, the Big House of the plantation. "Do your parents know I'm Black?"

FIGURE 1.1 Chris and Rose in *Get Out*. Screenshot by the author

comes the standard question in this circumstance, and with a suspiciously naïve, emphatic neoliberal answer. Rose Armitage empathically declares of his Blackness (sight unseen) that her parents are *not* reactionary racists. They're so non-racist, in fact, that they need not even know that Chris is, Black, or more deeply *Black-Black*. Thus Rose, the vamp, sets the scheme in motion.

Here, one must consider the other threads in the scheme of things that are brought into play: *blackpain* and its entanglement with scientific materialism and medical racism; the slave auction and the "ghost value" of the Black body.[2] One can trace the thread of *blackpain* through the metaphor of the deer, transitioning the story world, from doe to stag to buck. Besides the literal snatching of a Black body, that opens the film, on their drive upstate to the estate, the seemingly happy couple is impacted with an omen forecasting horrors to come. But this encounter is an unconscious thread leading to Chris's personal, buried *blackpain*. While driving, Rose hits a doe and Chris is deeply, emotionally, compelled to get out of the car to witness the agony of the doe slowly dying in the woods beside the road. Here, events stir the personal/political unconscious. Both Chris and Rose are rattled by the moment, but things go deeper for Chris, for this is the first hint of the buried and disturbing thread of *blackpain* that runs through the narrative, and that leads to his, soon to come, hypnotic bondage in the "sunken place," and the psychic chains that he must struggle to break.

As a relevant aside, it is worth noting that *blackpain* has a long historic, literary trajectory, as recorded by Chester Himes, apparent even in the titles of his two auto-biographies *The Quality of Hurt* and *Yesterday Will Make You Cry*; or by Alice Walker in *The Third Life of Grange Copeland*; or by Gayl Jones in *Eva's Man* and *Corregidora*. In this last stunning, *blackpain* novel by Jones, the protagonist Ursa is kicked down the stairs by her boyfriend, Mutt, hospitalized and castrated by medical science, via hysterectomy. Meanwhile, Ursa's prostituted and twisted Grandmother impels her to "make generations and tell the story" of their bondage and their Portuguese, slave master grandfather who pimped both Ursa's mother and grandmother in his Louisiana whorehouse. Black history, like real estate and much of the horror genre, is about "location, location, location." From ghetto to plantation, the scene of the crime is historically preordained. Once at the grand Armitage mansion/plantation, isolated with no near neighbors and cut off by a lake, Missy Armitage (Catherine Keener), a M.D. psychiatrist, hypnotizes Chris, "getting into his head" by route of his buried *blackpain*, the repressed memory of his mother dying by the side of the road, à la the doe, victim of a hit-and-run accident. Once in his head through impacted grief and guilt, Missy drives the paralyzed Chris into "the sunken place," the allegoric hold of the Middle passage slave ship.

Yet in the third thread of the scheme (perhaps the most important historic one), constructing the psychic chains of Chris's bondage and the horrific eugenic, fantasy of *transplantation* comes into play: medical, scientific racism and classism so brilliantly discussed in the work of a group of historians arguing fresh views predicated upon new research.[3] But also relevant here is Fredric Jameson's discussion of the architecture of the grand gothic, haunted house loosely charting a Freudian floor plan, with the top floors assigned to the concerns of the super ego, the ground and mid floors analogizing the ego and its consciousness of the "now," and the basement (where bad things happen) representing the Id.[4] Predictably, what we find in this basement is neurosurgeon, Dr. Dean Armitage (Bradley Whitford) and a completely equipped operating theatre. But also, here in the Id basement, the symbol and metaphor of the deer reaches its maturity. Chris bound to a large armchair, views an eerie video on a TV in front of him, forecasting, surgically what's about to happen: neurological transplantation. That is, an old white brain transplanted into a young, athletic body. The video ends with the command "Behold the Coagula!" then cut to a huge stuffed stag's head on the wall behind the TV. In ironic reversal, using the horns of the alpha male stag, Chris gores Dr. Dean Armitage, killing him. Then in a bloody "be Black, fight back" conclusion, Chris fights his way out of the house, killing the whole Armitage family, Mom, Grandma, baby bro, and finally Grandpa and his ex … Rose.

Important for this discussion are two things: one, the bro, Chris Washington escapes alive, horrifically so, and after much carnage; and two, medical dissection and experimentation on the Black body didn't start with the exposure of the medical horrors of the Tuskegee Experiment (for which President Bill Clinton apologized).[5] In slavery, the Black body from birth to death and well beyond, was chattel, a commodity and thus was fungible.[6] To feed the rising demand for bodies to stock medical school anatomy and physiology courses from the 18th century on, the Enslaved, poor white, and criminal bodies, were bought, sold, and traded according to a cadaver's "ghost value." As we see in the brilliant slave auction/garden party vignette that Chris's market value on the auction block tops out at $20 million, much to the admiration of all attending. There's another thing interesting about the film's dénouement: an alternate ending was revealed on DVD, one by which the local police show up and arrest Chris for the carnage at the Big House. Predictably, this alternative ending speaks to the wishful desire for a certain level of ideological containment, the old constitutional bamboozle for Blacks: "you are guilty until proven guilty" opposing the notion of perpetual "white innocence."

On the other hand, with *Get Out*'s present, resistant, ending circulating globally, and its cost-to-profit ratio coming in at an astounding $89 profit for every one dollar spent on production, in Hollywood, its political economy and box office hit status has greatly overdetermined much of what has followed for Jordan Peele.

Act II

Bad Dreams in the Master's House

Regarding the Afrofuture, while avoiding the stilted binary of Afro-pessimism/ optimism, we must hope that the Afrofuture will not be as horrific and twisted as the *Afropast* has been for so many with skin darker than white. So, for the immediate purposes of this essay, I would like to regard the Afrofuture, at least the near future as a haunted presence, carrying the ghostly tint and hurt of a troubled *Afropast*. In many ways, *The Master* (2022) is the complementary opposite of *Get Out* and for this reason, *The Master* completes the circuit between the past and future by dwelling on the haunting of the very near present. Whereas *Get Out*'s protagonist is Black male and of "movie star" status. *The Master*'s lead is a Black woman, Regina Hall, a fine actor, but not a household name in the movie business. *Get Out* is masculinist and horrifically violent, and blood-soaked. It spins a ribald, layered allegory with several implicated discourses. By comparison, *The Master* features a woman-centric allegory, a fairly straightforward tale following the lines of the Gothic, formulaic, Victorian ghost story. *Get Out* is industry mid-budget but resulting in mega-hit, box office money. In contrast, *The Master* is a "small film," an indie-streaming project earning substantial profits. Horrific, bloody racism drives *Get Out,* while *The Master*'s violence is interior, reflective, a curse with ghostly traces, an academic nightmare driven by microaggression, condescension, backhanded racist "love," "jokes," and insults cloaked as compliments. The horrors of *The Master* deeply scar the psyche and are as intense and as lasting as the action-adventure gore depicted in *Get Out*.

However, both films agree on the grand, overdetermining scheme of racism, overt or ambient in all of our institutions, including science, medicine, and education. *Get Out*'s conclusion is blood-spattered and suggests a grim present reaching into a dystopian, "near," Afrofuture, whereas *The Master*'s dénouement recycles the ghostly, elitist racist past haunting and maintaining the social hierarchies and relations of the immediate present.[7] Moreover, both protagonists defy dominant movie industry logic and escape their ultimate fates as hostages, tokens, or sacrificial slaves, as they literally walk away, escape from the terror of the "the Big House" of old. Chris Washington ultimately "gets out" by killing the whole Armitage family, thus disrupting the Coagula Process and escaping white retribution. Accordingly, considering the rewards of co-optation at the highest levels, the alleged "Master," Professor Gail Bishop (Regina Hall) does something rarely achieved by intellectual Blacks in the academy. Realizing that the academic game is haunted, rigged, and that the "house always wins," she simply quits, gets out, walks away, thus surviving

FIGURE 1.2 Professor Bishop in *The Master*. Screenshot by the author

the guilt and blowback of the witch's curse and the nightmare entrapping the Blacks of Ancaster College.

The Master opens, appropriately enough, with a view tracking across the green of a tony super-elite New England college campus and centering on "the Master's house," imposing and august, steeped in its historic splendor, and definitely the exclusive turf of the moneyed class. The fine elegance and chic charm of the building leave no doubt that the Master's house is the proverbial "haunted house" of Victorianism and before: smug in its privilege, arrogant and howling in celebration of its crimes. We are informed of how many Presidents, Senators, and so on had attended Ancaster, and those that didn't, as the joke goes, went to the second-rate Harvard. We are also made aware of one of those grand moments in the skilled practice of "tokenism," that is, using one subject as a marker to represent and hold off, the striving many. We learn that "the first" Black and female Professor of Ancaster College, Professor Gail Bishop, has been nominated to the prestigious title of "Master" of the Master's house. The irony and horror of this esteemed moniker becomes apparent as Professor Bishop takes the keys and swag, and the tale unwinds.[8]

The story world of Ancaster College charts the layered, triangulated struggles of three Black women: Professor Bishop, Liv Beckman (Amber Gray) a lecturer up for tenure, and Jasmine Moore (Zoe Renee) a first-year student, all facing the petty condescension and microaggressions of an elite white cultural and economic hegemony. All three Black women are vexed by a general feeling (à la Chris in *Get Out*) that they are being patronized, "set up," bamboozled, discriminated against, and being tolerated for the sake of Ancaster College's fake inclusive multicultural patina. While they struggle to be included, they are indelibly, phenotypically marked as outsiders that don't really *belong*. Commenting on the generalized malaise of racism and snobbery of the college, intertitles from the diary of "the first"

Black female student, who killed herself in 1968 under the haunted circumstances of the college's cyclical witch's spell, puts it literally: "*it's everywhere.*" Predictably in the cryptic *alchemy of whiteness*, privilege concentrates upward to the wealthy few, while containment, taxation, and discontent drip down on the consumer masses and underclasses, with a special importance on keeping all non-whites in their respective subaltern *places*. According to circumstance, each of these Black women come to realize their particular *place* as the tale darkens.

Of course, the three sites of true horror in the Black academic world are the faculty party, student raves, and parties, and the much-dreaded tenure review and its committee, usually chaired by Robespierre. All of these scenes are depicted with painfully eerie detail and insight. Professor Bishop endures a couple of stereotypic faculty parties: digs and jokes about her being "the first," being akin to Obama, adding "spice" to the soirée, mixed with the petty complaints and conversation of a cohort of smug, tenured mediocrities, with all this played out to the sound-scape of "classical" mortuary music, sonic wallpaper that no one could possibly dance to. One can describe the faculty party with a simple expression: stale, elitist, haunted *shit*. The metaphor is literalized when Professor Bishop starts seeing inter-loping ghosts at the bar, faculty faces morph and twist to reveal decadent monstrous interiors, and the portraits of the "founding fathers" as shape-shifting ghouls and devils. On the campus lawn at the end of one such festivity, the "temporary" lec-turer Liv Beckman, noting the disturbed, thinly repressed feelings on the face of the esteemed Professor Bishop, puts it succinctly, remarking that the faculty party experience: "Kinda makes you feel like a house nigger. Doesn't it?"

We must return here, to the "real estate" analog, "location, location, location" for Ancaster College was founded on a gallows hill, where a legendary local witch was hanged, thus setting the witch's curse in motion. Yet here we're dealing with double entendre, for in Black horror, location can mean your *place* in society, say status as maid or janitor, as well as *habitus,* places of servitude or containment such as a ghetto. Perhaps the most succinct example of "being put in your place" is inflicted on first-year student Jasmine Moore as she crawls through the lunch line. The Black cook serving the two ingénue white girls in front of her starts shuckin', coonin', and playing the mammy for their amusement. But when Jasmine's turn comes, the "food service worker" gives her the historic stink eye, the look of rejection and projected self-hatred found in every film with a gatekeeping Black servant or "mammy" housekeeper, from *Birth of a Nation* (1915) to *Guess Who's Coming to Dinner* to *Get Out*. The confluence of social status and Black locations reveals another subtle brushstroke backgrounded but persistent in the movie's broad mise-en-scene, where we see in the creepy campus shadows the exclusively Black "service workers," silent apparitions that mow, scrub, and sweep the insti-tution clean.

Jasmine's detective work in the eerie library archives leads her to find the diary of the "first Black student at Ancaster," the one who killed herself while under the witch's curse in 1968. So, being in the new "first" cohort of eight non-white students is not a fortuitous portent. Consequently, the focus of the witch's curse falls on the isolated, Jasmine Moore. She too has nightmares, sees interloping ghosts, sees the decadence and corruption of the place, maggots oozing out of pale, rotting faces of the portraits of the founders. From the jump, the story world sets her up as the witch's sacrifice, making her predicament much worse than the other two Black women in the tale. Jasmine is assigned to the haunted room 302 in the film's opening; she's marginalized at campus parties, and cheated and patronized by her wealthy classmates. In addition, she gets into a conflict with the only Black "temp-lecturer" on campus and officially grieves against her. Jasmine struggles to "fit in," but she can't outrun the rubric of alienation instigated by her pigmentation. Notably, her hair becomes an understated barometer of cultural resistance and her mental attitude. By mid-semester she signifies mental accommodation, assimilation by her hair going from self-assured nappy, to imitative straight/pressed, and then back again to rebellious nappy as the struggle for self-definition unfolds. Challenged by a series of nightmares, omens, insults, and condescensions, the repressed, nappy hair returns. But it's too late and one of "the first" Black students, again, fulfills the conditions of the witch's curse and hangs herself in room 302 at 3:33 a.m. on the dreaded witch's anniversary.

In a great culmination of horrors in the Master's house, Jasmine's hanging body is found in the jinxed room by the esteemed "Master" and Professor Bishop, and the threads in the narrative start coming together. Liv Beckman goes before the tenure review committee and comes up short on count: "thin research and pub-lication." She is rather smugly "put in her place" and reminded by the committee chair that promotion and tenure are a "privilege, not a right." Her case is further "stepped on" when Professor Bishop, naively, accidentally reveals that a "confiden-tial" grievance case is pending, against her. Of course, here, the kiss of death would be, that it's one of the few Black students at the college that has grieved against her. However, in a twisted law of racist compensation, in academic horror, real or otherwise, the suicide of a Black "first," Jasmine Moore, fulfills the sacrifice of the witch's curse, while Liv is granted tenure, in spite of a weak, thin case that would have doomed her.

However, at the final, sumptuous, and wonderfully horrific faculty party cele-brating Liv Beckman's tenure it all comes out. The two tenured Black women professors (now gladiators) come to struggle over issues of place, color, and ontology, as allegations about Liv "passing," in this case being white and passing for Black, are played out for the entertainment of the senior faculty, those present and the ghostly. In a twist of irony, it turns out Liv *is* Black, by identification and ontologic-ally so. Furthermore, the Master, Professor Bishop, in a cathartic dramatic moment reveals the horrific (and real) racist law of compensation by accusing that Liv's tenure compensates for Ancaster's guilt over the suicide death of Black student Jasmine Moore. So true; but a further deeper revelation comes as an epiphany that she shares with the faculty. All of the haunting of the honored Professor Bishop (aka The Master) has to do with putting her in her *place*, as previously argued, in the two senses that Black people view *place*. Signs of status as place constantly nag the professor: The pre-electricity servant's bells in "the Master's house" keep ringing, leading her into the lower floors, the kitchen and utility rooms behind, to answer and trace the ring's origins to her *place*, a servant signified by the servant's quarters. But it's also a haunted *place,* as in *the Id,* with its secrets typically located in the haunted attic, basement, or storeroom. She finds in storage old textbooks and research notes arguing scientific eugenic theories of Black sub-humanity and inferiority. In half-opened boxes and scattered about, old black and white and bronze tint pictures subtly hide (and reveal) the shadowy specters of the *Afropast* that still haunt, serve, clean up, and maintain the campus in the subaltern reality of the film's present.

Consequently, after the blowup at the faculty party, and this typically happens, one gets the "post-game analysis," where the faculty lounge around with stiff "real" drinks and pick over "what just happened." Now tenured professor, Liv Beckman, talks back, telling her story and exonerating herself. She is the bastard daughter of a *brother* and a white woman and born into an ominous, puritanical 18th-century New England, religious formation that condemns *all* Black people to hell: no appeals, parole, stays of execution, clemency, or pardons. As a result, she escaped the puritanical "white" world of her birth and opted for living her *Blackness*, both ontologically and culturally. Notably, while all three Black women feel the oppressive burden of the school's ghostly, stuffy old racism, Liv Beckman is the only one to say she finally "feels at home" at Ancaster. In understanding that now Professor Beckman has been for her entire career an itinerant lecturer, three jobs in the past three years, one can explain this feeling; she has found her *place,* as in promotion and tenure. But in Liv Beckman's case, *place* also means location, which points to Beckman's troubled, bi-racial origins, as she was actually born into the Ancaster community, its location, and therefore she is actually "home." This is signified when she leaves the faculty party smack down, in the same hooded cape of her alienated, white ancestors.

Meanwhile, in the post-party, stiff drink analysis, Professor Bishop makes a cathartic declaration, telling the faculty what she now understands about her *place* at Ancaster College, that *place* being totally ironic. She is not the "the Master" of the house, but more like its highest paid maid, much like all of the Black folks hiding in the shadows that haunt Ancaster's old grim portraits, its lawns, kitchens, dining rooms, its haunted subaltern spaces. She realizes that she is a Black academic servant, skillfully performing all the subtle tasks of tokenism while cleaning up and smoothing over Ancaster's racist, academic shit. Creepy forebodings of her *place* appear in the first moments of the film, when proudly approaching the Master's House and trying the key, the Master's door rejects her. The lock jams. And only after the house makes her wait and takes her measure, does the door, in a haunted cliché gesture slowly swing open on its own. After telling the faculty off, she walks out into the night, and on the way back to the Master's House, she is sussed out by campus security, who initially assume that she's faculty and asks to scan her I.D. card. In a final resolution, she tells the security guard that she is not an employee. He points the way out, and she, divested of tenure and honorific titles, walks off into the indeterminate night.

Act III

Twilight Civilization

At this writing, accurate divinations of the Afrofuture, cinematic or otherwise, are hard to come by; yet such views are deeply imbricated in the future of the planet, which is murky, ominous at best. One does not need the visionary, prophetic powers of an Ezekiel, or James Baldwin, or Nostradamus to see the warnings, signs, and disturbances in nature and the collective human psyche, to discern the bad things about the gathering planetary storm rapidly coming our way. Moreover, it is well understood from our newscasts, weather reports, and political projections that these "bad things" will happen to the darker peoples of the world first: famine, war, drought, plague, flood and fire, economic collapse. However, things that happen to the darker peoples of the planet and in the Afrofuture, are rapidly making their way towards the developed, industrial, technology-based and consumer-obsessed nations of the world, with all of these bad things underwriting the mounting catastrophe of the *Planetfuture.*

Black American cinema cannot resolve or save us from our calamitous planetary circumstances. Black cinema can only depict, reveal these circumstances, and perhaps edify, entertain, and enlighten us in small meaningful ways. One important, glimpse at this process discloses the philosophic differences between *Get Out* and *The Master* involving their approaches to depicting the illness of system-wide *racism*. These differences might lead us to some useful speculations about the Afrofuture. *Get Out* deals with the horrors of "scientific materialism" inflicted on the Black body, as in the real time horror of the "Tuskegee Syphilis Study," or the medical and commercial exploitation of the stolen cells of Henrietta Lacks, which were literally used to "transform medicine."[9] Meanwhile, *The Master* explores scientific materialism's binary complement, "idealism," as expressed in the ghostly haunted racist past and the ongoing experience of *blackpain* inflicted on the Black psyche. Nonetheless, both films agree on one focal theme: racism, as a horrific, scientific ideology, or as an idealist haunting, past and present, is atmospheric, ambient, and always here and now. And as Jasmine in *The Master* again reminds us, "*it's everywhere.*"

Without going off into a critical, deep reading of Jordan Peele's third feature *Nope* (2022), I feel that one of the things that Peele is tussling with in the film is the dialectical transformative tension between the "material" and the "ideal" rendered as a synthesis of his creative thoughts about the evolution of the horror movie. The peril, the threat of the monster in *Nope* is fluid, morphing between the scientific material of a giant mechanical UFO disk, and the idealist haunting of a black, horse training ranch by a giant, shape shifting, hungry, flying jellyfish. But beyond speculation about the Afrofuture, and its future forms in Black horror movies, there are a couple of things that are chillingly clear, the Apocalypse is real, it is here, and it is "From Now On." And, while James Joyce's "nightmare of history," as of this writing, is global and terrifyingly obvious, it bears special application to Chris in *Get Out*, in his "sunken place," as the repressed nightmares, uncovered and exploited by the "science" of psychoanalysis. But the nightmare of history also includes the haunted, creepy dreams of the three Black women entangled in *The Master's* "house." And racism is the American dream … and nightmare from which they, and I, are trying to awake, at the movies and in reality.

Notes

1 Deborah Walker King. *African Americans and the Culture of Pain* (Charlottesville and London: U. of Virginia Press, 2008). Throughout this prelude, I will deploy King's compelling neologism, "blackpain."
2 Diana Ramey Berry. *The Price for Their Pound of Flesh* (Boston: Beacon Press, 2017). Berry writes that

> "once an enslaved person died, whether buried of not they were given a ghost value. Some were sold or transported for sale to medical schools throughout the United States. …. In other words, since enslaved people's values were calculated regularly, it was easy to determine the value of their bodies at death—ghost values."
>
> *p. 7–8*

3 Here, I credit the fresh work of three historians: Diana Ramsey Berry, *The Price of Their Pound of Flesh*; Harriet Washington, *Medical Apartheid: The Dark History of Medical Experimentation on Black Americans from Colonial Times to the Present* (New York: Anchor Books, 2006); Kathrin Harkup, *The Making of the Monster: Mary Shelly's Frankenstein* (London and New York: Bloomsbury Sigma, 2018).
4 Fredric Jameson, "The Cultural Logic of Late Capitalism" pp. 1–54, in *Postmodernism or, the Cultural Logic of Late Capitalism* (Durham, NC: Duke U. Press, 1991).
5 Washington, *Medical Apartheid*.
6 Moreover, I would agree that this process, discussed in *Medical Apartheid* is ongoing, if only more broadly on a class basis.
7 Here, I borrow a concept from sci-fi, cyberpunk, novelist William Gibson who writes about the *near dystopian future* in such novels as *Burning Chrome, Pattern Recognition, Count Zero*, and not some cartoonish galaxy "far, far away."
8 Angela Y. Davis, "Black Women and the Academy," *The Angela Y. Davis Reader*, ed. Joy James (New York: Blackwell Publishing, 1998), Chapter 14. Here, Davis delivers an excellent historicization and discussion of the travails of Black women at all levels, working to gain a *place* "in the academy."
9 Washington, p. 158–185 for a discussion of the Tuskegee experiment; p. 355 for the story of Henrietta Lacks and the journey of her cells.

2

FEELING WHAT I'M SEEING, SEEING WHAT I'M FEELING

Herman Gray and Maya Iverson-Davis

Introduction

As we pondered the title for this chapter, two events brought together *Tongues Untied* (1989) and *Random Acts of Flyness* (RAF) (2018–present) prompting us to see RAF as a part of a radical concern with television, Blackness, and "putting people in a position to emotionally fight back" as Angela Y. Davis noted in a featured conversation with writer Maxine Gordon at the 2019 Monterey Jazz Festival.

We open our chapter on Blackness, seeing, feeling, and care with a few words on what makes this chapter and anthology urgent. We are writing from the early 2020s. The United States is in the middle of another reckoning around race and racism anti-Blackness and racial inequality centered on the experience of Black-Americans. The most recent Presidential election cycle gave us few options. Either we would let the slow but steady rise of fascism gain a deeper hold, or we would fight to maintain a system of governance, surveillance, and resource allocation that disproportionately affects and kills Black and brown people in the United States and around the world. With such an impossible choice, the 2020s are not business as usual, but an intervention that might keep us from deeply sliding into a political, cultural, and economic system incapable of recognizing Black people's right to a future. This moment is also conditioned by the possibility of a different future, one marked by a vision of abolition that reimagines Black freedom, equality, and justice.

We are writing in a moment where caring for Black people is not just a theoretical suggestion, play on words, or a trendy methodological concern, but an urgent call to protect the futures of Black people in the United States. As scholars, we are practicing what it means to write about television and media in a way that takes care of Black life and not just Black representation. Recent movements for social and economic justice and emerging scholarship about television, Blackness, gender, race, and disability have pressed us to consider how ours and academia's

DOI: 10.4324/9781003079682-3

commitments to media visibility and inclusion anchors a neoliberal project of civic participation that depends on the presumed transparency of the "other" as a fundamental requirement for social inclusion and representational diversity. Co-author Herman Gray has already made two interventions in media and television studies calling for different registers for thinking about difference in our fields. In 2013, Gray wrote "Subjected to Recognition," a piece that probed whether or not it is productive for media scholars and activists to continue to look to demographic parity, media visibility, and recognition as the only analytical basis for a cultural politics capable of engendering social justice and inclusion within neoliberal regimes of power.[1] Gray was interested in the cultural politics of representation especially where, in brand economies and digitally based social media platforms, the end game is so often the mere increase in visibility of difference itself. His work suggested that the goal of social parity, diversity, and inclusion, framed by the discourse of representation and waged in the glare of neoliberal markets and governance might be more productive if the focus of the industry, media scholars, and activists included a politics of concern about the life, death, safety, and security of Black people.[2]

What this means, we suggest, is broadening the analytic focus of our research first, from the longstanding methodological commitment of indexing progress on diversity and inclusion by empirically measuring demographic parity in industry participation of women and people of color; and second, moving away from our narrow focus on questions of accuracy, authenticity, and realness in television representation. If we do this, we might think about the way media content gathers audiences around what Gray calls—borrowing from science studies scholar Bruno Latour—matters of concern.[3] As we explore later in this piece, Black creatives foster narratives of care around how they construct narratives for food justice, racial disparities in health care, safety, police violence, mass incarceration, and more that challenge the ontological and epistemological assumptions we hold about Black life in the United States and elsewhere.

Concerned with the capacity of television to connect (with) viewers, forge alliances, and build a sense of attachment and belonging through the feelings and resonance that television can conjure, Gray identified a set of research questions foregrounding feelings and the affective register of television as a critical element in the politics of representation. Reckoning with these questions and the limits of conventional approaches, we are searching for ways of talking about television and Blackness in another theoretical and analytic register that resonates with how Black creatives call us to take care of Black life through their work.

In this chapter, attending to matters of concern also means caring about when, where, and how television gathers audiences around, cultural disputes and non-normative identities even when they appear in an unflattering light. This is an exercise in attending to what is on the screen even if it's not what we desire or feel comfortable with viewing. In addition, our framework of care acknowledges the time, creativity, legacy, vulnerability, and risk associated with telling Black stories that are explosive and expansive with no guarantee for how these articulations will influence the media industry, audiences, or other Black and non-Black creatives and the stories they tell. This is why we argue that Black creatives use television as a technology of Blackness. In doing so, we are writing in a tradition of Black speculative thought that understands that making space for Black life to exist in the future starts with how we imagine what it means to care for Black people in our intellectual and creative work.

We identify Terence Nance's *Random Acts of Flyness* (HBO) as a case study in how Black creatives call us to take care of Black life. As an exercise in writing with care, we start our analysis by considering how the visual relationship between Marlon Rigg's *Tongue Untied* (1989) and Terence Nance's *Random Acts of Flyness* exists within a legacy of Black creatives using film and television to augment how we care about Black life. We explore how *Random Acts of Flyness* demonstrates this care through opacity and the willingness to let Black expression exist within the space of television. We think about these moments of care as Nance and his team reaching out to Black viewers to say "I see us, I create for us." It's a type of validation that isn't only rooted in veracity or truth, but like Riggs, grounded in a tradition of using any means necessary to adjust our concerns over the condition of being Black in the United States.

We look to the work of Eduard Glissant (by way of Kara Keeling) to help disentangle the role of television in the nexus of liberal recognition, media transparency, and the production of (racial) difference as a problem of Black freedom.[4] For instance, using Glissant's concepts of transparency and opacity to look at selected programming in the Peabody Archive from the late 1940s to the 1970s, Gray found that as technologies of power in the classic broadcast network era both television, and the American discourse of race relations, constructed Black people, people of color, and immigrants as social problems; as such, to participate in the project of white liberal freedom, they had to prove themselves as loyal and trusted.[5] Glissant rejects this requirement of social transparency as a condition of recognition by the powerful in social and civic life. Instead, he demands that everyone be seen and known on their own terms and that we build social and civic relations on the ground of mutual respect, recognition, and equality. For Glissant, this condition of relationality is egalitarian and includes our relationship to the natural, social and cultural worlds.

Feeling What I'm Seeing: Nance and Riggs

At the time we suggested the title for this chapter, two events brought together *Tongues Untied* and *Random Acts of Flyness* (RAF) and prompted us to see RAF as a part of a radical concern with television, Blackness, and care. First, the Peabody Awards Jury on which Herman Gray sits recognized RAF with the Peabody Awards for its genre innovation and political courage to engage with Black life in the United States, as well as its ability to deliver withering cultural and social criticism. The Peabody Awards notes that RAF does this without "a preoccupation with white gaze or desire" and that "*Random Acts of Flyness* centers Blackness as a complex, productive historical fact and contemporary lived experience rather than a phobic-obsessed reaction to whiteness."[6] Second, the Brooklyn Academy of Music (and Pacific Film Archive and Berkeley Art Museum) featured a month-long retrospective of Marlon Riggs' work, including his innovative and seminal film, *Tongues Untied*. Debuting in 1989, *Tongues Untied* was one of the first publicly broadcast televised programs that prioritized the politics of care in the presentation of Black life in how it unquestionably demanded viewers exist in the same space as Black gay male love and desire. Framed by these two remarkable works, much has changed about Black cultural politics and television. As NPR television critic and former Peabody Juror Eric Deggans observed, there is more diversity on television than there was a mere 20 years ago. He counts *A Black Lady Sketch Show* (HBO), *South Side*, *Ramy* (Hulu), *Atlanta*, *Insecure* (HBO-Max), *One Day at A Time* (Netflix/POP), *This Is Us* (NBC), *Mixedish* (ABC), *Fresh Off the Boat* (ABC), *Vida* (STARZ), *The New Party of Five*, *All Rise* (CBS), *The Good Fight* (CBS All Access), *When They See Us* (Netflix), *Pose* (FX), *Sorry for Your Loss* (Facebook Watch), and *Undone* (Amazon). To this list, we would add *Sherman's Showcase* (IFC), *Lovecraft Country* (HBO-Max), *I May Destroy You* (HBO), and *Random Acts of Flyness* (HBO) as a part of this new wave of diversity on television.

With so many television programs about Blackness and involving Black people available in this third moment of Peak TV why look to RAF as an example of the politics of culture and representation in another register?[7] In our own case, we acknowledge the conventions of story, character, narrative, plot, and conflict in these other shows still guide our own critical responses and judgments about them and the strategies of representation and cultural politics they perform. As beautifully rendered, challenging and innovative as they are, our critical judgment about the veracity of their treatment of Blackness remain tied to the accuracy and resonance of their representation and such facts of the matter certainly inform our evaluations. In the end, of course, these shows reward with pleasure and identification. By contrast, RAF's conceit operates at the level of sentiment and feelings, knowledge, and meaning that exceeds the legibility and transparency of characters, genre, and critical exegesis; so while RAF dwells on the facts of all sorts of matters, it insists on a kind of opacity, ambivalence, and indirection that can be as confusing as it is edifying, and as knowable as it is mysterious. For us, this is its appeal and the source of its critical multiplicity and urgency.

This claim is no mere cultural politics of opposition. As an index of the "truth" of Blackness, the discursivity and concerns that Black TV representations mobilize can expand and enrich the range of cultural meanings and angles of vision that television representations of Black people offer. Moving outward from the facts of the matter of Blackness can prepare and make us receptive to different analytic registers like those expressed in the work of Marlon Riggs—the poetic, the playful, the oblique the opaque. For Black critical approaches to television, RAF and *Tongues Untied* starts from the idea that television can convene Black viewers around concerns as emotionally resonant and aesthetically rewarding as they are intellectually challenging and politically urgent; gathering viewers around the political urgency, ethical commitments, and emotional experiences of care and concern for each other and not just what we share as market consumers of brand identities is, we suggest, what is at stake.

The ethic of care and concern is one of the conceits of *Tongues Untied*. Much of Riggs' work, especially *Tongues Untied*, raises critical questions among Black viewers about Black vulnerability, loss, care, and love among Black gay men.[8] Using poetry, dramatic reenactments, direct camera address, confession, and music Riggs extends the innovative approaches to documentary by Lourdes Portillo, Lynn Hershman, and Trinh T. Minh-Ha. Riggs uses the documentary form as a call to action in response to the crisis of HIV/AIDS that was ravaging Black gay communities, especially Black men. In the news media and popular discourse when Black gay men were rendered visible, they were demonized and measured through the hegemonic framework of Black heteronormativity masculinity. Stigmatized as deviants, gay Black men were represented as living and loving beyond the acceptable boundaries of whiteness and hegemonic Black heterosexual masculinity. *Tongues Untied* can be understood, among other things, as a call to consciousness around the urgency of critical illness and death among Black gay men and a critical rebuke of this hegemonic framing of Black gay men.

Along with Riggs' radical critique of the normative masculinity required for Black visibility in television, Riggs staunchly rejected these terms of Black visibility and transparency as a condition of civic representation and social inclusion.[9] With *Tongues Untied*, he exposed and challenged the limits of possibility using the film to focus his concerns about beauty, love, loss, and care among Black gay men. Riggs overwhelmed the screen and filled national and local public television broadcast of *Tongues Untied* with Black men loving Black men, expressing regard, intimacy, joy, and care as a way of signaling his/our concerns. Riggs' narrative and visual framing gave voice to the fear and anxiety, courage and determination needed for him/us to take care with and of each other. With *Tongues Untied*, Riggs centered these concerns, disrupted dominant conceptions of Black (gay) men, and registered the absolute urgency of life and death facing the Black gay male community.

By pushing the limit of formal, stylistic, and visual conventions of documentary, Riggs deconstructed the form, infused it with performative and poetic elements, reassembled it, and bought these reimagined conventions to bear on issues critical to him and his community. The connections between *Tongues Untied* and RAF are not merely that one follows the other. Instead, as Racquel Gates and Michael Boyce Gillespie propose with their generative example of attending to the discursivity of Blackness, the two media texts operate within the same discursive field and make the point that in the hands of Black creative personnel as a technology of Blackness, television is capable of assembling us around Black concerns about care and vulnerability.[10]

RAF assembles viewers around concerns that matter for Black people—especially women, trans, and LGBTQ communities.[11] RAF can do this because the show has a definite point of view that draws from contemporary and historical elements including news footage and media archives that it merges with fictional performances, reenactments, lectures, activism, and criticism. As in *Tongues Untied*, the themes, sketches, and characters in RAF circulate within dense image and story worlds; stylistically and ontologically, the show uses humor and satire to foreground the intensity and absurdity of the emotional life of the show's characters. Because the creators are mindful of the representational weight of accuracy, legibility, and respectability that comes with struggling over television as a technology of race, including managing the gaze of whiteness as both ideological and market categories, they are free to pursue the different aesthetic and emotional registers open to them. For example, the willingness of the creative team to do a sketch on rape culture or violence against the LBGTQ community without eliding its specific harm to Black women or sanitizing it to capitulate to the white heteronormative gaze or worrying over Black respectability politics is certainly novel for a sketch series. Naming sources, consequences, and effects of this harm to Black women and members of the LBGTQ community are one of the defining elements distinguishing the show's discursive practice and circulation relative to the Blackness it engenders. This engendering and discursive circulation of televisual Blackness is an emotional (re)source of the show's resonance and stylistic distinction, especially its centering of Black women and their particular matters of concern about health, invisibility, and vulnerability.[12]

Moreover, the series' explicit and courageous intellectual commitment is to multiplicity: no one character is defined by any one identity. All are productive mixtures of distinct cultural experiences, histories, relationships, and locations. RAF also places Black women at the center of its world building, cultural critiques of gender and sexual injustices, and the show's vision of social justice. In this sense, RAF is one of the few programs on television to explicitly render Black characters and their social relations complexly and compassionately, and to do so without sentimentalism or exoticism. For instance, RAF uses Black endeavors with gaming, coding, and social media to showcase the linked practices of state surveillance of Black people and the critical response to that surveillance by Black youth. Using play, mockery, irreverence, and satire, RAF ponders what the gaze upon Blackness by power looks and feels like. It importantly returns the Black gaze upon power and gives us a sense of what the refusal of that gaze of state power feels like. In the context of movements for social and racial justice led by BlackLivesMatter (#BLM), this perspective on the "gaze" is an orientation, a way of taking the measure of the medium of television's demand to see, and Black desire to see and to be seen. RAF takes seriously the power relations of looking; looking at as well as looking back at the structural inequalities that create different social registers around social and cultural differences. As with the BBC's *Black Mirror*, Isaac Julien's *Looking for Langston* (1989), and Riggs' *Color Adjustment* (1991), some of the show's best moments manipulate these elements of screen politics and the looking dynamics that structure the history of Black looking relationships.

Television as a Technology of Blackness

RAF is quite the unruly television object within our contemporary wave of Black television. The series is billed as a sketch comedy though it does not wear this label particularly well. Because of its unconventional approach to narrative, its imaginative use of visual and sonic elements, its shifting poetic, affective and intellectual registers, its distinct aesthetic style, and its direct engagement with Black concerns. RAF's very unruliness is the means through which it critically reimagines, and in some cases challenges, academic, journalistic, and industry consensus on televisions' strategies of representation, economies of visibility, politics of parity, and inclusion of Blackness.

RAF and its contemporaries critically mobilize television as a technology of Blackness. Terence Nance and his collaborators use RAF's visual and sonic elements to organize our televisual sense of time and space by immersing viewers in Black emotional and psychological life, cultural imagination, and dreams. We suggest this makes RAF a discursive regime of televisual care organized by an approach to Blackness and Black life that moves in and across spatial, historical, and temporal registers of Black life. The grammar RAF uses to amplify these spatial, temporal, and historical registers exist within the historical context and cultural grammar of Marlon Riggs' poetry, Isaac Julien's performance, John Akomfrah's archive, Arthur Jafa, and Julie Dash's visual sensibilities, and Black diasporic cultural practices. Together they inspire the show's claims to Black space and care exemplified by how it looks, what it says, how it sounds, and how it feels.

What we find most promising about *Random Acts of Flyness'* take on television as a technology of Blackness is that it explores the relation between Blackness and technology, pressing both into territory and practices viewers rarely see on television. While this quality sets RAF apart, we want to be careful of this talk about relation and territory in this moment of Peak TV. It sounds and feels eerily familiar, like talk about previous booms of Black screen and media cultures: Blaxploitation, urban "ghetto" film, hip-hop, and Black rom-coms. In television, it certainly recalls some of the optimism generated by Black cast and themed shows from the Black block cycles, cable net-lets like the WB, UPN, Fox, reality programs, and later, Black cable platforms (including TVONE, OWN, and BET). RAF and the cluster of Black theme and Black cast content dominating Peak television at the moment owes some of its creative and stylist freedom to the possibilities created by shows like *In Living Color* (Fox), *MADD TV* (Fox), *Sponge Bob Square Pants* (Nickelodeon), *The Simpsons* (Fox), *Key and Peele* (Comedy Central), *The Richard Pryor Show* (NBC), *South Park* (Comedy Central), and *The Boondocks* (Cartoon Network).

That RAF appears in the same seemingly expansive content universe as *Sherman's Showcase, I May Destroy You, Watchman* (HBO), *Lovecraft Country, Pose, Atlanta* (FX), *Insecure* (HBO), *The Chi* (Showtime), *Dear White People* (Netflix), *The Duce* (HBO), *Vida* (STARZ), *She's Gotta Have It* (Netflix), *Blackish* (ABC), *Mixedish, The Carmichael Show* (NBC), *Empire* (Fox), *The Housewives* Franchise *(Bravo), How to Get Away with Murder and Scandal* (ABC), *Transparent* (Amazon), and *Orange Is the New Black* (Netflix) is by no means coincidental. When placed in the ecology of streaming services and platforms and the escalating competition among technology companies, legacy media companies, and digital content providers for control of distribution, content, and libraries one detects a sea change that is sure to impact Black cast and themed television content.

In the spacetime of RAF, Black knowledge and history set the epistemological and ontological terms of engagement and fashions a televisual world organized around the specificity of Black knowledge, experiences, and cultural assumptions. RAF's epistemology of Blackness, the representational strategies it uses, and themes it gathers is what interests us. That is to say we are especially fascinated by the way it assembles, probes, and mines the architecture and performance of television Blackness; engaging its Blackness without reducing it to a feature of television's historic optics, social problems, or cultural mimicry of whiteness. This allows RAF to populate its televisual worlds with technology-savvy Black people who navigate social spaces where Black thoughts and emotion are rendered discursively and aesthetically in the rhythm and language of Black-defined television space and time. The show demarcates Black spaces, which in turn set up sharp contrasts with some of the most familiar and revered spaces of commercial television—the living room and bedrooms, talk show sets, workspaces, and advertising where Black people are most often absent, at least in television's imagination of those spaces. The show's signifying practices enact a poetics of Black world making in the tradition of Black writers Toni Morrison and Paule Marshall, musicians George Clinton and Miles Davis, intellectuals bell hooks and Audre Lorde, and once again, filmmakers Marlon Riggs and Julie Dash whose approaches to language, perspective, rhythm, practices, and relations among Black people form the basis of their art.

Gathering Concerns, Monetizing Blackness

In the second decade of the 21st century of the American television and media environment, the major players, financing models, distribution systems, shifts in production models, especially in response to the global Covid-19 pandemic and movements for racial and social justice, viewing experiences, and content are quickly shaping the television landscape for the foreseeable future. Is it possible that for first time in the history of television and the debates about the politics of representation and diversity the conditions are ripe for disruption of the link between the television industry, racial politics, gender, and representation? Certainly, at the level of content creation, this potential disruption has as much to do with changes in the conditions of production, finance, distribution, and viewing, especially the transformation of mass audiences and appointment television, as well as the fortification of viewing silos, and the influence of social media. Because streaming capacities, access to content, and viewing experiences, stories heretofore imagined but unrealizable in the network broadcast era are now becoming fundamental to the definition and experience of Peak television, which seems to mean, as *LA Times* television critic Lorraine Ali put it, "more is better." Subscription-based funding models of streaming services like Hulu or Amazon (rather than exclusively advertising models) delink the fate of content and content makers from the make-or-break appeals to mass advertisers in search of broad audiences. For content makers, especially those whose stories have been marginalized and shut out of the television industry, streaming services are defining the new conditions of possibility for content creation and innovation. Paradoxically, while there are more spaces for heretofore marginalized stories and content creators these opportunities come with conditions whose impact, including the length of seasons and number of episodes per season, it seems the industry is still sorting out.[13]

The contest is to gain a competitive advantage, ensure access to the talent, to sustain brand appeal in the spaces where social media and streaming services meet, to grow subscriptions, and to add value to brand content. Algorithmic metrics measure site visits and audience demographics that guide investment decisions, predict breakeven thresholds, and calculate risks. In the calculus of risk, the value of content has shifted from licensing content, a practice started in the broadcast and cable era, to corporate ownership of creative content. Occasioned by the ubiquity of the smartphone, the tablet, and the computer as viable platforms for viewing in the streaming environment a key metric for measuring value is shifting from the number of hours per week to the number of hours per day. In the corporate brand and product environment, these changes in turn impact episode lengths, pricing, and shelf-life, which means lower breakeven thresholds that a given program must reach to add value; hence, the aim is not just to add new viewers for a given show but to expand the number of subscriptions and to entice visitors to exercise brand loyalty. These emerging models mean, so the reasoning goes, that tent-pole vehicles like *This Is Us, Killing Eve* (BBC), *The Handmaid's Tale* (Hulu), and *Orange Is the New Black* can co-exist in the same ecology as more unconventional shows like *Bo Jack Horseman* (Netflix) or *Claws* (TNT) without shifting the responsibility for profitability to any one of these.

Not surprisingly, the competition for viewers streaming services and content creators among the major media and technology players like Warner Media, Disney, ATT, Amazon, Apple, and Google is at a fever pitch. At first blush, this means that for Black content makers like Terence Nance and Issa Rae, Jordan Peele, Misha Taylor, Lena Waithe, and Robin Thede some of the previous aesthetic constraints and financial risks associated with program formats, length, style, and story, no matter how adventurous, are finding homes among digital streaming platforms like HBO-Max, Disney Plus, Netflix, Hulu, and Amazon.

This congealing ecology of streaming, digital platforms, and subscription-based valuation models, along with modifications in viewing experience, is making it easier to direct specific content to specific audiences and in turn making it efficient and more lucrative for content creators to develop shows like *I May Destroy You* and *Lovecraft Country* that push conversations around intergenerational racial and sexual trauma in Black communities, as well as the afterlife of slavery.[14] The hope among these creatives is that the subscription funding model for Peak TV creates financial interest, production conditions, talent pools, and creative collaborations where Black and brown writers, casting directors, and showrunners have the opportunity to bring their visions to the screen without having their work shaped or severely limited by that old broadcast era sawhorse of least objectionable content.

But there is another story of value operating here too. With the highly publicized success of Ava DuVernay's production and distribution platforms and lucrative deals by Shonda Rhimes and Kenya Barris leading the way almost every week industry trades, seemingly, announce a new deal, series, collaboration, and reboots with well-established content makers. Perhaps it would not be too much of a stretch, despite public commitments and lucrative investments in talent and programming content that the new ecology of streaming has wrought, to ask does it remain the case that the current push for greater diversity and inclusion is another instantiation (upgraded to be sure) of separate but equal niche environments of cable and broadcast television. What are the conditions of possibility that make this moment different? Recall too, that the cable television revolution spawned "quality" TV, its own version of peak and prestige TV; and that it too gathered slices of television viewers who no longer shared the emotional, psychic, and cultural life of fellow citizens through shared network viewing. RAF is an example of this holdover of television's marketing and industrial logic, but in the context of BlackLivesMatter (BLM), it also exceeds that logic since as the recent movements suggest, this concern with care and security is shared more broadly nationally and globally.

This version of Peak TV seems promising in the willingness of the new deep pocketed players to financially invest in culturally diverse content and to form a rich pool of talented Black and brown managers, writers, showrunners, and content creators. Our guess is that we are at the end of a cycle of creative and structural flux where unconventional stories and creators managed to work in the space of an industry in transformation and that we are settling into another phase of reconsolidating and restructuring by television industry leaders. Since this moment in the history of Black screen cultures and production resembles other film and television cycles, it is just as precarious and subject to the similar vagaries of personality, investment, profit, and competition. As RAF and the current staple of Black cast and themes suggest, the talent and stories have always been there among Black and brown creatives; less so, the political will and economic investment by the television industry. The question for now is this: With the new investment and valuation models and with the deep pockets of tech companies entering the television streaming ecology, making content to hail thinner and thinner slivers of the audience with a deep pool of talented and proven content creators and managers, and given the sustained cultural concern and political pressure for greater diversity in Hollywood, is the moment ripe for consequential and lasting change?[15] And, how will this change influence how television programs connect to the politics of care and feeling Black creators weave into their content?

Seeing What I'm Feeling

If Nance and his co-creators use television as a technology of Blackness to mobilize our concerns, around what kind of concerns does its viewers gather? As we have suggested, the series follows the adventures of Nance's character, our guide and narrator as he and his crew move in and out of Black spaces where "acts" and situations appear random and natural but of course they are anything but random. In these quotidian spaces of Blackness, we meet characters and roll with them as they confront the social, emotional, intellectual, and psychological challenges they face in the routine conduct of daily life. Some characters respond to the difficult situations and hostile attitudes particularly from whites. Other characters ponder how things got this way, and they take the measure of how these situation and conditions impact their futures and relationships. In one of the through lines of the series, our guide dwells on the consequence of the media's saturation of Black space with large and small acts of injustice, assault, and suspicion.

The ensemble moves through apartments, bedrooms, police stations, and houses with stops along the way inside video games; player fantasies populated by Black avatars; 1950s television ads and sit-coms with white middle-class families; and a Black family backyard barbecue. These weekly romps in Black televisual space put viewers in worlds where the sketches and the meanings they signify treat television entertainment as a technology of race (especially the dominance and longevity of the genre of situation comedy); that is, the sketches reveal and critique the practices, elements that render as natural, social assumptions about white (middle class) space in television fantasies. By imaginatively creating and emphasizing Black fantastical and surreal worlds, the sketches focus critical attention on the role of television in producing and sustaining these longstanding and pervasive fantasies of whiteness. In the case of news, RAF rehearses this criticism of television's historic role by replaying archival footage of assaults on Black people including television coverage of Emmett Till's murder and funeral; the 1992 Los Angeles rebellions; the FBI murder of Fred Hampton in Chicago; the rebellions in Ferguson, Missouri. All of this is packed into a tightly edited, fast-paced three-minute sketch.

RAF moves us through its imagined world of Black space amplifying the remarkable and mocking the absurdities of everyday life for Black people—a Black bike rider stopped and questioned by the police, Black men greeting each other in the park, women gathering in the beauty shop, a backyard barbecue. These signifiers of Black time and space, intimacy and relationships, anxiety and trauma open semiotic and affective portals to Blackness and Black worlds using its cut 'n mix aesthetic to address social concerns about Black men, women, and children. Exploring the fantastic dreams and powerful emotional lives of young Black people using animation, claymation, virtual reality, poetry, and intellectual discourse is both refreshing and compelling. For instance, the masterful way the sketches mine Black enslavement, mass incarceration, the plantation economy, and white wealth accumulation, weaving them into a compelling critique and demonstration of how race works as a technology of power.

The reference to "Flyness" in the title of the series is not really random so much as it is an invitation to celebrate Black stylization, the creative inventiveness of Black people, and the centrality of improvisation, humor, and poetics to the discursive circulation of Blackness across the political, cultural, media, and historical scape of American life; for instance, a sketch on Black food-ways at a backyard barbecue is hilarious on its face and yet sharp in its attention to color palette, texture, language, and presentation. Poetically, "Flyness" uses aesthetics, style, and improvisation to emphasize the seminal importance of the body, sensuality, and beauty to sexual life, non-normative identities, non-conventional relationships, and care. The expressions of care and concern that the series considers is neither compromising nor random. In one sketch, the writers use the trope of the (white) television game-show genre to concentrate our sights on Black vulnerability and early death among Black children; another sketch trains our attention on the relationship between the rape of Black women, police indifference to investigations and prosecutions, and disparities in health treatment, and the trauma Black women experience as a result.[16]

There are also powerful expressions of hope in some of the sketches as when Nance's character takes to the air and flies away from the dangerous clutches of a white policeman. The qualities of the series that are most unexpected is its imaginative assembly of styles, themes, topics, and sonic elements that constitute Black worlds. The series creatively uses the sketch format to mine in just the right balance the heuristic, entertainment, critical and emotional weight of the writer's concerns. Ranging across the genre boundaries of comedy, drama, satire, and critique, the series hits its marks with care and acuity dwelling in and exploring the spaces of Blackness constructed in a medium that has heretofore been hostile to, or at best, indifferent to Black people and our concerns. As a technology of Blackness the series commands the form, subjecting it to careful critical scrutiny, putting it in the service of explicating Black vulnerability, care, and concern.

RAF is a remarkable piece of television also in the sense that gathers us, grabs our attention, and trains it on matters of concern to Black people in ways that are poignant, funny, wise, and innovative. It does not shrink from controversy, bad objects, or forbidden topics but addresses them in ways that encourages alliances and connection with others, recognizing and dreaming through the optic of difference about new possibilities. Like *Tongues Untied*, RAF names, points out complicities, and trains our sights on urgent subjects like rape, homophobia, and misogyny in Black communities. It refuses to avert its gaze (and our eyes) or resort to visual and editing tricks to change the subject. It is critical of white liberal guilt and sentimentality as well as Black respectability, sexism, patriarchy, and homophobia that excuse harmful sexist, class, and gender behavior.

Some of the most sensitive elements of the series come in the close spaces of intimacy among family and friends. Like Riggs, sketches in RAF provoke questions, especially with regard to the Black discourse of respectability, that are hidden and silent among us about who we think we are and would like to be, how we love, and how we care for one another. Operating in such close spaces urges creators to deal with normative and taken-for-granted assumptions that imprison and silence, injure and marginalize, while it also engages practices of repair and regard that hold us accountable for homophobic, sexist, and colorist complicities and injuries enacted by people inside and outside of Black communities.

As with *Tongues Untied*, RAF is aware of large historical conditions and institutions like medicine and health care that deny, ignore, and belittle Black women's health needs, government immigration policy regimes that sanction violence against immigrants and people of color seeking safe harbors and refuge, criminal justice systems that warehouse Black and brown men, and corporate media where assumptions about truth and beauty, risk and profit, worth and value are at stake. The series does not compartmentalize elements of story, world making, character, and plot from one another; Black queer love, liberal guilt, and children's vulnerability exist in RAF's television universe.

Television and the Discursivity of Blackness

Random Acts of Flyness and its contemporaries demand media and television scholarship on race and difference that no longer analytically centers respectability politics as the primary critical optic through which to understand and challenge how race and television operate as technologies of power. We have exhausted the cultural, moral, and political investment in shoring up what "respectable and positive" images of Black people on television means for challenging racism and pursuing social justice. In their important provocation about new directions for Black screen studies, Racquel Gates and Michael Gillespie observe,

> Blackness in film and media is always already an incitement, a question and a process... New approaches must reckon with how the idea of Blackness in film and media (as an enactment of Black visual and expressive culture) can generate acute imaginative staging of the art of Blackness and the discursivity of race.[17]

This observation engenders critical questions about Black difference and the affective intensity of the meaning and experience of Blackness that is easily elided by the preoccupation with progress narratives, appropriate identities, factual accuracy, positive images, and exceptionalism. Moreover, Gates and Gillespie's provocation directs our attention to those formations and circuits where Blackness travels. Attention to the discursivity of Blackness charts the semiotic movement and performative expression of Blackness with and without Black bodies. As such neither embodiment nor identity is a precondition for understanding how and where Blackness operates in social, economic, cultural, and political discourse. This kind of discursivity is a powerful critical optic through which to analyze television and media. Gates and Gillespie thus urge scholars to reimagine television and media Blackness as not merely attached to Black bodies but as a discursive logic, aesthetic formation, and cultural politics.

By pursing the discursivity of Black television programs, scholars direct our attention to reality television, make-overs, house-hunting, housewives as well as rom-coms and melodrama set in Black cast series and serials. By so doing, they set their analytic sites onto the lifestyles, desires, and cultural practices and the relationship between the aesthetics and value of television Blackness, suggesting that we have much to learn about both television and race by shifting the focus of our gaze. Scholars like Ralina Joseph consider how celebrities use what she calls situational critiques and strategic ambivalence to navigate modern forms of racism and sexism in the media while protecting their image. Other scholars like Alfred Martin focus on production strategies, writer's rooms, and close readings of representational strategies to show how Black cast situation comedies shore up heteronormative Blackness by casting Black gay male characters in narratives where they are expendable.[18]

In *Double Negative*, Racquel Gates claims that the popular objects discursively understood as "bad objects" that dominate popular cable and broadcast television's landscape, by her reckoning invite critical interpretation as expressions of the meanings, feelings, emotional life, and Black structures of feeling.[19] For Gates, the critical potential of the idea of double negative opens pathways to analyze performances and practices of love, attachment, and care. Similarly Eva Hageman looks to HGTV house-hunting, make-over, and rehab franchises for insights into how Black consumers navigate the housing market, the racial machinations of banking and the real estate industry, and their effect on Black home buyers and the meaning of home ownership among Black people.[20] The racial and class contradictions she argues are on display in these popular shows.[21]

In *Queer Times, Black Futures*, film and media scholar Kara Keeling combines the insights of Eduard Glissant, Beth Coleman, Afrofuturism, queer theory, and Black feminist theory to advance a vision of cultural politics routed through queering or the refusal of Blackness to regard itself in terms of whiteness, heteronormativity, techno-utopia, and the liberal commitment to civic and cultural legibility demanded by the neoliberal state and market. Keeling's vision of Black futures turns instead on the Black and brown, queer and feminist radical social relations and cultural imaginaries that reside in (and circulate through) the sonic densities and sensibilities of embodied experience, Black epistemologies, freedom dreams, and relations of intimacy and belonging.[22]

The insights of Keeling, Gates, Hageman, Martin, Gates, and Gillespie open different itineraries for a critical politics of culture commensurate to the conditions of possibility in which we find ourselves. As we enter the second decade of the 21st century, we are especially sympathetic to Gates and Gillespie observation that "the new approaches must insist on reading the artistic and epistemological consequences of Black film and media: the very idea of Black film and media is defined by historiography over history, performativity over essential identity, affectivity over embodied truth."[23] Indeed, they proceed from theoretical and methodological view that "each creative work tacitly details a discursive conceit and a set of aesthetic choices that represent speculations and remediations of history and culture."[24]

In terms of Gates and Gillespie's suggestion to find new analytics, objects, and discursive strategies with which to see and experience television Blackness, what might we learn from RAF? What does the example of RAF teach television and media scholars, activists, and critics about the politics of representation and about the conditions of television production of Blackness, Black worlds, imagination, and care? In the end the show strikes us as a kind of love letter to Black people; one fashioned with hope, ingenuity, and courage. As with *Tongues Untied*, RAF stakes claims, tells stories, and makes images for Black people from within Black worlds of concern and regard. It is not just the distinctive style of telling stories, world building, and the quirky characters; nor is it the urgency of concerns that Nance and his collaborators gather that deserves our critical attention. Rather it is that RAF has the audacity and the intelligence to tell so many important stories over the course of just six 30-minute episodes in the process actualizing the potential of television not just to construct legible Black folk for the pleasures of whiteness or the legibility of Blackness but to insist on opacity as a resource and the potential of television as a technology for engaging the cares, desires, and fantasies of Black people.

Coda

Random Acts of Flyness emerges during a moment when the way we consume television and the way the television industry delivers television content to audiences has changed dramatically. These changes include the ways that technology companies and social media platforms shape our access to content, and how users of these platforms increase our awareness of the racial, gender, and sexual inequalities in pay, employment through hashtags like #BlackLivesMatter, #MeToo, and #OscarSoWhite. These technology-based interventions and movements call out the abuses of power in film, television, gaming, and the technology industry that reinforce the need to include care into our discussions of television. The creation and mobilization of these hashtags also indicate that television and media are also the objects of critical policy disputes, cultural criticism, and activism by Black, brown, gay, lesbian, and women activists. With the increasing entrenchment of digital technologies in our everyday lives and how these technologies impact social justice movements and our awareness of Black histories of struggle and resistance, we also see television as a cultural means for producing Blackness and a means of affirming Black people's conception of Black life and freedom. We live in an economy of visibility where television, as a technology of race, plays a crucial role culturally and socially in making class and race inequalities appear natural and an inevitable part of American life.

In this chapter we use RAF to probe some of the possibilities that are conditioned by the current circumstances of American media and television especially as they bear on issues of Black safety, security, care, and conceptions of Black freedom. We are particularly interested in the opportunities, strategies, and effects that *Tongues Untied* conditioned for Black show runners, directors, and writers, and how RAF engages with, perhaps even, advances, cultural politics that actualize the potential of media and television as technologies of Blackness. In other words, we want to think about *Tongues Untied* as a case study in the politics of care rather than just a strategy of representation concerned with questions of visibility, parity, and inclusion of Black images in the media. Furthermore, we want to think about RAF with *Tongues Untied* aesthetically and politically to help us see the terms in which RAF addresses Black concerns with care, love, vulnerability, death, and silence.

We have been suggesting that by elucidating some of the innovations Riggs introduced with *Tongues Untied*, RAF may offer media studies scholars and critics a way of thinking differently about the politics of representation and the representation of Blackness in the landscape of Peak TV. RAF's innovation is its command of sketch television to gather and engage concerns of Black people. As a text, RAF mobilizes and critically uses Blackness as a critique of television and race. RAF constructs a Black field of vision, epistemology, and ontology where the legibility of Blackness and the meanings it gathers does not depend on the authorization of whiteness and power. As such, RAF uses television and Blackness to mine another field of vision and register that constitutes a distinct ontology and different epistemology and affect through which to see, feel, and know Black imaginations of freedom. RAF's critical use of its form is brilliant, too, in its engagement with cinema theory, media studies, critical African American studies, women of color feminist, and queer studies.

We have not said very much about the reception of RAF, especially the range of positions and angle of vision that its mobilization and deployment includes and excludes. There is much more to say for instance about RAF strategies of representation and use of television as a technology of Blackness in relationship to some of its contemporaries—*Atlanta, A Black Lady Sketch Show*, and *Insecure*. The most successful of these series make their mark by bringing new content to the screen at a time when cracks in the system of production and industry practices from casting to writers' rooms are undergoing change. This and the recalibration of risks, financialization, and political expediency adds up to new opportunities for new voices and stories. We most certainly think RAF benefits from this crack in the system as well.

But here we want to try to go further than merely acknowledging the space of new voices that appear in the cracks and crevices of a reconfigured industrial system. This stance strikes us as the latest instantiation of a dance that scholars, critics, industry, and activists continue to dance in relationship to the politics of representation that are foundational to the stories we tell and see and the critical questions we ask of them. We would like to consider more carefully for a moment what it means to think with RAF about questions we ask about the relationship between a critical project of television as a technology of Blackness that mobilizes a different way of thinking about television at the limit of its depiction of Black people and a politics of representation and industrial change. Such questions involve fundamental issues of power and, therefore, exceed the limits and capacities of a cultural politics where diversity and inclusion, visibility and recognition are often ends in themselves. This managerial discourse of diversity in the media and the racial politics of recognition on which it depends directs critical scholarship and research away from the promise of critical projects like those that Riggs anticipated and toward technology of race, patriarchy, sexism, homophobia and which Black heteronormativity and visibility insures. Thinking critically with RAF stands to queer our times, as Keeling writes not only by producing a legible Blackness that we recognize, but by critically imagining a Blackness that demands a reckoning with Black difference and a critique television as a technology of race. Such an engagement helps make explicit the condition under which different kinds of Black imagination, concerns, and approaches to the role of television in cultural politics can be thought.

We point to Nance and Riggs not as exceptions in the struggle over the politics of representation of Blackness but as an example of what Angela Davis has in mind when she observes that culture "prepare[s] people emotionally for social change;" they help us see and understand the conditions of possibility for programs like *RAF, Insecure, Atlanta, Black Lady Sketch Comedy Show, I May Destroy You, Sherman's Showcase,* and *Lovecraft Country*. It is easy to say that these shows and others in this moment of Peak TV reflect the slow but steady liberalization and diversification of television, especially on questions of gender, race, sexuality, and ethnicity. In the end, our observations are not so much proscriptive as diagnostic so we are suggesting that RAF challenges us, insists really, to ask different questions about television as a technology of Blackness.

Why are we surprised, for instance, to see and hear the work of Audre Lorde, bell hooks, and feminist of color explicitly referenced in RAF and not be reduced to bad objects of liberal Hollywood condescension? This is what we mean by RAF insisting that we ask different questions of it and to ask them differently including interrogating our own expectations and surprises. So, we are saying that our work as critical scholars matter; the perspectives we ponder can help rearrange the order of our thinking, especially how we regard the objects of our work and the relationships in which they are embedded and those that they in turn help to conjure and structure.

Over 30 years ago, in *Tongues Untied*, Marlon Riggs said Black men loving Black men is a revolutionary act. To see Black men, people who are non-binary and/ or trans, Black children, Black women, gamers, and Latinx folks communing and making community with each other on television should not be a revolutionary act 30 years later, But it is. It is time we start to ask different questions about Black desire and care. *Tongues Untied* and RAF urge that in addition to the annual census and inventories of how many Black, brown, women, gay, lesbian and trans people are on television that we also interrogate what concerns, knowledges, and imaginations the latest instantiation of television mobilizes and asks us to care about and to what end?

Notes

1 Herman Gray, "Subject(ed) to recognition." *American Quarterly* 65, (4): 771–798.
2 This chapter is concerned with Black life. However, we acknowledge that our current political moment creates multiple registers of concern. For example, the alliance of neo-liberal market sovereignty, governance, and racial and ethnic transparency as a pre-requisite for civic membership and social value is most evident in the draconian measures of the Trump administration's immigration policy toward migrants from Central America and Mexico whose language, history, and culture mark their racial and ethnic differences as the source of suspicion by the Trump administration about their loyalty and trustworthiness for citizenship.

3 Herman Gray, "Race, media and the cultivation of concern." *Communication and Critical Cultural Studies* 10 (2–3): 253–258.

4 Kara Keeling, *Queer Times, Black Futures* (New York: New York University Press, 2019).

5 Achille Mbembe, *Black Reason* (Durham, NC: Duke University Press, 2017).

6 "*Random Acts of Flyness* (HBO)," PeabodyAwards.com, Accessed October 16, 2020. www.peabodyawards.com/award-profile/random-acts-of-flyness.

7 The 2020 television season also contained other shows that depicted complex narratives of Black life and care. Some of the shows we recommend viewing are *I May Destroy You* (BBC), *Watchman* (HBO-Max), *Lovecraft Country* (HBO-Max).

8 *Tongues Untied* was initially broadcast on public television and at the time created a storm of controversy in Congress and the media over its content. See, Frank Prial J, "TV film about Gay Blacks is under attack," *New York Times,* June 25, 1991, https://www.nytimes. com/1991/06/25/movies/tv-film-about-gay-black-men-is-under-attack.html.

9 Alfred Martin also shows homo-normativity in Black cast situation comedies. See Alfred L. Martin Jr., *The Generic Closet: Black Gayness and the Black-Cast Sitcom* (Bloomington: Indiana University Press, 2021).

10 Racquel Gates and Michael Boyce Gillespie, "An introduction," *Film Quarterly* 71(2): 9–11.

11 For more on "matters of concern," see Bruno Latour, "Why has critique run out of steam? From matters of fact to matters of concern." *Critical Inquiry* 30 (Winter 2004): 225–248.

12 Shows like *Insecure* and *Atlanta* also seem to share a similar relationship to the onscreen Blackness it imagines.

13 Lorraine Ali, "Commentary: Streaming TV sparked a creative revolution. Now it's at risk of losing its edge," *Los Angeles Times,* October 10, 2019.

14 Saidiya Hartman, *Lose Your Mother: A Journey along the Atlantic Slave Route* (New York: Farrar, Straus and Giroux, 2007).

15 Ali, "Commentary."

16 Other content programs in the shared brand platforms like HBO, Netflix, and FX occasionally explore similar conventions and topics. In Season 3, an *Atlanta* infomercial episode, Black and white hipster liberals with insider knowledge of Blackness and Africa make an appearance. Similarly, RAF stages an extended sketch about a liberal do-good filmmaker pitches a film about rescuing an imaginary Black child from some place in the "third world."

17 Racquel Gates and Michael Boyce Gillespie, "An introduction," *Film Quarterly* 71(2): 9–11.

18 Martin, *The Generic Closet.*

19 Raquel J. Gates, *Double Negative: The Black Image and Popular Culture* (Durham, NC: Duke University Press, 2018).

20 Ava C. Hageman, "Debt by design: Race and home valorization on reality TV," pp. 221-245 in Sarah Banet Weiser, Roopali Mukherjee, and Herman Gray (Eds.), *Racism, Postrace* (Durham, NC: Duke University Press, 2019).

21 Patrick Johnson, Assistant Professor at Sonoma State University, has been trying to make sense of the way that the generation of Black viewers raised on a diet of hip-hop and television reruns of Black cast programming from the 1980s cultivate novel viewing habits by locating themselves within the context of Black discursive practices and cultural meanings shaped largely by hip-hop and Black case re-runs from the 1980s and 1990s. According to Johnson these viewing practices and the meanings that they engender produce televisual memories anchored by the connection between the sonic grammar of hip-hop production, performance and consumption and the televisual world building

of Black situation comedies like *The Jefferson's, Martin, Girlfriends, The Fresh Prince of Bel-Air.* According to Johnson's account, these viewing practices among Black millennials is a way of remembering, producing, and re-ordering a cultural past about Blackness that they know and are able to creatively access by television and mixing it with the cut and mix sampling logic of hip-hop. When students in his study watched Black cast re-runs through the logic of sonic samples—they borrowed liberally from their sonic archive, their parents' memories, and popular culture of the moment recombining these elements into a new television experience now. Johnson suggests that this savvy logic and practice of textual production by his students requires deep knowledge and command of the archive of Black cast television and thus constitutes a kind of epistemology so often missing in our readings of Black television texts. Patrick Johnson (2018). *B(l)ack like it never left: race, resonance, and reruns* [Dissertation]. University of California, Berkeley.

22 Avery F. Gordon, *The Hawthorn Archive: Letters from the Utopian Margins* (New York: Fordham University Press, 2017), Keeling, *Queer Times, Black Futures.*

23 Gates and Gillespie, "An introduction," 10.

24 Ibid., 10.

3

BURY ME IN THE OCEAN

Marvel's Black Panther and the Politics of Performative Wokeness

Artel Great

The social and historical context surrounding *Marvel's Black Panther* (2018) is, in many ways, just as intriguing as the film itself. The movie arrived at a fascinating moment when several Black cultural producers were enjoying tremendous success in Hollywood. Television show creator Shonda Rhimes was at the height of her network powers with the smash hit *Scandal* (2012–2018) on ABC. Both Barry Jenkins' *Moonlight* (2016) and Jordan Peele's *Get Out* (2017) transcended the indie film scene to become commercial and critical darlings. Each film brought in significant financial returns at the box-office and each director snagged Academy Award wins. At the same time, Beyoncé's breakthrough visual album *Lemonade* (2016) enunciated her arrival as an artist of politically Black engagement. Of course, there was also Kendrick Lamar's magnum opus *To Pimp a Butterfly* (2015), which provided infectious hip-hop anthems for the movement for Black lives. Both records came on the heels of the reclusive musician D'Angelo's release of his long-awaited and critically acclaimed protest album *Black Messiah* (2014). During this same period, the hip-hop Pulitzer Prize winner Kendrick Lamar delivered a polemical performance at the 58th Grammy Awards ceremony that critiqued police violence and mass incarceration. While Beyoncé slayed audiences into "formation" both at Super Bowl XLVII and the Coachella Valley Music and Arts Festival with performances that foregrounded the celebration of unapologetic Blackness. Each of the above instances evinced the rising social and cultural energies around a renewed spirit of Black resistance; however, this 21st century phase of the civil rights movement also signaled lucrative commercial possibilities for major corporations eager to capitalize on the vast earning potential of politically Black artistic expressions.

Some cultural critics and media scholars quickly pronounced this moment as the dawn of a "new Black renaissance." Or, perhaps more apropos, what one might describe as yet another fleeting wave of hyper-Blackness in Hollywood.[1] Ironically, or perhaps, predictably, this "new renaissance" was birthed under a precarious cloud

DOI: 10.4324/9781003079682-4

of anger and disaffection in America, with Black protestors taking to the streets en masse. Outrage erupted across the country after the acquittal of the murderer of Trayvon Martin, the Black teenager who left a Florida convenience store with a bag of Skittles and a can of iced tea, excited to return home and watch the NBA All Star game on TV. But young Trayvon never made it back home; instead, he was gunned down by a white vigilante. What followed was a series of social uprisings that spread like wildfire across the nation. More rebellions were ignited months later as the response of furious citizens weary of watching a tragic parade of high-profile state-sanctioned police killings of unarmed Black men like Eric Garner in New York, Oscar Grant in California, Mike Brown in Missouri, and Freddie Gray in Maryland—each heart-rending loss gripping the nation more tightly by the throat. From this horrific loss emerged collective acts of resistance that thrust the movement for Black lives into the forefront of mainstream consciousness. Suddenly, rich and previously passive Black athletes and artists, across various sports and disciplines, boldly raised their voices and leveraged their celebrity platforms to call for social justice and align themselves with the Black freedom movement. It is within this equally depressing and scintillating context that *Marvel's Black Panther* activated a national and international wave of commercial excitement, rabid fandom, and mainstream celebration. Enthusiasm for the film revolves around common conceptions of the picture's "revolutionary" achievement as a landmark victory in Black expressive culture that broke through in dominant cinema.

Pundits and scholars alike applauded the film's employment of dark-skinned Black leading actors, Ruth Carter's sumptuous Oscar-winning costume design, and the symbolic depiction of the fictitious nation-state of Wakanda as a turning point in Hollywood. Yet, the film also conjures disturbing questions about its legitimacy as a radical product of Black cinema; and spur-of-the-moment laudatory assessments of the picture indicate, to some degree, a lack of acknowledgment. Most obviously, regarding the film's use of a vocabulary of Blackness born out of a complicated ideological register that is, quite frankly, antipodal to the emancipatory racial politics the film is said to espouse.

Underneath *Marvel's Black Panther's* "revolutionary" patina lies an aesthetics of racialization, an overly simplistic approach toward understanding otherness, and an ideology that upholds status quo ethics of racial hierarchies, which, regrettably, positions the film as yet another exercise in the furtive deployment of Hollywood's greatest superpower—the power of co-optation. It is true that entertainment juggernauts Marvel and Walt Disney Studios joined forces to bring the film to the silver screen at a social and cultural moment that perfectly coincided with a new, very public crusade for Black lives and the rise of the so-called woke movement in the popular (white) imagination. Mind you, this contemporary crusade for Black freedom occurred despite the mythical achievement of a "post-racial" society. Lest we forget how swiftly America was declared "post-racial" by countless talking heads and "experts" after the election of Barack Obama to the nation's highest political office. It should not be overlooked that during the eight years of the Obama administration, America's racial demons were savagely reinvigorated and unleashed with particular ferocity as the country was swept up by a flood of Black tears flowing from the previously described, seemingly endless, stream of police killings. Hence, the phrase "stay woke" rose from the streets of Black communities as both a mantra and a rallying cry for Black people who acknowledged the fallacies of a post-racial America. Or, more aptly, the phrase was invented by, as the great James Baldwin so eloquently put it, the Black-Americans who were now "alerted to the necessity of waking up."[2] Sadly, the pro-Black idiom, "stay woke" has subsequently been hijacked and truncated to just one word, "woke" and given a negative, non-Black, neoliberal connotation in the corporate media environment and popular imaginary.

Although the symbolic victories and material disappointments of the Obama years soon gave way to a reoccurring, visceral white backlash, one fact remained true—politically Black artistic expressions had successfully been monetized corporately and proven wildly popular and profitable, a fact that runs antipodal to the aims and outcomes of the 1950s Civil Rights Movement. Within this messy and complicated social and historical moment *Marvel's Black Panther* became possible and gave rise to what I call the politics of *performative wokeness*—that is, the exploitation and co-optation of the aesthetics of radical political-Blackness to drive financial profits and satisfy corporate incentives, as opposed to the sincere expression of, or veritable commitment, to liberatory Black cultural politics and principles. It is my contention that both Disney and Marvel Studios deploy the film as a profit-driven corporate strategy of performative wokeness, exploiting the signs, symbols, and music of the Black resistance movement without ever attaching the film's ideology to the movement itself. Nor do the studios wield their considerable corporate power and political influence to advance or support broader Black communities' demands for social justice.

This essay provides a reflective space that offers a more complicated reading of *Marvel's Black Panther*. To that extent, my analysis proposes a counternarrative against the grain of the standard effusive readings of the film and, most notably, its declaration as a "revolutionary" text in the canon of Black cinema. It is crucial to consider the broader cultural and industrial context of *Marvel's Black Panther* in order to understand the film's engagement with the politics of performative wokeness. In effect, the film represents the full embodiment of Hollywood's masterful self-fashioning and operates as a direct expression of the co-optation and cultural appropriation of the signs and symbols of 21st-century Black social protest. The aim here is to demonstrate the ways that Hollywood's dominant cinema not only shapes popular culture and notions of identity but how the industry itself, in so many ways, is dependent on Black expressive culture for its primary source material, co-opting, commodifying, appropriating, repackaging, and redistributing Black culture back to Black audiences—empty of any genuine social depth. From this perspective, *Marvel's Black Panther,* with a visuality that signifies "wokeness" (a term redefined and appropriated in mainstream media from the resistant Black vernacular, anti-racist expression "stay woke") offers the appearance of Black solidarity while still upholding the dominant cinema's racialized status quo. As a result, the film's underlying ideological register remains firmly rooted in the politics of safety for white consumers.

It is imperative to state that the object of study in this chapter will be referred to as *Marvel's Black Panther* rather than simply "Black Panther." This is intended to serve as a critical distinction between the fictional Hollywood film and real-life members of the Black Panther Party for Self-Defense, who rose to global prominence in the 1960s during the Black Power Movement. My aim is to circumvent the cultural erasure of Black history and contributions in the American social imagination and to preserve the legacies of freedom fighters like Huey P. Newton, Bobby Seale, Fred Hampton, Elaine Brown, Alprentice "Bunchy" Carter, John and Erica Huggins, Kathleen Cleaver, David Hilliard, Bobby Rush, Mark Clark, Geronimo Pratt, Lil' Bobby Hutton, and countless other *real* Black Panthers: many of whom were wrongfully imprisoned or lost their lives for the cause of Black freedom. Consequently, the name Black Panther must forever be synonymous with the influence of those comrades who fought vociferously against American systemic racism and exhibited a deep commitment to revolutionary love for Black people. The memory and legacy of the *real* Black Panthers must not be forgotten, no matter how many billions of dollars are generated from Marvel comic books or Hollywood tentpole films that appropriate their moniker.

At a time of surging anti-Black violence in a racially tense America, there are a deluge of prima facie interpretations of *Marvel's Black Panther* as a "revolutionary" cinematic text, both in academic and popular circles. One reason for this view is the symbolic arrival of the film within the aforementioned context of notions of a "new Black renaissance." The film's symbolic Blackness seems to challenge the social structures of embittered whiteness that were intent on flexing its political muscles to roll back Civil Rights–era voting laws, while white politicians turned a blind eye to state-sanctioned violence against Black bodies. This daunting reality coupled with an overwhelming sense of Black exhaustion with the endless physical and digital streams of vexing racial conflict led to modern echoes of Fannie Lou Hammer's poignant proclamation (re)appearing on protest placards, T-shirts, and Twitter hashtags—Black-Americans had, once again, become "sick and tired of being sick and tired."

Hollywood has long specialized in serving audiences heavy doses of escapism. From the very beginning, movies were marked as a working-class form of entertainment, and not surprisingly, movie-going peaked in the United States during the Great Depression. As Carlos Stevens reminds us,

> throughout most of the Depression, Americans went assiduously, devotedly, almost compulsively, to the movies...the movies offered a chance to escape the cold, the heat, and loneliness; they brought strangers together, rubbing elbows in the dark of movie palaces and fleapits, sharing in the one social event available to everyone.[3]

Over 60 million Americans per week flocked to movie theaters during the Depression. While the number of weekly movie-goers has certainly declined over the last 80 years, Black communities continue to overconsume motion pictures, composing nearly 23 percent of the monthly U.S. movie audience, while making up only 12 percent of the total population.[4]

At the heart of the Hollywood tradition of escapism lies the idea of spectatorial pleasure. The industry operates under the assumption that its pleasure-inducing film aesthetics, coupled with ubiquitous and aggressive marketing campaigns, can create mass audiences and drive enormous box-office returns. This Hollywood formula has been refined and systematized to bring in significant financial profits despite its movies' often regressive cultural politics. Todd Berliner argues that "Hollywood cinema offers viewers certain predictable psychological experiences, which, at a general level, include processing fluency, cognitive challenge, emotional intensity and variety, imagination, and arousal."[5] These characteristics compose what Berliner calls the "Hollywood aesthetic." One crucial aspect of the popular reception of *Marvel's Black Panther* is derived from the film's ability to elicit aesthetic pleasure for Black audiences. The film successfully generates in Black viewers a specific type of thrill-seeking gratification that is the trademark of slick, big-budget Hollywood movies—an experience historically reserved for white films that cater to white audiences.

Marvel's Black Panther, on the other hand, offers the same trademark Hollywood aesthetic; however, it does so, with its sights trained on Black cultural specificity. For many Black movie-goers the film soothes a deep sense of dissatisfaction and alienation felt while watching Hollywood films that traditionally devalue or ignore Black experiences altogether. In this sense, the film is rather significant. Yet, one cannot escape the reality that *Marvel's Black Panther* is based on a comic book character manufactured in the white imagination: an invention of two white men, Stan Lee and Jack Kirby. In the 1960s, Lee launched his "Black Panther" character as a minor spin-off of the *Fantastic Four* comic book series. When considering that Stan Lee is responsible for creating the African nation of Wakanda and its warrior king T'Challa (portrayed in the film by Chadwick Boseman), the white origins of *Marvel's Black Panther* provoke pertinent questions about artistic perspective, creative ownership, and cultural appropriation.

The film is lauded for its originality, although its narrative content and structure are ironically quite conventional. At the heart of the motion picture lies a father–son drama set in a technologically advanced distant land where the son, T'Challa, must endure the "hero's journey" to realize his true purpose beyond the shadow of T'Chaka (John Kani), his powerful father. Upon further scrutiny, with an eye toward film history, *Marvel's Black Panther* bears striking similarities to George Lucas' seminal creation, *Star Wars* (1977). Both films engage larger-than-life operatic tales of tangled father and son dynamics. Each son must ultimately reject the father's identity to realize his true power and carry on the family legacy in his own unique manner. While *Star Wars* is set in a galaxy far, far away, the lush beauty and fantastical technology of the isolationist, never colonized, uber-wealthy, militaristic African monarchy of Wakanda feels light years away from the earthly realities of modern Africa and its Diaspora. Both films feature epic battles with exotic spaceships and innovative flying aircraft, high-tech weaponry, obligatory romantic subplots, and emphasize world-building philosophically tinged mythologies.

Star Wars' mythology is rooted in the philosophy of the Jedi. The Jedi Order is a monastic, military institution with an ascetic spiritual tradition. The Jedi Knights wield an extraordinary power known as the "Force," an all-encompassing, ubiquitous metaphysical energy present in every aspect of the universe. The Jedi's ability to employ the Force comes with great responsibility and requires years of intense training of the mind. On the other hand, *Marvel's Black Panther's* mythology is grounded in the fictional world of Wakanda and the philosophy of Afrofuturism. Like the Jedi Knights, the warrior monk guardians of peace and justice in the *Star Wars* universe, "Black Panther" is a title earned by Wakanda's warrior king and supreme leader upon emerging victorious from the battle against those who seek to oppose his reign.

In the far distant past, Wakanda was struck by Mena Ngai, a powerful meteorite composed of a rare element known as vibranium, a fictional metal noted for its ability to release and store massive amounts of kinetic energy. This valuable natural resource is only found in Wakanda. It has enabled the country to build the most technologically advanced society on earth—that has deliberately concealed its resources and isolated itself from the rest of the world. The desire among many Black-Americans to escape into an Afrofuture where we are no longer "targets" but rather the arbiters of our bodies, resources, and social destinies is not a new phenomenon. Black artists have long envisioned alternative worlds where they are fully empowered, self-governing, and experience themselves beyond the white gaze and in the absence of white affliction. Mark Dery describes this form of cultural expression as Afrofuturism or "speculative fiction that treats African-American themes and addressed African-American concerns in the context of the 20th-century technoculture—and, more generally, African American signification that appropriates images of technology and a prosthetically enhanced future."[6] Afrofuturism encompasses literature and philosophy, music, fashion, film, television, and ever-expanding forms of cultural and critical thought. From the brilliant literary worlds achieved by writers Octavia Butler and Samuel R. Delany to the sacred soundscapes of musicians like Sun Ra and the funky mothership connections of George Clinton's Parliament, the philosophies and visual aesthetics of Afrofuturism have played a significant role in Black-American culture and its self-fashioning. Alisha Acquaye argues that by "making use of Afrocentricity; African magic realism; African mythologies; African aesthetics and traditions; all of which are intertwined with technology, sci-fi, and social awareness, Afrofuturism narrates a parallel or distant reality that is empowering and effervescent."[7] The mythology of *Marvel's Black Panther* also engages ancestral reverence and rites of passage ceremonies as a part of ancient African practices and spiritual traditions.

Likewise, *Star Wars* and *Marvel's Black Panther* both represent significant markers in the development of what Justin Wyatt calls the "high concept" film. This term describes a production model and brand of commercial filmmaking that originated in the 1970s post-classical Hollywood period when marketing and economic factors became the driving force behind greenlighting a studio picture. At the core of a high-concept blockbuster is its condensability into a simple 25-word "pitch" that expresses the film's themes and captures the audience's attention. Studio executives then deploy massive film marketing campaigns derived from the pitch to ultimately reap enormous dividends at the box-office. Wyatt argues that high-concept movies are "a form of differentiated product within the mainstream film industry. This differentiation occurs in two major ways: through an emphasis on style within the films and through an integration with marketing and merchandising."[8] Ironically, this undiluted advancement of commercialism in Hollywood motion picture production was super-charged during the 1970s by a motley crew of American independent directors subsequently labeled the "Film School Generation," "Movie Brats," or "New Hollywood." This network of filmmakers that includes Francis Ford Coppola, George Lucas, Brian De Palma, Steven Spielberg, and Martin Scorsese were classically trained in university film programs and were inspired by the pantheon of European art film directors during the 1960s like Bergman, Truffaut, Fellini, and Godard.[9]

Hollywood's industrial focus on high-concept blockbusters is inextricably linked to the mega-success of two pictures helmed by Film School Generation directors: Spielberg's *Jaws* (1975) and Lucas' *Star Wars*. Both films elicited major strategic changes in Hollywood production practices. In recent years, high-concept movies have been described as franchise films, blockbusters, or tentpole films and have become the rage among Hollywood executives clamoring for scripts with simple narratives that are easily communicated through marketing in a way that more complex, harder to explain films are not. The studios' overemphasis on advertising campaigns and marketing strategies increased their potential to generate higher profits from merchandising and ancillary revenue streams.[10] Ironically, the high-concept mode of production runs antithetical to the independent spirit of the Film School Generation directors who were driven by a passion to express an iconoclastic vision of American auteurism. Some critics argue that Lucas and Spielberg are largely responsible for the deterioration of mainstream American cinema. David Thomson has long attributed the film industry's oversaturation of childlike movies (now repackaged as superhero blockbusters) to the brand of cinema spurred on by the films of Spielberg and Lucas, particularly movies dependent on computer-generated imagery and spectacular special effects technology as their central quality of attraction.[11] The recreation of adolescent pleasures like uncomplicated fun and fantasy, coupled with the fastidious attention to art design, production design, and costuming at the heart of *Star Wars*, distinguishes the film as the progenitor of the world-building, comic-book-style movie aesthetic from which *Marvel's Black Panther* descends. Unlike any film before it, *Star Wars* gripped the global popular imagination and launched an array of wildly successful sequels, merchandising opportunities, toys and video games, clothing, books, and beyond.

Marvel's Black Panther extends the cinematic tradition of *Star Wars* and modernizes the high-concept film by adopting an aesthetics of racialization. This is most notable in the film's foregrounding of Black characters and themes within a genre, budget range, style, and mode of production typically reserved for white directors and white movies. The film's arrival at a cultural moment that collides with increased mainstream acceptance of politically Black visual aesthetics functions to enhance *Marvel's Black Panther's* resonance with audiences. Marvel Studios and Disney executives strategically conflated their profit-driven interests with the ambitions of Black creative talent, both behind-the-scenes and on-camera. Hence, the film stands out as a differentiated product in a marketplace where American cinema has historically normalized white male superhero movies through countless recycled depictions of *Batman, Superman,* and *Spider-Man* dating as far back as the early 1940s.

While *Marvel's Black Panther* is by far the most profitable Black superhero movie, it is not the first. The earliest Black superhero films emerged during the Blaxploitation era in Hollywood when films like *Shaft* (1971), *Foxy Brown* (1974), and *Abar: The First Black Superman* (1977) combined inner-city street iconography with action-adventure themes and superhero motifs. In the 1990s, Black superhero films took a comedic turn with Robert Townsend's social comedy *Meteor Man* (1993) and the big-screen adaptation of *Blankman* (1994), based on Damon Wayans' popular character on the breakout sketch comedy series, *In Living Color* (1990–1994). Both *Meteor Man* and *Blankman* were major financial flops. And in 1997, Hall of Fame NBA player Shaquille O'Neal took his turn starring in the Black super-hero film *Steel*, which also bombed at the box-office.

However, the 1990s ended with two popular Black superhero movies *Spawn* (1997) and *Blade* (1998). Each film showcased the martial arts talents of actors Michael Jai White and Wesley Snipes. Both pictures were helmed by white dir-ectors as adaptations of Black comic book characters created in the white imagin-ation. *Spawn* grossed nearly $90 million for New Line Cinema on a $40 million budget. Wesley Snipes' *Blade* grossed over $130 million on a $45 million budget and generated two sequels, *Blade II* (2002) and *Blade: Trinity* (2004), each bringing in over $130 million at the box-office. The *Blade* series is a crucial marker that set the stage for Marvel Studios' future success in comic book feature film adaptations—a fact that is largely overlooked in superhero film discourse. Rounding out the 2000s, *Hancock* (2008), starring Will Smith as a disreputable superhero with a pen-chant for self-destructive behavior, became the most successful Black superhero film prior to *Marvel's Black Panther. Hancock* was produced by Columbia Pictures for $150 million and raked in a remarkable $630 million at the box-office, making it the fourth highest-grossing film of the year. It is worthy to note that *Spawn, Blade,* and *Hancock,* three highly profitable Black superhero films, highlight Black male protagonists that are deeply flawed and disconnected from Black social issues, politics, and communities and, in many ways, reinforce racist ideology of Black men as socially troublesome—despite their superhero status. In that regard, *Marvel's Black Panther* stands out among these Black superhero pictures with its deep reson-ance with audiences. It is the only such film that manages to engender the type of pageantry and cult following of major franchises like *Star Wars, Harry Potter* (2001), and *Pirates of the Caribbean* (2003).

It is also instructive to point out that *Marvel's Black Panther's* employment of Afrofuturist mythology offers entertainment value by activating a scopophilic pleasure for Black audiences. For the first time, a Hollywood film openly targeted Black folks with the big-budget, state-of-the-art cinematic special effects treatment, and the mega-marketing usually reserved for white films. The formal beauty and visually stunning elements of aesthetic value in the movie captivates viewers with an ornate world of advanced technology and the splendors of Black fantasy and science fiction witnessed on the big screen—in IMAX. Yet, *Marvel's Black Panther's* sense of cultural achievement, aesthetic arousal, and intense audience pleasure is troubled by the film's complicated ideological impulses. In fact, the film has been blasted by African critics and scholars like Patrick Gathara and Paul Tiyamba Zeleza for endorsing regressive racial politics and a reductive view of the African continent. Gathara argues *Marvel's Black Panther* is nothing more than a well-executed marketing stratagem.[12]

At the same time, Zeleza critiques the picture's engagement with colonial discourses and tropes. He points to the film's diegetic description of Wakanda as a "tribal nation-state." Zeleza astutely distinguishes such description as a form of cultural denigration. He argues that the employment of the term "tribe" or "tribal" in many African societies represents the colonial equivalent to the "n-word."[13] Put differently, the film's emphasis on tribes and tribalism evokes a white-imagined sense of "African authenticity" and conjures atavistic assumptions and the politics of the primordial that are inherent in colonial discourses. African scholars also draw attention to the film's overreliance on colonial tropes like "tribal" body markings, spears, shields, and wild animalistic chants of the film's African characters. Salim Washington contends that *Marvel's Black Panther* espouses a highly problematic romanticization of African feudalism and patriarchal notions of monarchy that reify Western values and ideals. Washington argues that *Marvel's Black Panther* follows a similar pattern in contemporary Western films about Africa like *Blood Diamond* (2006) and *Last King of Scotland* (2006), which depict African nations and cultures as "exotic but backwards, endowed with riches but mismanaged by superstitious anti-intellectual leaders and cultures, tradition-rich but impotent in the power dynamic of the modern world."[14]

From this perspective, *Marvel's Black Panther* seems to offer a reductive vision, engaging colonial tropes rooted in Hollywood's racist history of atavistic portrayals

FIGURE 3.1 Battle scene in *Marvel's Black Panther.* Screenshot by the author

of African peoples that date back to 1918 and to the *Tarzan* films of the 1930s and 1940s, which helped crystallize white-manufactured images of Africa as the brutal and primitive "dark continent" within the American social imaginary. Patrick Gathara argues that *Marvel's Black Panther* leans on destructive mythoi to depict Africa as a "divided, tribalized continent, discovered by a white man who wants nothing more than to take its mineral resources, a continent run by wealthy, power-hungry, feuding and feudalist elite."[15] For Gathara, Wakanda is depicted as a nation devoid of thinkers and philosophers or intellectual leadership who can aid in the development of a more peaceful transition of power that would eliminate the ultra-violent, intracommunal, fight-to-the-death bloodshed required to ascend to the country's highest leadership position.

On the other hand, one of the film's counternarratives is forged in its depiction of women in the nation of Wakanda. The film's Black women characters assume positions of power in the country, particularly Okoye (Danai Gurira), who is the chief of the Dora Milaje, Wakanda's mighty all-women army of bald Grace Jones–like warriors, and Shuri (Letitia Wright), princess of Wakanda and the nation's innovative lead scientist and technologist. The centrality of women in the film attempts to subvert heteronormative narratives that limit the role of Black women to the margins of the cinematic frame. Such privileging of women in Wakanda emphasizes the film's efforts to engage with Afrofuturism as a critical lens, reimagining African futures and its place for women as a means of resistance. Rosemary Chikafa-Chipiro argues that the film reconfigures representations of Black womanhood through its employment of an Africana womanist perspective. For Chikafa-Chipiro, Africana womanism is "also a reclamation theoretical perspective that seeks to reclaim Black women's identities and subjectivity in the face of western feminist hegemonies."[16] She further argues that *Marvel's Black Panther's* depiction of women represents

> a return to the source of sorts which recalls African women warriors who have been celebrated in the African past but seem to have lost the significance of their prowess over time but still have prospects in a re-invented Africa.[17]

The premise of Africana womanism is central to the film's position that Wakanda is an enlightened nation because it has managed to evade the historical traumas suffered by the rest of the continent.

However, despite Wakanda's vibranium-based techno-wizardry, the scientific genius of the royal Princess Shuri, Angela Bassett's regal strength as Queen Ramonda, and the deft military prowess of the Dora Milaje, the film's efforts to engage a liberatory vision for Black women are hampered by the film's politics and myth-building that remain rooted in the all too familiar Hollywood archetypes and formulas of tokenism. That is to say, the centrality of Wakanda's women represents the tropes of archetypical sidekick characters, occupying space in the mise-en-scène yet remaining subordinate to the more powerful male figures. The film's theoretical positioning of Africana womanism is troubled by the fact that the women in Wakanda appear to play significant roles, yet they do not rule. Instead, their primary purpose is to exist in service of the patriarchy and its methodologies of domination.

Although Okoye leads an all-women battalion of warriors, they still function at the pleasure of T'Challa, the supreme male leader of the Wakandan monarchy. Nakia (Lupita Nyong'o) holds dual roles as a Wakandan spy and T'Challa's fiancée, who, while a capable fighter in her own right, must still be rescued by the Black Panther during an undercover mission. Likewise, Shuri, the embodiment of the Africana womanist ethos in the film, is the light-hearted genius inventor behind Wakanda's technological innovation. Yet, her character's liberatory potential is wasted, relegating her to a female version of Q—aka James Bond's "gadget guy" colleague—whose sole purpose is to supply her brother T'Challa with the latest flourishes of techno-wizardry. Derilene Marco astutely points out that

> despite [*Marvel's Black Panther's*] strong characters, the positioning of this womanhood is never explored further; for example, we never learn why Wakanda has an all-woman army, nor what do we learn why or how Shuri knows everything she knows. A rather powerful intention then, feels somewhat misplaced, as though the film comments on patriarchy without really following through on anything.[18]

Thus, while offering the appearance of subversion, the film's Africana womanist frame of reference ultimately functions as yet another aesthetic prop that maintains Hollywood's traditional representational practices and reifies heteronormative patriarchy.

Given this context, *Marvel's Black Panther,* as a product of the dominant cinema apparatus, establishes an elaborate façade of performative wokeness that elicits a cognitive overreaction from audiences to the film's superficial traits and computer-generated visual spectacle. By virtue of its $200 million budget, the film's visions of Blackness are squarely cemented in social and political-economic parameters that are controlled and produced within the specter of whiteness. Notwithstanding the presence of Ryan Coogler and the wealth of Black talent working on the creative team, *Marvel's Black Panther's* ideological underpinnings do not operate against the grain of dominant society, which continues to repress actual Black liberatory culture and its expressive potentialities. Instead, the film's employment of racial phenomena denotes a strategy of co-optation that engages the concept of performative wokeness by distorting the critical links between aesthetics and politics.

Such distortions are quite pronounced, for instance, in the film's employment of Hollywood's tired and well-worn "white savior" trope, which is embodied in *Marvel's Black Panther* in the form of a Central Intelligence Agency (CIA) operative, no less. The character Everett Ross (Martin Freeman) is a known CIA agent and one of the few white characters in the movie. Ross is initially presented as an adversary to T'Challa. However, during a botched assignment in South Korea to apprehend the villainous arms dealer Ulysses Klaue (Andy Serkis), T'Challa, Shuri, and Nakia choose to rescue Ross, the CIA operative. At this point in the film, the Wakandans form an alliance with Agent Ross even after Shuri, the nation's resident tech genius, derisively describes him as a "colonizer." Regardless, Ross is afforded access into the inner sanctum of Wakanda, and he is freely educated on the advanced technological wonders of their futuristic civilization. Ross' alliance is strangely permitted and easily accepted as a normality despite centuries of Wakanda's deliberate efforts to keep foreigners and the white Western world from entering the borders of its isolationist kingdom. Ross becomes the obligatory white sidekick to T'Challa. And by the end of the film, the CIA operative emerges as a hero. He is deployed to the battlefield and remotely maneuvers a Wakandan fighter jet (which he instantly masters) to shoot down enemy planes transporting hazardous vibranium weapons. Through his valorous actions, Ross, the film's perfunctory "white savior," effectively rescues Wakanda from imminent destruction.

Given the violent and disdainful history between the CIA, the continent of Africa, and progressive civil rights organizations like the Black Panther Party, it is rather suspicious (and frankly appalling) to bear witness to *Marvel's Black Panther's* narratological efforts to ignore, or perhaps erase this murky and brutal legacy. The film demands that we ignore the role the agency played in the assassination of revolutionary African leaders like Patrice Lumumba in the Democratic Republic of Congo, Thomas Sankara in Burkina Faso, and the overthrow of Ghana under Kwame Nkrumah. The picture also requires that we disregard the agency's role in neutralizing and destabilizing the Black freedom movement in the United States.[19] *Marvel's Black Panther's* promulgation of the benevolence of the CIA, however, is a factor that must be critically interrogated. The film compels Black audiences to ignore the disruptive tradition of the agency in Africa, which for decades secretly armed American-friendly regimes, pitting African nations against each other in support of American foreign policy. In her book, *The CIA in Hollywood: How the Agency Shapes Film and Television*, Tricia Jenkins details the historical partnership between the agency and studio executives in Tinsel Town, dating back to the Cold War era of the 1950s. Jenkins unpacks how the agency has long offered scripts and storylines to Hollywood studios to help win over audiences and drum up support for U.S. foreign policy both at home and abroad. Jenkins also poses serious questions regarding the legal and ethical dimensions of U.S. citizens being subjected to agency propaganda or outright "CIA recruitment" efforts through the vehicle of Hollywood films.[20]

Former 1960s activist Tom Hayden, a leading voice in the anti-war movement, points to recent films like *Argo* (2012) and *Zero Dark Thirty* (2012) as "productions the CIA has influenced in the 15 years since the agency opened its official liaison office to Hollywood."[21] Paul Barry, a CIA entertainment industry liaison officer, stated that "Hollywood is the only way that the public learns about the agency."[22] However, Hayden argues that

the agency is looking to plant positive images about itself (in other words, propaganda) through our most popular forms of entertainment. So natural has the CIA–entertainment connection become that few question its legal or moral ramifications… [and] the truth of its operations is not subject to public examination.[23]

The question is, how has such a robust association between the Hollywood industrial complex and the nation's premier institution of spies not been brought under critical public scrutiny? Hayden rightly contends that "when the CIA's hidden persuaders influence a Hollywood movie, it is using a popular medium to spin as favorable an image of itself as possible, or at least, prevent an unfavorable one from taking hold."[24] From this vantage point, *Marvel's Black Panther* endorses thinly veiled propaganda that recycles dangerous cinematic tropes. In effect, the Agent Ross character encourages Black audiences to sympathize and identify with a white CIA operative, which functions to undermine the film's symbols of Black liberation.

Perhaps nowhere else in the film are the tangled webs of white-engineered visions of Blackness more acute and disturbing than in the complicated and messy renderings of the character Eric "Killmonger" Stevens, portrayed masterfully by Michael B. Jordan. Killmonger is presented as the atomic rage-filled villain of this Marvel cinematic tale. Born in Oakland, California, Killmonger's father, N'Jobu (Sterling K. Brown), is a royal prince of Wakanda living in America. His brother, T'Chaka, ultimately murders N'Jobu while Eric is still a child. After the murder, T'Chaka abandons young Eric, his nephew, in the United States and returns to the lush beauty and riches awaiting in Wakanda. This act renders the young boy fatherless and alone, left to fend for himself in the harsh realities of the U.S. inner city, disconnected from his royal lineage.

Killmonger's origin story is an account of personal trauma and the struggles of poor and working-class Black-Americans desperately yearning for a lost ontology. Moreover, he possesses a distinct vulnerability, and a backstory that Tia Tyree and Liezille Jacobs might argue holds the fundamental building blocks for the making of a quintessential superhero. Tyree and Jacobs posit that in traditional superhero lore, an origin story like Killmonger's "spur[s] the need to do something about the world. The hurt of a family member or friend or a sense of internal brokenness fuels the need to become a savior of others."[25] However, in *Marvel's Black Panther*, Killmonger is positioned as a threat to Wakanda and to the world at large, and his objective to help Black people around the planet is condemned as unstable and unsafe.

We are introduced to the adult Eric Killmonger in the Museum of Great Britain as he studies rare African artifacts. In this explosive scene, Killmonger speaks with the museum's "expert" on African history (a white woman) who attempts to educate him on the artifacts assumed seductively primitive origins. However, he is not impressed; he knows the truth. He easily dismantles the white curator's "rhetorical strategies of empire" with all of its European powers of invention. Killmonger understands, as David Spurr aptly put it,

the anxiety of colonial discourse comes from the fact that the colonizer's power depends on the presence, not to say consent, of the colonized. What is power without its object? Authority is in some sense conferred by those who obey it.[26]

Hence, Killmonger refutes the curator's colonial discourse by refusing to adhere to her authority over the artifact in question, in turn, rightly calling out the West's strategies of plunder, domination, and appropriation.

Killmonger casually inquires of the historian/curator, "How do you think your ancestors got these? You think they paid a fair price? Or did they take it, like they take everything else?"[27] His questions swiftly trigger a swarm of museum security. However, Killmonger's objective is to reclaim the artifact and liberate its true purpose and potential, shattering the manners in which "the colonizing imagination takes for granted that the land and its resources belong to those who are best able to exploit them according to the values of the western commercial and industrial system."[28] In this brilliant sequence, Killmonger manages to destabilize status quo discourses concerning European plunder of African nations, which is, by virtue, an insurgent act. He represents an unspoken "Black truth," a counternarrative, if you will, regarding who shall inherit the earth.

Eric Killmonger's primary aim in the film is to use Wakandan resources to aid in the liberation of Black people worldwide. Like many Black-Americans and Africans throughout the Diaspora, he has grown weary of centuries of incessant suffering, trauma, and pain that tends to mark the lives of those living while Black. However, the dominant cinema apparatus, wielding the might of its Hollywood powers of co-optation, utilize the cloak of "street cred" afforded by Ryan Coogler as a Black director, to furtively disseminate the ideology of white hegemony. In effect, the film positions Killmonger as a morally bankrupt anathema, an ultra-violent "*super-thug*," the quintessential vitriolic angry Black male in America stained by the scourge of his enslaved ancestors and forever robbed and separated from the enormous wealth, pride, virtue, and "pure" blood so bequeathed to his first cousin T'Challa in the Motherland.

FIGURE 3.2 Killmonger and the curator in the Museum of Great Britain. Screenshot by the author

By associating Killmonger with violent and regressive traits, *Marvel's Black Panther* coerces audiences to root against him for striving to liberate Black people—by any means necessary. This not-so-subtle shaping of perception coaxes Black audiences into rooting against Black-American interests. The binary between T'Challa and Killmonger's worldviews drives the primary dramatic tension in the movie. Both characters are wrapped in the thorny vines of respectability politics: one deemed "legitimate" and the other "illegitimate." And audiences are carefully guided to align themselves with Boseman's restrained performance as the respectable T'Challa. While Jordan's electric performance as Killmonger leaps from the screen, dripping with charisma and magnetic intensity that must be ultimately rejected. The two characters' contrasting ideological impulses speak to age-old dichotomies in Black political thought, that is, Black-American identity versus continental African identity and cultural nationalism versus Pan-Africanism.

Putting the politics of respectability aside, the psycho-social complexity that undergirds the character of Eric Killmonger extends traditional filmic vocabularies of renegade Blackness and the worn-out Hollywood tropes of *bad* Black male "bucks" that represent a central theme in American cinema's racist ideologies.[29] Such movie characters are easily identifiable by their abject brutality, and buffed and "dangerous" Black bodies, teeming with hypersexuality. At the same time, the film morally contrasts Killmonger with a white CIA operative, who is ultimately redeemed while the Black-American male is condemned. The fatal flaw of *Marvel's Black Panther*, and the true indication of its ideological register, that is, its allegiance with the hegemonic structures of whiteness, lie in the film's pitting Killmonger against T'Challa, while elevating the status of the token "white savior." Such an alignment quells any notions of emancipatory potential but instead reifies the racist status quo to the impairment of Black-American social and political interests. As a result, the film squanders an enormous opportunity to have Killmonger and T'Challa join forces, as allies and blood relatives, to activate a glorious tapestry of intracommunal brotherhood and unity between Africa and Black America on a mission to rid the world of the persistent evils of global whiteness and its hegemonic domination.

Instead, the film reduces Killmonger to a "super-thug" whose uber-violent tendencies appear haphazard and centered on bloodlust. However, this rendering oversimplifies and mischaracterizes his objective of global decolonization. The question is, what is the real nature of Killmonger's violence? He understands, quite simply, that he and his Black sisters and brothers around the world are the "*wretched of the earth*." His approach toward global decolonization puts into daring practice the philosophical treatise of Franz Fanon, who wrote eloquently about Black liberation through the processes of decolonization. Fanon points out that "colonialism is not a thinking machine, nor a body endowed with reasoning faculties. It is violence in its natural state, and it will only yield when confronted with greater violence."[30] In this view, Eric Killmonger is acutely aware, as is Fanon, that in order to truly liberate Africa and its Diasporic peoples from brutal regimes of western colonialism, one must adopt the *lingua franca* of the colonizer.

In other words, Killmonger recognizes that the only language the colonizer truly understands is that of force and violence. Franz Fanon succinctly describes this relationship in his landmark text, *The Wretched of the Earth*, revealing the nature and uses of violence in the colonial context.

> National liberation, national renaissance, the restoration of nationhood to the people: whatever may be the headings used or the new formulas introduced, decolonization is always a violent phenomenon. Decolonization is a historical process. It cannot be understood, it cannot become clear to itself except by the movements that give it form and historical content. Decolonization, which sets out to change the order of the world, is, obviously, a program of complete disorder. But it cannot come as a result of magical practices, nor of a natural shock, nor of a friendly understanding. [...] The native who decides to put the program into practice, and to become its moving force, is ready for violence at all times. From birth it is clear to him that this natural world, strewn with prohibitions, can only be called into question by absolute violence.[31]

From this vantage point, Killmonger's prescription of violence is not frivolous, diabolical, or haphazard. Instead, it is the measured embodied action of Fanon's recuperative and self-redeeming philosophies intended to serve as the breakthrough vaccine to eradicate the social pandemic of the Western global colonial project once and for all. Yet, *Marvel's Black Panther* demonizes and reduces Killmonger to the film's villain, the force that must be vanquished from the earth—instead of, ironically, the global forces of whiteness, which he is fighting against. This ideological position robs the film of its radical potential. Moreover, it diminishes the movie's potency in the minds of some Black audience members, as evidenced by the viral hashtag #TeamKillmonger, which revealed widespread support for, and the mishandling of, perhaps, the film's most intriguing character.

It should come as no surprise that *Marvel's Black Panther*'s botched treatment of Eric Killmonger, its overreliance on the outdated "white savior" trope, its absolving of the CIA's sins in Africa, its reductive renderings of the tropes of African tribalism and atavism, coupled with the film's dependence on white visions of Black intracommunal violence, communicates overly simplistic and essentialist conceptions of racial identity. The film embraces the subject position and ideologies of colonial oppressors, instead of uniting T'Challa and Killmonger against them. These are but a few reasons that warrant a critical reassessment of the film and its politics as, perhaps, unsafe for Black consumption. We must be careful to safeguard our history—Black history, and preserve the legacy of our ancestors, who were the actual "superheroes" that walked the earth and managed to overcome seemingly insurmountable odds. It is our duty to remember the *real* Black Panthers. The young, swashbuckling Black women and men wearing black berets slanted atop of immaculately shaped afros, adorned in leather jackets and dark shades, with Black fists raised defiantly in opposition to oppression. We must remember so that 30 years from now, the mention of the name Black Panther does not conjure images of Marvel comics in the popular imagination, nor in the minds of our youth. Let us forever remember the sacrifices of the *real* Black Panthers. Say their names.

The cultural politics of *Marvel's Black Panther* are not liberatory, despite the movie's significant aesthetic appeal. As audiences and critics have celebrated the visually stunning cosmos of the Oscar-winning tentpole film, the trailer for the sequel *Wakanda Forever* (2022) racked up over 120 million views on YouTube 24 hours after its release. However, it is important to remain vigilant and "stay woke" regarding Hollywood's time-honored practice of using the slippery chimeras of co-optation and the prestidigitatory powers of performative wokeness to conceal regressive political and ideological agendas. While the film's Afrofuturist aesthetic, big-budget, and technical prowess are noteworthy, and the billion-dollar box-office returns are undeniable, one cannot dismiss the film's function as a capitalistic cultural production that utilizes mega-marketing strategies to exploit Black buying power, while undermining Black political interests.

Following the dark cloud of sadness that formed as news broke about the death of the film's talented lead actor Chadwick Boseman, studio executives soon announced that another actor would not replace the role of T'Challa in the film's franchise. Such a pronouncement, at first glance, may seem to honor the life of Mr. Boseman. But given the popularity and profitability of the film, this remains an odd decision. What have Hollywood studios historically done when white lead actors in popular franchises have died? The first modern star of the *Superman* franchise, Christopher Reeve, made four *Superman* films from 1978 to 1987. He was paralyzed from the shoulders down after a tragic horse-riding accident in 1995 and later passed away in 2004. Since his death, five *Superman* films have been produced from 2006 to 2021, with the titular character being portrayed by two different actors, Brandon Routh and Henry Cavill. Likewise, the first contemporary Joker character was brought to life on screen by Jack Nicholson in *Batman* (1989). Years later, actor Heath Ledger delivered a hauntingly virtuoso performance as the Joker in *Dark Knight* (2008). Six months after the film's release, Ledger succumbed to an overdose at age 28. Ledger's depiction was so explosive and acclaimed that he was posthumously awarded the Academy Award for Best Supporting Actor in 2009. Since Ledger's death, the Joker character has appeared in three Hollywood films portrayed by two different actors, Jared Leto and Joaquin Phoenix, with Phoenix winning the Academy Award for Best Actor in 2019. One might also look to the *James Bond*, *Spiderman*, and *Batman* franchises as key examples of beloved lead actors being recast in Hollywood seemingly ad infinitum. The question is, what makes *Marvel's Black Panther* the exception?

It is clear, however, that *Marvel's Black Panther* is a profound film—one that should be studied and appreciated for its spectacular visual elements and Afrofuturist orientation. On the other hand, the film should also be challenged and critiqued for its overreliance on racial tropes and its ideological positions that align against Black socio-political and cultural interests. The film provides an interesting case study that reveals how major corporations co-opt Black cultural aesthetics to engage the politics of performative wokeness, ultimately exploiting Black audiences to maximize white financial incentives. The success of *Marvel's Black Panther* is fundamentally bound up in the "politics of thirst," which is a cultural theory that posits,

> in the absence of a variety of voices and interlocution that speaks to the plurality of experiences of a particular group, members of that group will cling to any emergent voice that is heard and appears familiar even if that voice goes against their own interests.[32]

In other words, *Marvel's Black Panther* embraces the sign of Blackness, providing the appearance of inclusivity while upholding the politics of whiteness as its foundational underpinnings. Likewise,

> having been deprived, rendered invisible, and undervalued for so long Black [audiences] in many communities have developed a "thirst" for Black voices, images, and stories so insatiable that they are willing to "imbibe" any mainstream product that is made available, in order to quench their thirst.[33]

Thus, any commercial product featuring Black talent created and consumed within the complicated dynamics of the politics of thirst should be subjected to deep critical scrutiny, especially if said product employs signs and symbols associated with Black emancipatory aspirations.

The desert landscape of Black films in Hollywood continues to intensify Black audiences' yearnings for Black images and stories, especially while bound up in the politics of thirst. For this reason, serious cinematic interrogation should always occur to determine if Black filmic aesthetics have, in fact, been embezzled by the industry and divested of insurgent energy to the detriment of Black political and socio-cultural needs, while conveniently satisfying the profit-driven imperatives of multi-billion-dollar conglomerates. Without a doubt, movies that offer intergalactic visions of the Black fantastic create a space for dreaming and expanded representation. However, it is also true that the theft and appropriation of Black *"dopeness,"* be it in fashion, vernacular street slang, cultural objects, aesthetics, and other distinctly Black practices, remains an active part of Hollywood's global imperialism and a frequently deployed tactic in the perpetuation of the long and wrenching winter in our unceasing American dream/nightmare.

In short, we must think critically and challenge the entangled ramifications of new, emerging, deceptive cultural strategies born from dual pandemics in a post–George Floyd society, where the aesthetics of racialization and corporate acts of performative wokeness have given way to a terrain of depoliticized *nouveau*-activism fraught with the unabashed ambivalence of empty gestures, viral hashtags, and duplicitous catchphrases like "end racism" shamelessly emblazoned on the fields of billion-dollar NFL stadiums, while Colin Kaepernick remains intentionally exiled by the NFL for speaking out—against racism. And so it goes, acts of performative wokeness, on the surface, may seem progressive—even a step in the right direction, but ultimately, these deeds lack meaningful substance and do not amount to much more than resounding social placebos intended to placate a deeply traumatized and fractured Black America, while the rich get richer and strange fruit keeps swinging from the poplar trees, and—nothing truly changes.

Notes

1 Hollywood also engaged in the "hyper-production" of Black films and TV shows during the 1970s and again in the 1990s. Ultimately, both moments generated financial profits for studios, but did little to create sustained opportunities for Black entertainment creatives.

2 James Baldwin. *The Devil Finds Work* (New York: Vintage Books, 1976).

3 Carlos Stevens. "From the Crash to the Fair the Public Theatre," 1979. http://xroads. virginia.edu/~ug03/comedy/historicalcontext.html

4 Julia Stoll. "Frequency of Going to the Movies in the U.S. 2019 by Ethnicity." January 13, 2021. www.statista.com/statistics/538268/frequency-going-to-the-movies-ethnic ity-usa/ Accessed June 2, 2021.

5 Todd Berliner. *Hollywood Aesthetic: Pleasure in Cinema* (New York: Oxford University Press, 2017), p. 15.

6 Mark Dery. "Black to the Future," *Flame Wars: The Discourse of Cyberculture* (Durham, NC: Duke University, 1994), p. 180.

7 Alisha Acquaye. "Black to the future: OkayAfrica's introduction to Afrofuturism," *OkayAfrica*. www.okayafrica.com/african-future-okayafrica-introduction-afrofuturism/ Accessed June 1, 2021.

8 Justin Wyatt. *High Concept: Movies and Marketing in Hollywood* (Austin: University of Texas, 1994), p. 7.

9 Although prominent members of the "Film School Generation" Spielberg and De Palma never attended film school. Spielberg's applications were rejected for poor academic performance, and De Palma studied theater arts.

10 Wyatt, *High Concept*, pp. 8–10.

11 David Thomson. "Who Killed the Movies?," *Esquire,* December 1996, pp. 56–63.

12 Patrick Gathara. "'Black Panther' offers a regressive, neocolonial vision of Africa," *Washington Post,* February 26, 2018. www.washingtonpost.com/news/global-opini ons/wp/2018/02/26/black-panther-offers-a-regressive-neocolonial-vision-of-africa/ Accessed July 17, 2022.

13 Paul Tiyamba Zeleza. "*Black Panther* and the Persistence of the Colonial Gaze," *Medium,* April 3, 2018. https://medium.com/@USIUAfrica/black-panther-and-the-persistence-of-the-colonial-gaze-6c093fa4156d Accessed July 17, 2022.

14 Salim Washington. "You Act Like a Tho'wed Away Child: *Black Panther*, Killmonger, and Pan-Africanist African American Identity," *Image & Text*, Number 33, 2019, p. 11.

15 Gathara, 2018.

16 "The Future of the Past: Imagi(ni)ing Black Womanhood, Africana Womanism, and Afrofuturism in *Black Panther*," *Image & Text*, Number 33, 2019, p. 2.

17 Ibid., p. 1.

18 "Vibing with Blackness: Critical Considerations of *Black Panther* and Exceptional Positionings," *Arts*, number 7, 85, p. 9.

19 For expanded discussions, see Susan Williams' *White Malice: The CIA and the Covert Recolonization of Africa* (London: Hurst Publishers, 2021), Ray and Schaaps' *Dirty Work 2: The CIA in Africa* (London: Zed Press, 1980), and Tom Burgis' *The Looting*

Machine: Warlords, Oligarch, Corporations, Smugglers, and the Theft of Africa's Wealth (New York: PublicAffairs, 2015).

20 Tricia Jenkins. *The CIA in Hollywood: How the Agency Shapes Film and Television,* (Austin: University of Texas Press, 2016).

21 Tom Hayden. "The CIA Goes to Hollywood: How America's Spy Agency Infiltrated the Big Screen (and Our Minds)," *Los Angeles Review of Books*, February 24, 2013, http://tomhayden.com/home/the-cia-goes-to-hollywood- how-americas-spy-agency-infiltrate.html, Accessed July 16, 2022.

22 Ibid.

23 Ibid.

24 Ibid.

25 Tia C.M. Tyree and Liezelle J. Jacobs. "Can You Save Me?: Black Male Superheroes in Hollywood Film," *Spectrum: A Journal on Black Men*, vol. 3, no. 1 (Autumn 2014), p. 17.

26 David Spurr. *The Rhetoric of Empire: Colonial Discourse in Journalism, Travel Writing, and Imperial Administration* (Durham, NC: Duke University Press, 1993), p. 11.

27 *Marvel's Black Panther*, dir. Ryan Coogler (2018).

28 Spurr, p. 31.

29 Donald Bogle. *Toms, Coons, Mulattoes, Mammies, and Bucks: An Interpretive History of Blacks in American Films.* (New York: Bloomsbury, 2016).

30 Franz Fanon. *The Wretched of the Earth* (New York: Grove Weidenfeld, 1963), p. 61.

31 Ibid., pp. 35–37.

32 Artel Great. "Bring the Payne: The Erasure of the Black Sitcom and the Emergence of *Tyler Perry's House of Payne*," *From Madea to Media Mogul*, eds. Russworm, Sheppard, Bowdre (Jackson: University of Mississippi Press, 2016), p. 175.

33 Ibid., p. 175.

4

LISTENING RATHER FOR THE TONE THAN THE LYRICS

A Memoire of Afrosurrealism

Terri Francis

Afrosurrealism, as implied by the 2009 manifesto by D. Scot Miller that heralded its arrival and explicated its concepts, is intrinsically social and emphatic as it outlines a series of critical departures from surrealism, from negritude in so far as it is surrealist, and from Afrofuturism. As a manifesto in structure, it is a public declaration of a set of shared values expressed in specific tenets such as the following: (1) Afro-Surreal presupposes that beyond this visible world, there is an invisible world striving to manifest, and it is our job to uncover it; (2) Afro-Surrealists use excess as the only legitimate means of subversion, and hybridization as a form of disobedience; and (3) Afro-Surrealism is intersexed, Afro-Asiatic, Afro-Cuban, mystic, silly, and profound. As a genre of protest and collectivity, the manifesto addresses "we." We? Who? You know it if it's you! If it doesn't speak to you, then it's not calling to you. The manifesto, as a genre, is at its core a call to action addressed to those who hear it and Miller's exemplary manifesto goes on to issue and memorialize a catalog of "first steps in an illustrious and marvelous journey," among them "[*Marvel's*] *Black Panther* will grace the silver-screen."[1] In his 2016 reflection on the manifesto, "Afrosurreal: The Marvelous And The Invisible 2016" Miller recalls:

> When I wrote the Manifesto at the behest of SFBG [San Francisco Bay Guardian] editor Johnny Ray Huston, I had not envisioned anyone actually applying it to actual events. To me, it's a piece of art first and foremost; a declarative and evocative poem meant to speak directly to the first Futurist Manifesto, written by the Italian poet Filippo Tommaso Marinetti, published in the Italian newspaper Gazzetta dell'Emilia in Bologna on February 5, 1909. [He] had engaged with that manifesto, and my many others, as I researched the arts manifesto in form and function through Mary Ann Caws definitive work: Manifesto: A Century of Isms. The rage and lust for speed, war, and misogyny spoke to pre-fascist Europe and influenced many of the artistic,

DOI: 10.4324/9781003079682-5

social, and political movements for the last one hundred years. Though the first Surrealist Manifesto came fifteen years later, if you placed Futurism against Surrealism, it's clear that Futurism and the illusion of progress overcame Surrealism.[2]

Through the circulation of the manifesto, "being passed around on social media, being published in scholarly journals, discussed on panels, and has subsequently inspired artists and theorists to produce works through an Afrosurrealist lens" the concept of Afrosurrealism asserts itself as both a way of life and a critical practice, a way of viewing, selecting, and curating creative materials for the imagined public. It offers a syllabus that provides multiple starting points as well as edges to explore and to go beyond.[3] The challenge of the manifesto comes through its ironies where it is both an article of resistance, and to the degree that it, or rather its author, seeks social change as well as a collective with whom to pursue that change, a document of institution-building in a sense. Some of Miller's own ambivalence about the success of his "poem and evocation" is expressed here where he writes:

> I've lectured in major cities at their most prestigious undergraduate and graduate programs, and was given the time and the space to truly examine this work under the support from one of the most respected museums in the world, and have had the singular pleasure of watching a concept that I introduced get co-opted into the mainstream by attaching it to movies like [*Marvel's*] *Black Panther*, *Sorry to Bother You*, *Get Out*, *Us* and television shows like *Atlanta* and *Random Acts of Flyness*. Some knew that I did that, some didn't, some acted like they didn't, some claimed that they'd done it instead. Let's just say that brought it's [sic] own set of problems. If you've been with me since 2009, when this all began; you've witnessed them.[4]

One of the true gifts of the 2009 manifesto is the connections it invites as it helps to make visible concepts, as delineated by Miller, such as "Negritude, Black speculative, the absurdity of Black life being lived in real-time, and so much more," however much Afrosurrealism might question their inclusion. It can bring the seemingly marginal and the avant-garde into view, but as Miller suggests in 2019, there are problems that come into play when the term becomes so expansive it seems to include so many diverse forms, topics, themes, and eras, that it lacks the specificities of its initial insight. Not that the 2009 manifesto did not have global implications but it was also rooted in San Francisco. It has particular aims and it was Miller's vision. Yet he could not entirely control where it went from there.

In 2013 when I wrote my "Introduction to Afrosurrealism in Film and Video," I paraphrased something I had heard a long time before about how when you name a thing it goes underground. "Name a thing, watch it flee underground," I wrote.[5] At the time, I meant (I think) that it would disappear if it was named at all or too narrowly. I was conceding to defining Afrosurrealism as a necessary act of scholarship, but I wanted to recognize the limits of defining and theorizing the term—although that is exactly what I had done in the preceding pages. My introduction and the research it represented were creative actions on my part. I gathered the works I most wanted to look at, that most profoundly challenged what I had been taught to see, and lovingly organized them with the instruments available to me: the call for papers, the academic journal, citations, and the process of scholarly publication itself. Looking back, I now think that my use of the term "underground" conveyed my fragile and thus secreted optimism in that I might have meant that I hoped it would flourish underground away from naming. Though I sought to make this work and my work visible, I also seemed to have hoped that this visibility would not be encumbering or detrimental—or maybe I was ambivalent about bringing an academic lens to what appeared to be anti-establishment films, although almost all the filmmakers I write about are university-educated. Like Miller I perceived the bind of classification, or in Elizabeth Alexander's wonderful phrase "edifying conundrums."[6] I am now in this essay retracing my steps and rethinking my chants of Afrosurrealism as a method of reflection and re-imagining my current habitudes of reading, teaching, viewing, and exhibition in a time now, when either questioning everything matters more than ever before or questioning everything won't matter at all. That is a lot of pressure but when I re-read this ten years from now, I want to remember how it felt to be writing during the Covid-19 pandemic and in the wake of the 2020 uprisings and how this was my own act of mourning, of deciding to go on.

There have been sporadic treatments of experimental poetics in the media such as "From Beyoncé to Sorry to Bother You: The New Age of Afro-surrealism" by Lanre Bakare (*The Guardian*, December 2018), "Afro-Surrealism: Embracing and Reconstructing the Absurdity of 'Right Now'" by Keirsten Alexis (Medium, September 2019) or "A World Reimagined, Afro-surrealist Films for Surrealist Times" by Alex Smith (*ArtBlog*, July 7, 2020.) The term as used in these articles helps to identify essential elements of the experimental other-worlding and the introspective nature of the type of filmmaking that finds itself referenced as Afrosurrealistic. Yet what is often left out of discussions of Afrosurrealist filmmaking and media is that Black experimentations in film and film writing predate the re-animation of this important term and its application to contemporary media today. Few mention Afrosurrealism's lineage, including its early formulation in a 1988 essay by poet Amiri Baraka.[7] In this essay on "Afro-Surrealist Expressionism, with Baraka's references to Zora Neale Hurston and Toni Morrison, I found critical vocabulary for naming the unique sensory features of the visual avant-gardes I wanted to discuss. Despite his own distancing from surrealism, I do look at Miller's manifesto in connection with that of surrealism's co-founder André Breton, whose aim was to create from the unconscious. I still want to trace the philosophy of Afrosurrealism through the key texts and their connections to surrealism and négritude as explored by Léopold Senghor, Suzanne Césaire and Aimé Césaire, but Suzanne is the true genius of it all for me now. That Baraka's essay on Henry Dumas appeared in a literature journal shows that surrealism and Afrosurrealism are naturally multidisciplinary and intertwined, which offers the necessary prismatic framework for thinking through the intertextual relationships between films, films and paintings, songs and paintings, film and dance, within a Black expressive matrix. Looking for that internal formal mythic.

Mostly confined as we are to our individual screens, at this writing in the early 2020s, it has become important to me to recall the means by which these types of alternative films are usually encountered, particularly now when the sudden shift to streaming has brought a wide range of independent, avant-garde, museum-only, or gallery-only pieces to the public. The main difference in Afrosurrealism, when I published the collection in 2013 and now, is the participation in popular and commercial media success. *An Oversimplification of Her Beauty* (2012) had to be seen in person for an arranged screening back then. I merely read about it on *Shadow and Act* before going to New York City to see it and eventually bringing its director Terence Nance and the film to New Haven. He discussed the blues in his post-film comments at Lincoln Center and that's what made me decide on the importance of the blues in thinking through his work and potentially that of others. Influenced by Nance's comments, I started to think of the blues as experimental, as a mode of transforming experience. Fast forward to now artists like Nance who seemed somewhat obscure in the early 2000s or even in 2013 even in art cinema circles now has a much wider audience through his work on the HBO series, *Random Acts of Flyness*.

My work in Afrosurrealism began with my informal and formal study of experimental and avant-garde films as a part of my everyday life while researching my dissertation in Paris, France, around 1999. In Paris, watching experimental films seemed easy and avant-garde film culture seemed to be one of many forms of film exhibition I could walk to. Going to the movies in Paris was social, haptic, and accessible to a newbie like myself. Back home in the United States, I often hear people speak of film snobs and being intimidated or put off by art cinema and the people who would use a term like that. But in Paris it was cool. I got to know film through going to screenings in bars, on the river, in the street, in all-night screening affairs, at the mall, as part of theater, in the park. There were museum, gallery, and theater screenings too but looking back the proximity, variety, and convenience of screening venues helped make avant-garde films seem not at all removed or alien to me. I could walk to screenings within a few minutes or bump into them so I felt I shared the landscape with my newfound delight in going to the movies and in particular going to experimental or avant-garde movies.

Thinking back to 1999 and 2000 in Paris, it strikes me that the experimental film scene was cozy and also pedagogical. The screenings involved substantial conversation before and after the films were shown, where artists talked about what they made and where they saw it in dialogue with the wider world of images in cinema, theater, dance, literature, or visual arts. I had never considered film study before but through these experiences in Paris, I fell into it or walked into it and wanted to continue to learn more and participate.

On returning to Chicago in 2000, I saw Christopher Harris's thesis film, *still/here*, which he had produced at the School of the Art Institute of Chicago, in an audience at the University of Chicago's Film Study Center. My explorations of the avant-garde took off from there. Whatever else I saw, be it Black film, silent film, film noir, westerns, musicals, romantic comedies I saw everything through the experimental lens as the product of a practice, whether by the actors, the filmmaker, the cinematographers or the editors, an effort to make use of available materials, and an assemblage of sounds and images that have been cut and edited. Experimental films taught me to see film structure. I viewed any films, especially early ones and definitely Black films as experiments in using resources and innovations in how to represent the relationships between time and space. *still/here*'s use of duration, the pacing, use of sound, and the person of the director as the first Black filmmaker I had seen in the context of experimental Black film at that moment, opened up a pathway to a new way of thinking for me. But in an academic context, I had to relate it to what was known and more familiar. I presented a paper on *still/here* in 2003 by distinguishing it from other films about economically depressed cities in terms of its focus on structures, absence, and space over performance or human representation. Rather than looking at Blackness, in *still/here* we look through Harris' perspective as a Black filmmaker and contemplate the spaces, the absences and ironies that mark his relationship to the locations he captures in the viewfinder and presents back to himself first and then to the audience.

After discovering film study through discovering experimental films, I came upon Afrosurrealism about 10 years later thanks to D. Scot Miller's Afrosurrealist Manifesto, which provided an animating principle for my work in distinguishing the work of Black experimental filmmakers within the avant-garde world and connecting it to experimentations in literature and music. I wanted to look at film through the lenses I had acquired in my study of literature. The idea of Blackness as itself an experimental mode of survival, resistance, and invention was uncommon in film studies, but knowing that processes of migration, ingenuity, and rebellion were fundamental to the formations of Black art and the sustenance of Black life, I committed to Afrosurrealism as a defining yet expansive mode of gathering, ana-lyzing, and centering particularly unusual, materially surprising, and formally "out there" films by Black filmmakers in my research, teaching, and curating.

Viewing new experimental films, particularly by Black filmmakers, however, proved challenging in that it meant learning this area of filmmaking slowly through travel, building relationships with individual artists one by one, and being limited to the specific physical spaces and venues where these types of alternative often short films would be shown for a limited period of time. Some of the main venues included New Directors/New Films at Lincoln Center, Projections, the "sidebar" of the New York Film Festival, the Rotterdam Film Festival, the New York African Film Festival, and the Ann Arbor Film Festival. If I did not manage to travel to see films, I would write to filmmakers I had read about to request tapes or DVDs or arrange a meeting if they were within driving distance. Based on scouring festival programs, news from *Shadow and Act*, as it was then edited by Tambay Obenson and Sergio Mims, as well as person-by-person introductions, I created events in order to screen material and discuss the work with the makers. I learned about avant-garde films directly from filmmakers who introduced me to the work of their colleagues. Programming then became as much a research practice as close analysis, historical synthesizing, and archival mining. My research involved convening public discussions such as our 2005 (Sunday, April 3, 12:00–1:45 p.m.) panel on "Black Abstraction and Cinema" at the Society for Cinema Media Studies in London. Panelists included Christopher Harris presenting on "Toward an Avant-garde Poetics of Black Cinema," Kevin Jerome Everson on "Recognition as Motif," and Kevin Bell discussed "Exposures of Black Alienation Mythology: The Wig, *Chameleon Street* and Critical Detournement." As chair of the panel, I presented a piece titled "Carnivalesque Filmmaking: The Nottinghill Carnival, Violence and Black Spectatorship in Isaac Julien's *Territories.*" And Julien attended, being in fact one of our only attendees. I later organized screenings of Harris' *still/here* (2000) and *Reckless Eyeballing* (2004) at SCMS as well as (with Miriam Petty) a special showing of William Greaves' *Symbiopsychotaxiplasm* (1968) with Mr. Greaves and members of the cast in attendance. I was studying what I liked and I sought to create public spaces where that material could be part of the formal study of cinema, even at the heart of our professional meetings.

I have written that Afrosurrealism like the films I discussed in that rubric was both invented and found, made and recuperated. Following the lead of the filmmakers whose work I watched, wrote about, and programmed in the early 2000s, I became enamored with the variety of visual techniques. The delicacy of the images struck a chord with me, and I worked to find various ways of writing them. The diversity of forms I gathered under "Afrosurrealism" was as challenging as it was beguiling. One moment I defined Afrosurrealism through Christopher Harris' rephotographed excerpts of a 35 mm trailer for *Foxy Brown,* but it could also be done through an equally illuminating analysis of Akosua Adoma Owusu's needle-sharp pauses in *Me Broni Ba* or Kevin Jerome Everson's anti-representational portraiture. The films I was drawn to in the Afrosurreal offered a quality where they seemed to hearken to a cinematic past but one that was missing from our historical record, so it appeared dreamlike. There was also a materiality to this work in that as a viewer I found myself looking at the film, as though it were an object, rather than through it to the story, which there was little of, or its "about-ness." If there was a story it was about the film material, or how the filmmaker engaged the physical film material: painting on it, scratching at it, rephotographing, using obscure technologies that felt futuristic nonetheless. These films to me foregrounded the construction of the image itself or as Everson put it "recognition as motif" rather than an end in itself but a transport back into the artwork, like a painting or a sculpture that is recognizable but not a literal reproduction. With moving images, particularly of African Americans, there is that tendency to make recognition the core and purpose of representation. These artists began from the clarity of Blackness—or from multiple mysteries of Blackness—or from contradictory notions of Blackness as a cinematic phenomenon and then applied questions of Blackness to the medium of film. Not only do experimental Black filmmakers expand upon the conventions of narrative independent cinema, they create an acute awareness of the process of making film and draw our eye to the frame itself, raising questions of what is left out and what is cut in and why. For me, Afrosurrealism now was an interrogatory rather than declarative process.

I embraced Afrosurrealism as both a mode of definition and as a set of questions. It was a mode of curiosity. And I drew inspiration from it to cut a path through what then appeared to me to be the central debates both in scholarship and in the general press overrepresentation. In a sense, I simply wanted something beautiful for its own sake in its own way, peculiar, intriguing, delightful. Paraphrasing Arthur Jafa's words in his essay "69," I wanted a Black film that moved like Black music. In my mind, it was necessary to move beyond anti-Hollywood critiques and it was clear that representation, while very important, was not itself a victory. There were and remain with us even deeper structural considerations that reach beyond the manifest image.

Instead, the films that concerned Afrosurrealism questioned in their form and use of the image the fundamental expectations for what a film should be. Jafa's key question: well, if this work is supposed to be Black film, why does it use what is essentially strictly classical Hollywood spatial continuity? Where he was often told that Oscar Micheaux's work was "incompetently realized" Jafa found in the prolific race filmmaker a profound and alternate paradigm: "It just got badder and badder and badder."[8] In the essay, Jafa reflects upon cultural retention, as a precursor perhaps to his "notion of treatment," which he discusses a decade later in an interview with Pearl Bowser published in *Oscar Micheaux and His Circle*. Here he makes a remarkable observation that sheds light on the question of originality and identity in experimental visual Black art that speaks directly to form and formations. He says: "Afro-American creativity has this totally reactive dimension. ... Much of the heaviest stuff is situated in the space of treatment rather than the space of material."[9] In arguing that Black creativity arises from or is most potently visible through re-use, re-vision, re-deployment of existing materials and circumstances, is Jafa locating the Afrosurreal—that combination of (re)made and found several years before the term would be applied to film?

He goes on to explain that

> African-American creativity has been shaped by the specific circumstances Black people found themselves in; we weren't generally able to dictate the materials we were given to work with. When we were brought to the Americas as slaves we were generally seen as seen as material ourselves. You don't really have the leeway to go out and select your own materials. So, a lot of our creativity coalesced around the notion of treatment, that is transforming in some meaningful fashion, given materials.[10]

In "69," Jafa lays out his theories of constructing Black cinema. He reflects upon

> Black pleasure (not joy): what are its parameters, what are its primal sites, how does Black popular culture or Black culture in general address Black

pleasure? How does it generate Black pleasure? How do those strategies in Black music play out the rupture and repair of African-American life on the structural level?

He then presents an original term "polyventiality," which means multiple tones, multiple rhythms, multiple perspectives, multiple meanings, multiplicity." He's talking about "analyzing the tone, not the sequence of notes." Not what was sung but how they sang. Not the lyrics but the sound. Not the meaning but the means. Jafa calls this "Black Visual Intonation," which consists of using "irregular nontempered (nonmetronomic) camera rates reminiscent of the hand-cranked camera of silent film whose rough visual textures replicate the tendency in Black music to 'worry the note'—to treat notes as indeterminate, inherently unstable."[11] The engagements of Jafa, Isaac Julien, Valerie Smith, Kobena Mercer, and so many others in the 1990s, film criticism and expressivity with the project of Black film, opened up the whole field of Black film studies in a definitive yet open-ended and strategically unfinished way. My evocations of their work and contributions here mark both past and present tense of film study.

Black time is long time. In the something made, something found aesthetic by which I mark the Afrosurreal, the contemporary frameworks of recent cinema automatically imply a historical perspective as thinkers, Black experimental filmmakers and scholars, theorists all, continue to navigate the very long unfinished reconstructing process of integrating unthinkingly white institutions. I love when Miller says Afrosurrealism is right now. But I also feel like right now is still back then, the unfinished things shaping the present. Jafa's thoughts and his work as a filmmaker in *Love Is the Message, The Message Is Death* (2016) exemplifies this temporal back and forth at the same time-ness in its form. The quick cuts, use of slow motion, the wide variety of "worried" imagery appear to fulfill his vision of "badder and badder and badder" cinema. He has copied and recycled and re-recorded a selection from the vast mesh of our media landscape to find transcendence and trauma in their duet on Black life. Jafa draws on multiple sources and the work is both a unique object made for museum and galleries and, during the Covid-19 pandemic it has also streamed as bootleg and as limited available program. But for much of 2021 there has been a bootleg of *Love Is the Message, The Message Is Death* video on YouTube, so it has aptly returned to its source(s) in vernacular everyday media. Today as I write this the distinctions between museum, film festival, are blurred, maybe temporarily due to the Covid-19 safety protocols in place, maybe for a long while mixed into in-person screenings.

I view the relative inaccessibility in the early 2000s and mid 2010s of the films I wanted to write about with some nostalgia now as I see films by Kevin Everson, Camille Billops, Terence Nance, Akosua Adoma Owusu and more streaming for a few dollars per month any time of the day or night throughout the United States, during the pandemic and in the wake of increased and thoughtful programming that followed the Black Lives Matter 2020 protests. What I wrote about almost as lost films are now much more easily viewed and available in a variety of contexts like a supercharged art house cinema. They once had the aura of a special object to which I as academic writer or as a curator had special access. My writing then was necessarily descriptive, almost a form of ekphrasis, and I worked to convey the films to readers in words while also embedding them within their conscious or unconscious influences. Describing and theorizing worked together in my mind.

My early engagements with Afrosurrealism fulfilled my initial curiosities that had been sparked in Paris in that I found filmmakers eager to talk to me about their work. Planning screenings seemed easy and hassle-free. It seemed to be something unique I could offer students and colleagues, even if my work in Afrosurrealism was getting in the way of my book on Josephine Baker. Unlike the tedious and lonely work on the computer that revising a dissertation into a book required, the experimental film world felt human-scale and vibrant. The research like the films themselves felt organic and suited work that is often handmade and shown in small gatherings such as microcinemas. It felt exclusive yet accessible.

I framed my special section in *Black Camera* as an intervention in writing about both "Black film," which often neglected experimental work and white avant-garde cinema as a whole that tended to disregard the work of Black thinkers and artists. Photographer Dawoud Bey and others commented on the indifference to abstraction in the work of Black artists and the seeming incompatibility of Blackness and abstraction in the minds of some white critics and perhaps Black critics as well.

I deployed Afrosurrealism as a way to both mark out a space for Black experimentation and also Black alienation. Afrosurrealism for me was a navigational tool that for me seemed to capture our inside/outside frustration while it placed their work within long-standing global Black innovations in literature illustrated by works such as Jean Toomer's multi-genre *Cane* (1923) and M. NourbeSe Philip's historical book-length poem *Zong!* (2011), a textual sculpture on paper. Whatever critical or filmic approaches I intended to gather under the rubric of Afrosurrealism or something else, it was clear that in my scholarship and in their filmmaking, we had enacted the usual tenants of avant-garde movements in that I sought to deeply engage with the film medium and its languages, initiating hopefully, dialogues within and against institutional norms in film expectations that would bring about reflections upon underlying philosophical questions about how film history was rendered and needed to be revised and retold. Yet the "Blackness" of the inquiry, whether in the vessels of our racialized bodies or the intellectual traditions we claimed, seemed to provide gatekeepers a potent mode of dismissal, marginalizing the essential(izing) work of criticality and experimentation that is in fact central to the continued relevance of the humanities, particularly in American universities since the revolutions of the 1970s that saw the formation of Black Studies, Native American Studies, Asian-American Studies, women and gender/sexuality studies, and film studies. But there is also the material need to belong.

While research and teaching scholars in these fields provide knowledge and frameworks that recover histories that have been erased, the ways they can make whiteness visible and crack through the veneer of white non-identity and neutrality is perhaps a legacy as tricky as it is transformative due to the slippery "delusions of whiteness."[12] It initially appeals, even, or maybe even more to racialized people that identity might be something to slip in and out of "like a video game avatar" as Cathy Hong put it in her essay on whiteness in experimental poetry. One resists the rigid stereotypes and tropes of Black performativity for instance yet one wants to be grounded in a community. It's the cultural appropriation that is so scary. Is abstraction the getaway? As cited by Elizabeth Alexander in her essay "Who can LOOK at this?," Thelma Golden attributes the term "post-Black" to the artist Glenn Ligon who spoke of artists who rejected being labeled as "Black artists" while "their work was steeped, in fact deeply interested, in redefining complex notions of Blackness. … at the end of the 1990s … Post-Black was the new Black."[13] Although this particular discussion of "post-Black" and what to do with the quotations around race, or what Alexander describes as the "romantic language" of terms such as "my people" certainly informed my attraction to the term Afrosurrealism.[14] I was primed for Afrosurrealism by lines such as "BLACK is an open umbrella. I am Black and A Black forever" from Gwendolyn Brooks' poetry.[15] Afrosurrealism returned me from the constructed notions of race in quotation marks to *my people* with the awareness of the expansiveness of Kerry James Marshall's painterly "Black-Black: a Black that is deep, potent, and alive in its density."[16]

Alexander's work here and her work upon me as a reader is not a naïve romance but readiness to think through what it means to study experimental Black film—films that resist representational satisfaction—within institutions that want representational satisfaction. Her critique of the 1990s "tricky trend" where Black studies was institutionalized

> to so theorize and construct and deconstruct identity "categories" that some were apt to forget women and people of color themselves, in bodies, who wrote things that we urgently needed to read and who remained grossly under-represented among the professoriat, women and people of color whose voices and actions in historical, political, and cultural life, were too often marginalized, trivialized, forgotten, or erased

is a caution.[17] The "ism" in Afrosurrealism does the work of indicating a specific practice, system, or philosophy while surrealism and "afro" (un)ground the concept in Black dreaming, dreaming in Black, the transcendence and the trauma in the joy and the history we carry in our flesh but still must learn. By entering into institutions, Afrosurrealism can make a space to integrate curricula and create greater educational opportunities for everyone in the study of the arts. But success takes it out of our hands.

The complex negotiations of the inside/outside existence that Black intellectuals experience within white institutions draw on faith in cultural retentions, however tenuous, and not exactly shared experience but the shelter of listening for the through lines and variations in experiences in the roles assigned within institutions, maybe, maybe not. If Blackness is to be recognizable (does it not have to be though?) as material for tone and sound rather than lyrics and sequence, then the project of Black cinema (which does remain a specific enterprise, right?) is necessarily ever reaching toward the Afrosurreal, "Blackness as an entryway to the infinite, an idealized radiating Black subject."[18] How to claim Blackness but in a way that is different from institutional expectations as it is different from community expectations. What of the fraught communities within? How to account for the variation in these experiences and in how people decide to or feel they must inhabit (or not) their difference, or their non-difference and indifference, and how it plays out on screen? If the Afrosurreal taps into dreamspace, know that it is as much horror as paradise.

Notes

1 Scot D. Miller, "Afrosurreal Manifesto," May 20, 2009, http://dscotmiller.blogspot.com/2009/05/afrosurreal.html Accessed May 18, 2021.
2 Scot D. Miller, "Afrosurreal: The Marvelous And The Invisible 2016," October 4, 2016, *SFMOMA's Open Space*, https://openspace.sfmoma.org/2016/10/afrosurreal-the-marvelous-and-the-invisible/ Accessed May 18, 2021.
3 Ibid.
4 Scot D. Miller, "The Tenth Anniversary of the Afrosurreal Manifesto," May 20, 2019, http://dscotmiller.blogspot.com/2019/05/the-10th-year-anniversary-of.html Accessed May 18, 2021.
5 Terri Francis, "Close-Up: Afrosurrealism: Introduction: The No-Theory Chant of Afrosurrealism." *Black Camera: An International Film Journal*, Vol. 5, No. 1 (Fall 2013), 95–112.
6 Elizabeth Alexander, *The Black Interior* (Minneapolis, MN: Graywolf Press, 2004), 205.
7 Amiri Baraka, "Henry Dumas: Afro-Surreal Expressionist," *Black American Literature Forum* 22, no. 2 (1988): 164–166.
8 Arthur Jafa, "69" in *Black Popular Culture*, eds. Gina Dent and Michele Wallace (New York, NY: Dia Center for the Arts, 1992), 251.
9 Arthur Jafa, "The Notion of Treatment: Black Aesthetics in Film" in *Oscar Micheaux and His Circle: African-American Filmmaking and Race Cinema of the Silent Era*, eds. Pearl Bowser, Jane Marie Gaines, and Charles Musser (Bloomington: Indiana University Press, 2016), 27.
10 Jafa, "The Notion of Treatment," 28.
11 Jafa, "69," 254.
12 Cathy Park Hong, "Delusions of Whiteness in the Avant-Garde." *Lana Turner*, November 2, 2014, https://arcade.stanford.edu/content/delusions-whiteness-avant-garde. Accessed May 19, 2021.
13 Alexander, *The Black Interior*, 204.
14 Alexander, *The Black Interior*, 175.
15 Qtd. In Alexander, *The Black Interior*, 202. Gwendolyn Brooks, "I Am a Black," in *Children Coming Home* (Chicago, IL: The David Company, 1991), 5.
16 Alexander, *The Black Interior*, 203.
17 Alexander, *The Black Interior*, 202.
18 Christopher Harris, "Discussion of Reckless Eyeballing" (Zoom, Cinema and Media Studies at Indiana University, virtual, April 27, 2021.

5

THE PHILOSOPHONIC LABOR OF *THESE HANDS*

Fred Moten

> *La Petite Vendeuse de Soleil* (1999) begins not so much by introducing its individual characters but with a mini-documentary on Dakar going to work at dawn. This becomes a study of the very unequal means people have to make their way through an increasing globalized economy: La petite vendeuse on her crutches, a legless boy in his wheelchair, horse carts, bicycles, jitneys, Mercedes all heading to the market. Mambety's ultimate symbol of this contrast is a man methodically splitting a pile of rocks with a hammer while jumbo jets take off over his shoulder. In fact, Mambety intended to call the third, never completed part of his *Tales of Little People, La Tailleuse des Pierres* (The Woman Who Chipped Stones) and Flora M'bugu Schelling made this mind-numbing task the sole content of her remarkable documentary *These Hands*.[1]

In almost 30 years of approaching *These Hands* (1992), what I keep stumbling upon—in the broken dance of thinking, near touching, in seeing and listening—is a philosophonomy of percussion that's neither given nor held by the false alternatives of documentary and fiction. Schelling's cinegraphic study bears savor and aroma, too, so that sound's role in the sensual ensemble is not dominant but atmospheric. It surrounds, infuses, and insinuates. Moreover, song comes out of nowhere, in and out of everywhere, ensuring that approaching there is there and not quite there in inappropriable affirmation of the intrastitial, fleshily sentient sociality of ensemble as whorled not-in-between and scarred under-circumference. So that for the anaconceptual dramatis impersonae and their theatricum phonosophicum, we sound the seers' nonlocal sense of feel and field. Because forced migration and plotless refuge are at stake, certain instances of all but falling toe-tapping, always more and less than voluntary, are required in this science of the word's displace/ meant, which is what happens when labor and field theoretical practice bear the

DOI: 10.4324/9781003079682-6

animation of *musiké* considered as that optimal, non-optional instancing of beaten breath—a woman's club and its incalculable rhythm, in and out of any normative imagining.[2] Here, Schelling describes the film's preformative provenance:

> One day I went to Bahari Beach in Dar es Salaam. There is this huge quarry where a lot of poor women toil crushing stones in order to make ends meet. Many of them are refugees who fled the civil war in neighbouring Mozambique. I tell you, when I first looked at them slaving away I thought of those schizophrenic paintings by Salvador Dali. I told myself there and then that I must bear witness to this. I must make this movie. I did *These Hands* first and foremost for myself. It was so painful, yet at the same time, strangely beautiful to observe those women at the quarry. At Bahari Beach I saw death but I also saw life. Everything was there, sadness, joy...[3]

What is life? This question concerns poise or what it is to be poised. What is it to be positioned as waiting; patient but also looming, pending, and impending. Black study is always about to lose its composure. It is about what it is to be posed, as a question, and then explode. Is there a problem? Yes, and it's given in broken ground. With confidence in deprivation, we arrive at a place of emphasis we immediately leave, emphatic step and apophatic lift off scale, precise disequilibria of hand dance, percussion's open book of perlocutionary acts. Rhythm is (the discovery of immeasurable irregularities in) continuous interruption. Rhythm is undecipherable dyscryption, which is foregiven even and especially when what's interrupted is the exposure of truth that is somehow both buried and on the move. While such exposure wracks the nerves of those who have had to embrace quicksand existence, it throws off into smooth brutality the ones who swear their ground is solid. Those who are not the ones keep open the secret that's walked and whispered in emphatic, all but aphasic seizure. If you ask them, they could wrong the book. Theirs is the experience of shared experience, which is evidence of a nether world. Life is another whorled in and out of this one, under it and on its edge. Life is existence's tendency to fall, to stumble, to stutter, to scat, to break. Cinema, at the level of its fundamental apparatus, is an effect of this though cinema, as an effect of metaphysical antipathy to its apparatus, is rarely about this.

In any possible instance of figuring all that out for the fun of mourning and irreverence and war, a philosophonomy of percussion must break the melody of the iron system in order to record (its own) irregularity, informality, and disequilibrium. Its everyday interruption of the everyday works to preform a question; and those who are not but nothing other than drummers take the question's form. The cut is also a beat and a fractured roll and it's ok that in the mobile indigeneity of our Blackness we love to hear them call us (re)percussive philosophers. Do it pianissimo, as punkish quietude, in Cecilian insolitude, for off-mimetic, intrajective, auto(ana)lytic improvisation. Soloists who are neither one nor many, call up these hands in here, too, inside or outside the gloves. The rhythm of their labor and the rhythm of history lead to questions concerning (the) film's time: some people say it takes too long, that its length is a function of its repetitiveness, that there is, in the end, a monotony, a temporal and rhythmic regularity that is oppressive; that reading is a lot like Theodor Adorno's dismissal of Black popular music, which he reduces to "the rhythm of the iron system," understood as the negative effects of a kind of deindividuating sameness. He was not attuned to this music, however, in the same way that those who think the film too long are not attuned to its refusal of normative time and its microfracture of normative tone, and to the plying of pulse given in that pantonality, and to the nuance which thereby so powerfully marks it and what it represents as in construction, as in the midst of organization, as complex and ensemblic in ways that force a rethinking of our understandings of sameness and difference, totality and singularity, community and individuality or, as Sylvia Wynter famously puts it, *l'etre et l'etant*. The chance to rethink this, to reimagine the world as structured by that which is other than these formulations, is what art sometimes gives us. Not very often does it give it as clearly as in *These Hands*, whose articulations are so sharp, moving precisely by way of the rough transition from *verité* to fiction, which instantiates a narrative some might think is unfulfilled, unfinished, a movement from the unstaged to the staged, from the behaved to the performed, as when a worker dies and mourners dance, and the camera and what the camera does is acknowledged either openly or accidentally. Moreover, the organizing of the film—note the productive ambiguity of the genitive—is always given in the same way, from before the beginning to after the end, in the same way the philosophonic labor of the music in preformance is simultaneously given as and with the product or artifact or recording, the sound produced always in holoesthetic ensemble with its (re)production. Openly, *These Hands* assert cinema's fundamental surreptitious repetition: that narrative arc and melodic emplotment are unmade by the breaks and cuts and beats that make them. *These Hands* tells the story of narrative's interruption, tolls the ongoing story of the break in the story like a bell. It gives the liberatory force of the cut, which filmic form gives us too freely to be noticed, not only as an effect of the apparatus but also as an effect of affect's disruption of the ethnographic attitude, as in the small, uneven spectacle of a self-conscious smile whose gift indicates the continual setting of the scene, its interinanimation of prescription and dyscryption. (This) film lives in the imperfect, with its imperfections on its head, as the discontinuities at its heart. *These Hands* offers this anthological generativity in extra-ethno-cinegraphic practice. The ethnographic attitude depends upon suppression of the seam, in overdetermination of the seme, as overvalorization of an artificial seeming. Neither this nor narrative fiction is what Schelling and her colleagues have in mind.

When the women of/in the film sing of wounded kinship and motherless children, when they play in abandon and on abandonment, they hold (out) (for) another organization. There is no delusion of the therapeutic, no illusion of recovery. The film is about organization, which is to say new music. It is a sophonomy, a thinking-in-sounding, of new music. It breathes a percussive poetics of work against work and against the work. The women sing: *Do not disappear in vanity; yes we see you, we really see you*. That these phrases, these praises, are sung is more than everything—it's all. In *These Hands* sound considers how sound creates and amplifies and then improvises through the very idea of (interpersonal, international, economic, spatial) relation. When the women sing, *We remain in silence*, knowing silence will have never been the absence of sound, or the negation of the practice of sounding, they do so with Wynter, before and after her in cinegraphic time, announcing common, imprevisionary company.

Having discerned and articulated the need for a mode of intellectual ceremony that would bring to its proper end the era of man, Wynter has begun the experimental practice of developing and enacting that ceremony in a body of work that constitutes a powerful, intricate, carefully wrought charge against the last five hundred years of Western thought whose detonation will have caused modernity's foundations to collapse. One of the most important features of Wynter's explosive and expansive body of work—manifest with particular clarity in her extraordinary "Towards the Sociogenic Principle: Fanon, The Puzzle of Conscious Experience of 'Identity' and What It's Like to be 'Black'"—is its ongoing inhabitation of a necessarily interdisciplinary field in which contemporary literary critical and theoretical work on "identity" that takes up questions and protocols established in European continental philosophy must share ground with the discourse on identity that emerges from the intersection of the biological and physical sciences, cognitive science, and Anglo-American analytic philosophical inquiry. Wynter's inhabitation of this Trans-Atlantic, interdisciplinary intellectual current and territory exemplifies the imposed but radically improvisational erudition that animates a lived history of abduction, flight, and grounding. Such erudition is rigorous intellectual embodiment, a choreographic form of critical life inscribed with Wynter's unique literary and performative signature. Her elaboration of Fanon's "sociogenic principle" is just such solicitation, just such punctuation and troubled, trembled, trebeled emphasis. For me, her thinking is inseparable from her physical presentation of it—in particular, the one instance in which I have been in her presence, at a talk she gave at the University of California, Berkeley, in which she scored the urgent gliss and variation of her formulations with the analectical report of keen-toed shoes of mauve on a wooden floor. What does such auto-accompaniment mean? What's held and released in tapped and overflowing social principle? This double movement—which Gilles Deleuze might describe as a manifestation of "the extreme taste for principles" or "the identity of the principle and the cry"—might be better understood as that anarchic disruption or unfolding of principles that is afforded by what remains unregulated and unenclosed in the cry and, deeper still in a step of the dance. It is characteristic of a productive and precisely situated restlessness in thought, which is to say, by way of Wynter's terminology, a peripheral utopianism, which Deleuze would call baroque and which I would like to think of, again by way of Wynter, respectfully, if perhaps against her grain, as Blackness, given always most emphatically in Black women's beat and beaten song. If I imagine Wynter tapping her toes to the rhythm of *These Hands*, it is with the mournful pleasure of recognizing her kinship with the women who work a sonic philosophy of enjoyment's terrible beauties.

If *These Hands* is the aftereffect of an incomplete trilogy (the more + less than third of a trio including Mambety's *La Petite Vendeuse de Soleil* and, before that, his *Le Franc* (1994)), the film is both prosthetic and antithetical. It's intra-action of montage and work song resists reduction to signification by way of the insistence, rather than neutralization, of the phonic substance. Signs, and, as such, reductions of the complex totality of convergence, which they iconically perform and constitute, are cut here. To describe that totality, and to improvise through the descriptive and its other, the law of idiom, the hegemony of the signifier, and the oppositions they engender (history/theory—aesthetic [ideological]/scientific) must be broken. Such work requires a mind of Wynter and Schelling's capacity for seeing with the crushing felicities of deadly life allows us to understand such mind and such visual accompaniment as foregiven in the social entanglement of Black women's aesthesis, Black women's thought, and Black women's work. *These Hands* preforms an incalculable liturgy of rupture in its (re)organization of the cinematic apparatus so that we remain in the sounding silence of what's radical and elemental: the multiple presence and present and presencing of the cut. The necessarily dehiscent trauma that the signification of trauma imposes is anticipated in the extra-signifying reverb of a field of unrepresentable, unspeakable sets and institutions. The world system is active in the space between Samora Machel and his absence, Julius Nyerere and his absence, African socialism and its absence, and the looming presence of the remains of Apartheid South Africa, the imprisoning presence of the International Monetary Fund, the restless presence of exile, and the ghostly presence of coloniality in the postcolonial. If the world system is where these women work, then what is the project in and which these women work? Captive to abandonment and displacement in the world, they work through work to truncate and exceed the world in the broken unison of social and sensual ensemble. The chorus's serrated edge serenades itself.

The women have no drums yet their hands, their tools, make chouses of the rock. Their music's content, in contradistinction to its meaning, shifts in the sand they sift like resonant shells ornamenting, augmenting, and disrupting a proper instrument. They make music and the sound conveys and exceeds or takes out meaning. They make music, which is to say they are engaged in the formation of a mode of organization; they have organized themselves and their labor in aesthetic sociality and the track they sound is never separate from the image track it differs and differs from, the whole held not-in-between the senses. Rhythms are voiced like chords and then they speak over them. They sing a story that breaks and accompanies their unnarratable labor. Their misery, the difficulty and danger of their lives, is open. They sing its causes, with deep understanding of the political forces that have shaped their expulsion from narrative in the narrative arc of global racial and sexual capitalism whose periodization is itself made complex by the structures and effects of the very idea of development. That idea always belies the ecstatic copresence of the pre-capitalist and the precolonial, the industrial and the imperial, the postmodern and the postcolonial, which the film conveys, which is held in the conditions of its making, distribution, and reception but which, above all, the women work through in their philosophonic labor.

I'm interested in the way the image-track cuts are shadowed, complicated by continuities of the soundtrack, moving into later dissolves. The cuts allow the relation/interval between the work of the women and the macro level within which that work operates, the larger operations of the mine as a whole. The cuts keep percussively moving from micro to macro, the images complicated by a certain mixing of the sounds, the sounds of the big machines fading into the rhythm of the drumming/sifting/pounding, toned, tuned, attuned, and then the reversal of that fade, the acoustic drumming overwhelmed by the mechanized rhythm of the large machines, the machines in whose preparation they work, signifying Tanzania's larger industrial projects and intentions, the "digital" sounds of global capitalism's industrialization and urbanization. The cuts invoke modernity, but a modernity which, in the midst of its overwhelming force, is, in a real sense, though never enough, improvised in the kind of anticipatory ex- or underurban counterorganization that AbdouMaliq Simone has long seen and heard and studies. And then modernity's national organization dissolves. And then the film's tracks dissolve. And then I dissolve in what Gerard Raunig might speak of as the film's "condividuate" tracking, what Karen Barad might speak of as its "cutting-together-apart" inside and out, allows palimpsestic diffusion, a kind of video-phono-graphic depth of the non-synchronous, the approach of a drum roll heard and seen. This felt perspective is a function both of exhaustive and ecstatic habitation in the cinematic apparatus and in the regional and global political economy. Not-in-between its cuts and shots there's something more and less than suture that is held in *These Hands*.

What's held in and what holds together the film is percussive dehiscence. This is to say that questions of spectatorship/audition/reading, and of their place in the formation of (racial/class/sexual) identity, and in the (racial/class/sexual) division of labor that is registered at the intersection of the political and the aesthetic, which are operative within the kind of psychoanalytic frame that feminist film theory offers, are only part of the breaking, broken story. They must be augmented by another analytic, an analytic of the lingering fall into a pan-tonal, pan-dimensional field of largesse and reception in deprivation, which the film preforms and prefers. Such an analytic will have honored what Fredric Jameson once called "an aesthetic of cognitive mapping" in the breach because something happens when, in sharing, we follow Schelling's attention from the women working in a way that might be mischaracterized as pre-technological to the machines which, in their size and volume, seem to signify a technological order that grinds these women-as-raw-material in much the same way that they grind rocks. Moreover, something else happens to what is given in those cuts as the contrast between the pre-modern and the hand-me-down remnants of an industrialized modernism. The machines are like monsters from an unexperienced past the women live and work in every day, where both the filmmaker and global capital, one perhaps resistantly, the other aggressively, provide for us an inevitably ethnographic—which is to say regressively and oppressively temporizing—optic. And then, what else that happens is precisely this: a sounding of the deep solution that surrounds, infuses, combs, and braids a cinematic tracking that abrades the normal temporal sequencing of narrative film and the conventional historical syntax of political-economic. A displacement is forged within the experience of the film itself. It opens out from the internal difference of the technical apparatus, wherein we feel, paradoxically, the totality of that apparatus. A certain mechanical content is given not only in the cut from the women to the machinery, but in the cut between sound/image/text even when the machinery is not there. The sign of gender in the experience of film is reorganized by this second cut, this refusal of suture, and the intra-active force of the film's tracking does not mitigate against a sensual experience of it in which sound surrounds and disperses, complicating all notions and wishes of mere showing, enriching what is shown through the opposition of the in/visible, the politics of the film's form, its invention and organization of music/labor always paralleling what the women consciously and creatively do in the generativity of their engagement. The film, and what it holds (out), and what it (with) draws, intimates how we might practice our own socioaesthetic organization. It shows and proves what passeth show and tell.

The film clocks in at an all but endless 45 minutes, within which the supposed space between *verité* and fiction appears to have been traversed. This endlessness, an effect of percussion's varied and continuous entanglement of repetition and interruption, is the ground in and upon which (a) narrative is laid that tells or tolls or tallies the unfulfilled, unfinished, movement from the unstaged to the staged, from the unperformed to the performed, from the indeterminate to the overdetermined, when a woman worker dies and her fellow women workers dance, and when the camera's views and movements are acknowledged either openly or accidentally. (The) story charts the buried emergence of a subjected object held in death's individuating grasp. She becomes a person, now that she has a story, but she's gone. *We remain in silence.* The film's organization—a productive ambiguity of the genitive—is always given in the same way, from beginning to end, in the same way the labor of the music in performance is simultaneously given as and with the product or artifact of recording, the sound produced always in holoesthetic ensemble with its production: an ongoing staging then, an ongoing narrative interruption of narrative, the story of narrative's interruption, the ongoing narrative of the cut of narrative, the liberatory force of the cut that filmic form gives us so clearly, the cut as effect of the apparatus but the cut also as an effect of affect—of what is held in a smile out of time. These solicitations, in which staging and the unstaged are one another's blurred effect and disappearance, indicate a continuous flow of discontinuities that form the perfect way of the imperfect, the "been gone" of a soloist interred. The perfect of way of cinema's ongoing discontinuities is marshalled by Schelling so that we can know, by way of their unmarshalled showing, what these women work to know—the rhythmic timelessness that development comes, in uniform tradition, to ensnare. Insofar as they defend what they know in their practice of it, the imperfections of *These Hands* are somehow gracefully on its head. The film lives (in) the imperfect. Its machinery is revealed at the site of its breakdown and we know that its music depends on those generative cuts. The film is situated in and prompted by the destruction and reconstruction of social organization, opening once again, as ritual, the ongoing possibility of the improvisation of ritual. The ethnographic attitude depends upon the suppression of the seam, the overdetermination of the seme, and the overvalorization of an artificial seeming (of community in and as tranquility). Such repression is not what the makers of and in *These Hands* had in mind. Rather, even before the music strains against the narrow space between the true and the fictive, the women work this sound: *Do not disappear in vanity; yes we see you, we really see you.* We really see with you.

Notes

1 "Description of *Le Petite vendeuse de Soleil (The Little Girl Who Sold the Sun)*", *California Newsreel*, www.users.interport.net/n/e/newsreel/films/petiteve.htm, accessed August 12, 2022.
2 Judy, Wynter, Baraka, McGregor, Philip, Spahr, Bashir, Du Bois.
3 Olyango Oloo, "I Am a Film Maker. Not a Geography Teacher." http://onyangooloo.blogspot.com/2004/05/music-views-reviews-and-interviews.html

6

TO BUILD A TABLE

The Rise of Tyler Perry in African-American Cinema

Brandeise Monk-Payton

Introduction

At the June 2019 Black Entertainment Television (BET) Awards, multi-media mogul Tyler Perry became the third recipient of the network's "Ultimate Icon" Award. Despite criticisms of problematic images of Blackness in his films and television programs, one cannot deny Perry's impact on African-American cultural production within and outside of Hollywood through the creation of his own production studio. Since his humble beginnings creating stage plays on the so-called chitlin circuit, he has amassed a huge following with Black audiences, and especially churchgoing women in the South. In 2020, he received the "People's Champion" award at the People's Choice Awards as well as the prestigious Governors Award at the 72nd Emmys. During all of these events, Perry has made inspiring speeches on topics as varied as digging wells and sewing quilts, which act as short sermons that contain life lessons. Perry enacts the power of storytelling through preaching.

This essay explores Perry's influence on Black cinema and media through the vernacular of faith. Perry's faith goes beyond religion and infuses his entrepreneurial spirit as a writer, director, producer, and actor. Such faith manifests as a resistance to catering to the white gaze of Hollywood. Perry eschews fighting for a seat at the table in the mainstream entertainment industry, which has historically been inhospitable to African-Americans, in favor of building his own table for popular media that, as he stated in his Black Entertainment Television (BET) Award acceptance speech, "God would prepare [it] for me in the presence of mine enemies." This use of Bible scripture from the Book of Psalms exemplifies his own roots in the Black church and also gestures toward how faith functions as a brand for his media empire. Through intimately investing in Black audiences and valuing their unique ways of knowing, he has cultivated a loyal fanbase for his steady stream of content. Perry

DOI: 10.4324/9781003079682-7

has built not just a table, but an entire infrastructure for Black folk storytelling in an unprecedented spiritual striving for creative autonomy.

I do not aim to uncritically praise Perry in positioning him as an important force in African-American cinema, and especially a force predicated on religiosity. While he has accomplished a vast and groundbreaking amount in his fifteen-year film career, Perry's success is due in part to his keen capitalization on a moment in which a scarcity of film (and TV) projects by Black creatives allowed for him to saturate the market for African-American media representation. Thus, Perry's projects tended to be understood as representative of Black popular film within mainstream media discourse, a development that critics and scholars alike had to contend with in their past fraught engagement. In terms of scholarship, two academic edited collections published in 2016 centered on the entertainer: *The Problematic Tyler Perry* and *From Madea to Media Mogul: Theorizing Tyler Perry*. The former attends to the pernicious use of stereotype in Perry's body of work and questions his influence in popular culture and on African-American audiences in particular.[1] The latter delves deeper into the representational logics at play with his public persona as they connect to media history, industry, aesthetics, and spectatorship.[2] I build on the insights presented in these two anthologies and offer both a retrospective examination of Perry that is also future-oriented as he embarks on the next phase of developing his media empire. Ultimately, this essay is not meant as a definitive take on Perry but rather contributes to the ongoing process of studying his career, analyzing public discourse on the star, and coming to terms with his significance to Black film in theory and practice.

On Acrimony and the Perry Paradox

Perry released his 19th feature film entitled *Acrimony* in 2018 starring longtime muse Taraji P. Henson as the protagonist Melinda Moore—a hardworking and dedicated, but vengeful woman—who has a fatal attraction to her ex-husband. The movie is initially told in flashback structure as Melinda recounts to her therapist how she met Robert Gayle (Lyriq Bent) at college and fell madly in love. Through voiceover, she details their fairytale courtship that turned into a tumultuous relationship and marriage as she attempted to help him achieve his professional dreams despite financial woes. Perry makes use of five intertitles to segment the film, with each one displaying the definition of a different word that, taken together, reflect the spectrum of Melinda's emotions: acrimony, sunder, bewail, deranged, and inexorable. The first term, acrimony, is defined on screen as "bitterness, anger, rancor, resentment, ill feeling, ill will, bad blood, animosity, hostility, enmity, antagonism, waspishness, spleen, malice, spite, spitefulness, peevishness, venom." The psychological thriller's title mirrors public conversation about Perry, who has been the object of ire in African-American film and media.

Though Perry has a devout following, he frequently receives vitriol from those peers, reviewers, and academics not quite as enamored by his creative output. The "complicated significance" of Perry at the current juncture reflects the friction between his popular appeal among an audience demographic that recognizes itself in his imagery, and those non-fans that assert he profits off peddling harmful representations of race, gender, and sexuality.[3] Specifically, Perry's perverse treatment of Black women in his films and television programs has come under fire among Black cultural critics and feminists alike.[4] In *Acrimony*, when Melinda's therapist presses her on her anger issues, she retorts: "I'm sick and tired of hearing that. Every time a Black woman gets mad, she's a stereotype." Indeed, the film seems to comment on the critique that naysayers have levelled at Perry about all of his projects. However, even with this heightened awareness of the problems associated with "controlling images" (per Patricia Hill Collins), Perry still subscribes to the story logic that Black women must be punished for their sins and what Robin Means Coleman describes as "narratives that exploit women's suffering."[5] Thus, Melinda becomes scornful and slowly unhinged, the price she must pay for not believing in her husband's potential to succeed. By the end of the film, her volatility must be contained to spectacular effect. *Acrimony*, which was shot in only eight days, received a 17 percent rating on Rotten Tomatoes. In addition to the use of tropes, the film's poor quality is exacerbated by limited character development and confusing diegesis. For example: "How does Melinda get on the boat?" It is a question audiences periodically ask in jest on social media that references the final act of the film in which the villainess seems to magically appear onboard a ship to exact revenge on her ex-husband and his new bride. Complete with plot holes, shoddy dialogue, and a heavy-handed use of Nina Simone's musical oeuvre, *Acrimony* is exemplar of Perry's productions in not only content but also cinematic form.

Seven years before the premiere of *Acrimony*, film critic Wesley Morris called 2011 the "Year of Tyler Perry." Morris labeled him as "hardly the best black filmmaker in America" but the most popular and, thus, most important. Writing further, he comments: "Tyler Perry saw and filled a void—for colored audiences who have considered suicide when the lack of options is enuf."[6] The remark is in reference to Perry's film adaptation of playwright Ntozake Shange's beloved choreopoem *For Colored Girls Who Have Considered Suicide When the Rainbow Is Enuf*. The movie version of the theatrical work—abbreviated to *For Colored Girls* (2010)—takes liberties with the original text as Perry excruciatingly attempts to experiment with his storytelling craft through embracing an "unruly dramatic structure."[7] In their unabashed penchant for melodramatic messiness, even the filmmaker's purported cinematic failures like *For Colored Girls* become successes in the context of a dearth of Black representation in mass-marketed media during the decade of the 2000s. Indeed, Perry made his mark in movies before the rise of critically acclaimed feature-length films by African-American directors like Ava DuVernay, Ryan Coogler, and Barry Jenkins. At the time in which *Madea's Family Reunion* (2006) hit the big screen to great fanfare, notable Black male writer/director John Singleton had only released a few projects since his Oscar-nominated and widely praised debut *Boyz 'N the Hood* (1991). And Perry's past artistic nemesis Spike Lee, while putting out a steady stream of films every –two years at the turn of the new millennium, did not reach the heights of Perry's independent hits. In fact, as has been well documented, Lee once criticized the depiction of Black people in Perry's film and TV work as contributing to the racist history of "coonery and buffoonery" in American culture.[8] For Lee, Perry does not offer complex and progressive portrayals of African-Americans, but rather trades in damaging caricatures of Blackness. Yet Perry's activation of not a politics of respectability, but rather *dis*respectability, fuels his adoration.[9] His perceived low-brow material (in terms of aesthetic taste) and lack of acceptance within Hollywood as well as among auteurist elite like Lee contributed to the conditions that allowed him to triumph.

A large part of Perry's success can be attributed to his fandom of predominantly older Black women that are drawn to his stage plays and films that include his iconic Mabel "Madea" Simmons character. Played by a cross-dressing Perry, she is described by him as being "tough-talking and "truth-telling," a homage to the African-American women he spent time with during his childhood days in Louisiana.[10] The no-nonsense Madea is thus a "signifier of nostalgia" for not only Perry but for Black and working-class female moviegoers in the South who identify with her as a symbol of African-American folk culture.[11] These audiences trust Perry to speak to their circumstances as Black women living in the South through the character of Madea and her eccentric family. As I discuss later, this trust is secured by a common faith in a higher power and, specifically, a belief in God. Madea's presence in his films as a God-fearing and wise-cracking matriarch affirms a traditionally neglected population of viewers and they derive spectatorial pleasure from her behavior and attitude on screen.

Perry retired the Madea character with *A Madea Family Funeral* (2019) becoming her last cinematic appearance.[12] In addition to being the final film released that features the matriarch, *A Madea Family Funeral* was also the last movie produced through Perry's "first look" pact with Lionsgate. The mogul had a long-running partnership with the studio for the distribution of his projects. That same year, he also ended his exclusive multi-year deal with Oprah Winfrey's OWN (Oprah Winfrey Network) cable network after seven years of bolstering the channel's ratings through the development of scripted television programming. Currently, Perry's lucrative deal with ViacomCBS allows him to expand his media market and reach a wider audience by producing films through Paramount Pictures and television shows for Black Entertainment Television (BET) as well as the network's new subscription streaming platform BET+.[13] All in all, Perry has written, directed, and produced over 18 feature films and 7 television programs, an impressive output of material from someone who never received training in the field. With these business moves, Perry sets the stage for a broader industry takeover as he builds an entire media enterprise that finds its headquarters at the historic Tyler Perry Studios.

Welcome to Tyler Perry Studios

The city of Atlanta, Georgia, is integral to Perry's entertainment empire. As Miriam Petty comments, "Atlanta has occupied 'Black Mecca' status for African Americans, existing in the popular imagination as a place where African American dreams thrive and prosper."[14] The collective fashioning of Blackness emerging in the city through cultural production like Southern rap music can be extended to film and TV production. Perry's rootedness at the nexus of African-American urban, sub-urban, and rural experience manifests itself through employing geographies of Atlanta for his movies and acquiring property for his economic gain removed from Los Angeles and, specifically, Hollywood.

While 2008 marked the opening of his smaller studio in southwest Atlanta (consisting of two former Delta Air Lines affiliated buildings), the 330-acre lot now known as the site of Tyler Perry Studios was bought by the mogul in 2015 for $30 million. Formerly a Confederate Army base, Perry transformed Fort McPherson into a gigantic complex for film and TV production that is "larger than Paramount, Warner Bros. and Walt Disney's Burbank Studios combined."[15] The complex is now even integrated into the official geography of the city with its name emblazoned on an Atlanta highway sign. The studio contains a variety of neighborhood sets (such as the "Maxineville" community named after his deceased mother that houses the iconic residence of Madea) and even his own replica White House to shoot the primetime television soap opera *The Oval* (BET, 2019–present). The expansive site functions as his own homage to Black Hollywood. Indeed, the soundstages built on the complex are named after African-American entertain-ment icons who have made indelible contributions to cinema: Ruby Dee and Ossie Davis, Cicely Tyson, John Singleton, Della Reese, Diahann Carroll, Sir Sidney Poitier, Spike Lee, Harry Belafonte, Whoopi Goldberg, Will Smith, Halle Berry, Denzel Washington, and, of course, Oprah Winfrey. The dedication ceremony for the soundstages that also served as the grand opening of the renovated studio on October 5, 2019, was an extravagant affair complete with a glamorous red carpet and fireworks display to celebrate Perry's historic accomplishment. The guest list for the opening reflected an array of Black media movers and shakers; attendees in the film and media industry included Viola Davis, Samuel L. Jackson, Tiffany Haddish, Ava DuVernay, and those alive who were paid tribute. Even despite their past feud, Spike Lee also attended and took part in the pageantry of the moment. Politicians like congressman John Lewis as well as former President Bill Clinton and Secretary of State Hillary Clinton graced the red carpet along with athlete-activist Colin Kaepernick. Music royalty Beyoncé and Jay-Z also appeared for the festivities. Documenting her experience at the event, Beyoncé posted on Instagram: "I could feel our ancestors' presence." Here, the superstar speaks to how the studio fosters intergenerational communion through the invocation of Black elders who have passed on but remain tethered to the land in spirit.

Indeed, the land that is home to Tyler Perry Studios becomes a symbol of African-American liberation after enslavement. Perry reflects on the impact of his exclusive ownership of the studio and specifically the ground on which it stands:

> I can go outside and take this dirt and put it on my hands and know that there were Confederate soldiers here walking this land, plotting and planning everything they could to keep us Negroes in place…The very fact that I am

here on this land, the very fact that hundreds of people—Black and brown people—come here to make a living, that is effecting change.[16]

Here, Perry's newfound possession of territory occupied by those who fought for the continued subjugation of Black folk during the Civil War serves as a kind of poetic justice. If the name of Lee's production company, 40 Acres and a Mule, signaled the fight for reparations for slavery through material compensation in the form of a modest amount of land, Perry's studio exceeds this size eight times over. Thus, the piece of real estate takes on value as a testament to the potential of Black independent cinema to financially flourish outside of the machinery of white Hollywood.

It should be noted that Perry is not the first African-American media maker to own a studio. In fact, he is part of a long tradition of Black entrepreneurs in U.S. cinema starting in the early 20th century with filmmakers like the brothers Noble M. and George P. Johnson as well as Oscar Micheaux. Founding the Lincoln Motion Picture Company and the Micheaux Film and Book Company, respectively, these men were pioneers who made and independently distributed "race films." It was even announced that Perry is set to play the latter filmmaker in a HBO biopic.[17] A press release for the future film on Perry's website states: "A trailblazer in his own right, Tyler Perry is the perfect choice to play Micheaux. Similar to the filmmaking legend, Perry combines his written prowess with his mastery behind and in front of the camera."[18] In drawing parallels between their careers, Perry is also seen as a self-made Black man whose status as outsider allowed him to claim autonomy from the mainstream movie industry that marginalized people of color.

On his studio grounds, Perry can create his own version of Hollywood that is even complete with a Black "Walk of Fame," which recognizes lesser-known actors who have contributed to Perry's film and TV projects and places them into the history of African-American media culture. Performers he has worked with such as Keshia Knight Pulliam (formerly a child star of *The Cosby Show*) and Crystle Stewart, a supporting actress in *Acrimony* and main cast member on *For Better or Worse* (TBS, 2011–2012; OWN, 2013–2017), have stars on the Walk of Fame at Tyler Perry Studios. "My name is immortalized," commented Patrice Lovely, who starred in the OWN sitcom *Love Thy Neighbor* (2013–2017) and various Madea movies. Perry provides encouragement to individuals who have not been validated by the entertainment world and supports them by creating professional opportunities:

> In my 'finding a way' there were a bunch of people that were coming through the door with me. The doors and the tables that I was building for myself, they were allowed to sit at and create…That's why I tell people when they come to work for me, this is a place for you to come and build your base, a great audience that will support you. [19]

Perry believes in the act of paying it forward and that people can thrive under his wing when given the chance to be seen.

The literal cementing of Perry's legacy extends to the studio's assistance with the development of movie projects important to Black folk. The superhero hit *Marvel's Black Panther* (2018) was the first film partially shot on one of the soundstages, turning it into the beloved fictional African nation of Wakanda. Additionally, the facilities have been home to Black blockbuster productions like *Bad Boys for Life* (2020) and *Coming to America 2* (2021) with photographs on the studio lot of the casts of both cult classic franchises circulating on social media to great fanfare. Eventually the site will offer public tours and become a tourist destination. Beyond its status as a cultural landmark, Tyler Perry Studios even hosted a Democratic primary debate in November 2019. Outside of commercial ventures, a future phase of development includes the construction of a compound for displaced LGBTQ youth, battered women, and sex-trafficking survivors.[20]

Frequent collaborator Michael Jai White has remarked on Perry's distinct "talent as a builder."[21] The icon who has built characters, stories, an audience, and a brand, is now committed to leaving an inheritance for not only his son, Aman Tyler Perry, but also Black media culture. To return to his BET Awards "Ultimate Icon" speech, Perry preaches the spiritual and moral imperative of helping folks "cross," that is, lifting people up and aiding them across a threshold to get to their desired destination. Thus, the creation of a studio provides a viable path forward for those marginalized in the industry. Not content with fighting for a seat at the table through demands for inclusion such as the #OscarsSoWhite hashtag campaign, he built a table of his own. In his refusal to conform, Perry has established a kingdom with seemingly overflowing resources as part of his media mission.

Prosperity Gospel and "Walking by Faith" in the Entertainment Industry

If Perry sees Atlanta as "the promised land," a Biblical reference to the land of Canaan that God gave to Abraham and his descendants, then his studio in the city exists as an extension of such a paradise for African-American media producers and audiences. The logo for Tyler Perry Studios consists of two sideways "T" letters that resemble the Christian cross. The entrance to the grounds includes a fountain, manicured lawn, and a modern black-and-white edifice. Its landscaping and architectural features telegraph the aesthetics of the megachurch. Indeed, the studio seems to invite those who enter to "worship at the altar of Perry" and become the congregants of his contemporary media mecca.[22]

Perry's brand of Black Christian populism as epitomized by his gospel cinematic endeavors infuses his relationship to the entertainment industries.[23] The language that he uses to frame his extraordinary achievements consistently relies on his fundamental belief in a higher power that will sustain him as a creative. For example, when describing his fandom of older Black churchgoing women and their loyalty, he comments that "When they are with you, you can move heaven and Earth."[24] Perry links his ability to manifest projects, materially and spiritually, to his audience's devotion to him and the work. This viewer demographic has an unwavering belief in both Perry and Jesus Christ. The passion involved in preaching the gospel of Perry's media content corroborates Alfred J. Martin's description of Black fandom as "evangelistic."[25] Displaying an image of the Tyler Perry Studio freeway sign on his Facebook page, Perry shares Bible scripture from St. Mark 9:23–25 in which Jesus relays the power of belief to make "all things" possible. Having faith is crucial to the construction of his table and its abundance of offerings to consume for those seated. Embracing stewardship as an economic model for his success, Perry states: "It's a business…and key in this business is to deliver to this audience, to super serve them and give them everything they want that you can give them."[26]

In many ways, Perry's trajectory in show business has been predicated on elements of prosperity gospel. In this theological worldview, "money, health, and good fortune" are considered "divine."[27] Specifically, teachings promote how prayer and sheer faith will manifest financial blessings from God. An October 2020 *Forbes* magazine profile of the media mogul announced Perry's current status as a billionaire. The underdog of Hollywood who is persistently underestimated by critics has amassed an amount of wealth that rivals his industry colleagues. In another pseudo-parable, Perry divulges:

> When I was young, my father worked as a sub-contractor. He would build these houses and he would come home so happy with $800. But then I watched the man that he built the house for sell the house and make $80,000. I always wanted to be the man who owned the house and not the man that he paid to help build it.[28]

Perry uses such a story to indicate his interest in the accumulation of capital. An ethos of bootstrapping underlies his investment in capitalism as he overcame hardship as a poor person to become someone with a net worth of one billion dollars. His earnings over the years become a testament to the ideology of the American Dream and to his religious beliefs. For Perry, due to his unwavering faith, God has bestowed favor upon him and anointed him with the capacity to foster creative projects and people. Yet he sees himself as an exemplary figure in which "No one, black or white, has been able to do what I've been able to do."[29] Perry unabashedly insists on being a one-man-show in contrast to the focus on collaboration so central to traditions of Black independent cinema such as the L.A. Rebellion school of filmmakers. His individualism fundamentally reflects a conservative agenda of producing media despite an image of communal uplift. Even worse, as Aymar Jean Christian and Khadijah Costley White warn, when Perry "guards creative ownership" and becomes a "One Man Hollywood," it constrains risk and innovation in Black media culture.[30]

The rhetoric of creative control is apparent in Perry's performance of ownership. The entertainer proudly asserts that he pens the scripts for all his films and television programs by himself after noting in an interview with *Essence* that having a writer's room in the past was a "nightmare."[31] In early 2020, he displayed through social media his outsized personal work ethic by posting a video clip of multiple scripts he wrote singlehandedly and a picture of himself alone in his grand home seated next to a roaring fire in a large leather chair with his laptop. The caption on the photograph reads, "My writers room!!!" Perry's insistence on sole authorship of his projects allows him to retain intellectual property, but also comes at a cost; namely, his demand to be at the helm of his projects renders him resistant to critique.

There is a moment in the fifth episode of the Netflix comedy series *#BlackAF* (2020–present) in which TV writer/producer Kenya Barris, playing himself, pays Tyler Perry a visit to seek his advice on the cultural politics of criticizing Black media creatives who he thinks produce terrible content that he sees as regressive.[32] While Barris is clearly anxious about negative public (read: white) perceptions of African-American representation in film, Perry confidently relays to Barris, "I don't care what white people think." He continues his pep talk by emphasizing his connection to "us" Black folk. Perry delivers a monologue that serves as a direct message to his naysayers. Their disapproval means nothing and does not constitute the worth of his projects. Thus, the cameo reflects a man confident in his ability to provide content for his niche viewership. Moreover, Perry relies on his critics' lack of comprehension of his fandom's tastes and uses it as an alibi for his widely panned aesthetic. He doubles down on this explanation in interviews, once commenting:

> Do you understand that the audience is in love with this?…Because if you're complaining about my writing, you're not the audience. My audience loves the way that it's done and the way the stories are told. And from the beginning, it's always been about being true to them.[33]

Here, Perry attempts to insulate himself from critique because of the success of his formula for storytelling; if one does not "get" that his film and television work is popular, it is simply because the work is culturally illegible to critics and deemed irrelevant. Such an excuse gives him license not to take feedback and improve his capabilities as a writer, director, and producer.

Though he has cultivated an image of self-efficiency and sufficiency, Perry does have a vast amount of employees that work for him under precarious conditions. His exploitation of labor through union-busting has been well-documented. Four staff writers on the television series *House of Payne* (TBS, 2007–2012; BET, 2020–present) were fired and accused Perry of unfair treatment.[34] In 2015, the Actors Equity Association placed Perry on a "Do Not Work List."[35] Perry's aversion to unions affects his workers' ability to fight for fair wages, health insurance, and other benefits. As Samantha N. Sheppard notes, his "corporate practices reify the institutional pattern of exploiting (invisible) Black labor in the film industry."[36] However, he has also provided opportunities for continued employment in the industry come hell or high water. For example, Perry made news when his casts and crews returned to set during the Covid-19 pandemic. The producer managed to create a bubble called "Camp Quarantine" and miraculously shot seasons of four different TV programs at his studio in a three-month period over the summer of 2020. Amidst the global public health crisis, he also purchased groceries for needy families under the name "Atlanta Angel."[37] Thus, there are tensions evident in his acts of goodwill that are connected to class politics.

Conclusion

At the opening of Tyler Perry Studios, Viola Davis praised the billionaire media maker as "a Black artist taking control of their artistic life and the vision that God has for their life."[38] From a modest start, Perry has amassed a fortune in the entertainment industry and extended his original reach in stage plays to film, television, and now streaming content. Indeed, his entire library is archived on BET+ for audiences to watch at home and on demand. Perry didn't learn within the Hollywood system and his projects still "operate with little need for white eyes."[39] This feat has sustained him even though he remains a polarizing figure in Black film. Indeed, Perry's mythic "brand of Blackness" produces a "structure of feeling" that conjures up strong positive and negative affects that publicly circulate.[40] While a sense of acrimony pervades the reception of his still growing media empire, he has also created a filmic language that spiritually resonates and brings joy to audiences that have been historically ignored as valued cinema-goers. As recent accolades bestowed upon him recognize his social and cultural impact, this essay has considered his ascent in African-American cinema with an eye toward how Perry attempts to honor God with his storytelling platform.

Over 15 years after Tyler Perry's entrance onto the film scene with *Diary of a Mad Black Woman* (2005) and most importantly, *Madea's Family Reunion* (2006), the conditions of possibility for Black media makers in the entertainment industry have expanded. Content produced by a diverse array of African-American creatives currently spans across film, television, and digital media. Perry is no longer rendered exemplar of all that African-American cinema has to offer to audiences. Even if Perry's outsized significance to Black cultural production has arguably waned with respects to representation, it is noteworthy that his success seems to have given other Black filmmakers a newfound confidence in terms of artistic possession and empowerment. On October 10, 2019, Ava DuVernay tweeted:

> Meeting at a Hollywood studio today. Walked in with new eyes. What used to seem supersized + untouchable to me was now—not so much. Tyler's lot is more than quadruple in size. And solely owned by a Black man. Felt proud of him + happy for a new outlook."[41]

DuVernay takes inspiration from Perry's milestones. In his faith-based efforts to build a table in Black film and media, the mogul has claimed a definitive spot within its history and allowed for a renewed attention to the power of heritage in the entertainment industry.

Notes

1 Brian C. Johnson, ed. *The Problematic Tyler Perry* (New York: Peter Lang, 2016).

2 TreaAndrea M. Russworm, Samantha N. Sheppard, and Karen M. Bowdre, eds. *From Madea to Media Mogul: Theorizing Tyler Perry* (Jackson: University Press of Mississippi, 2016).

3 Taryn Finley, "The Complicated Significance of Tyler Perry" *Huff Post*, November 15, 2019 www.huffpost.com/entry/tyler-perry-studios_n_5dc9ad5de4b0fcfb7f6ae9a6.

4 For example, Black feminist historian and cultural critic Brittney Cooper rails against Perry's disrespect of Black women in a 2013 blogpost on her Crunk Feminist Collective website titled, "Tyler Perry Hates Black Women: 5 Thoughts on *The Haves and the Have Nots*: www.crunkfeministcollective.com/2013/05/29/tyler-perry-hates-black-women-5-thoughts-on-the-haves-and-have-nots/.

5 Taryn Finley, "The Complicated Significance of Tyler Perry."

6 Wesley Morris, "The Year of Tyler Perry. Seriously America's Most Important Black Filmmaker." *Film Comment* 47, no. 1 (2011): 61.

7 Ibid., 60.

8 *Our World* with Black Enterprise, hosted by Ed Gordon (May 18, 2009; Black Enterprise, Inc.)

9 For more of a discussion of Tyler Perry and disrespectability, see TreaAndrea Russworm's introduction in the edited collection, *From Madea to Media Mogul: Theorizing Tyler Perry*. A robust theorizing of negative images in Black popular culture can be found in Racquel Gates, *Double Negative: The Black Image and Popular Culture* (Durham, NC: Duke University Press, 2018).

10 Tyler Perry, "Madea Honored the Strong Black Women I Grew Up With, but It's Time to Move On," *The New York Times*, February 28, 2019, www.nytimes.com/2019/02/28/movies/tyler-perry-madea.html.

11 Miriam Petty, "Old Folks at Home": Tyler Perry and the Dialectics of Nostalgia," *Quarterly Review of Film and Video* 34, no. 7 (2017): 589.

12 Though Perry stated that Madea would be retired, the character returned to the spotlight with the film, *A Madea Homecoming*, which premiered on Netflix on February 25, 2022.

13 Nellie Andreeva, "Tyler Perry Inks Mega Film & Television Deal With Viacom," *Deadline*, July 14, 2017, https://deadline.com/2017/07/tyler-perry-viacom-film-tv-deal-with-viacom. Perry is now poised to do unscripted and variety television in addition to sitcoms and drama series.

14 Miriam Petty, "Old Folks at Home": Tyler Perry and the Dialectics of Nostalgia," *Quarterly Review of Film and Video* 34, no. 7 (2017): 595.

15 Greg Baxton, "Tyler Perry Studios, the House Madea built, Becomes a Landmark for Black Hollywood," October 2, 2019, www.latimes.com/entertainment-arts/tv/story/2019-10-02/tyler-perry-studios-atlanta-dedication .

16 Madeline Berg, "The Rise and Rise of Tyler Perry," *Forbes* (October 2020): 116–122.

17 Cynthia Littleton, "Tyler Perry to Play Pioneering Filmmaker Oscar Micheaux in HBO Biopic (EXCLUSIVE)," *Variety*, June 29, 2017, https://variety.com/2017/tv/news/tyler-perry-oscar-micheaux-hbo-biopic-1202482378/.

18 "Tyler Perry to Star in as Oscar Micheaux," Tylerperry.com, accessed December 8, 2020, https://tylerperry.com/tyler-perry-to-star-as-oscar-michaeux-in-hbo-biopic/.

19 Angelique Jackson, "Man of Action: Tyler Perry on Producing During the Pandemic and Why He's Weighing in on Politics," *Variety*, October 2020, https://variety.com/2020/film/news/tyler-perry-producing-pandemic-politics-1234811061/.

20 CBS News, "Tyler Perry's Atlanta Studio to Include a Compound for Displaced LGBTQ Youth and Trafficked Women." CBS This Morning. October 8, 2019. Video, 0:42. www.youtube.com/watch?v=YJNmWC2B5Ek.

21 DJ Vlad. "Michael Jai White, Who Worked with Tyler Perry, Breaks Down Why He's a Billionaire." Vlad TV. September 30, 2020. Video, 3:17. www.youtube.com/watch?v=_DeZLFV5Qrs.

22 Brandeise Monk-Payton, "Worship at the Altar of Perry: Spectatorship and the Aesthetics of Testimony" in *From Madea to Media Mogul: Theorizing Tyler Perry*, eds. TreaAndrea M. Russworm, Samantha N. Sheppard, and Karen M. Bowdre (Jackson: University Press of Mississippi, 2016): 72.

23 For more discussion on Perry and Christianity, please see Ron Neal, "Spike Lee Can Go Straight to Hell! The Cinematic and Religious Masculinity of Tyler Perry," *Black Theology* 14, no. 2 (2016): 139–151 and Keith Corson, "Tyler Perry, T.D. Jakes, and the Birth of Gospel Cinema" in *From Madea to Media Mogul: Theorizing Tyler Perry*, eds. TreaAndrea M. Russworm, Samantha N. Sheppard, and Karen M. Bowdre (Jackson: University Press of Mississippi, 2016): 52–71.

24 Baxton, "Tyler Perry Studios."

25 Alfred L. Martin Jr., "Fandom While Black: Misty Copeland, *Black Panther*, Tyler Perry and the Contours of US Black Fandoms," *International Journal of Cultural Studies* 22, no. 6 (2019): 739.

26 Cara Buckley, "Tyler Perry Builds a New Kingdom, With Madea Behind Him," *New York Times*, October 14, 2019, www.nytimes.com/2019/10/02/movies/tyler-perry-atlanta.html.

27 Kate Bowler, *Blessed: A History of the American Prosperity Gospel* (New York: Oxford University Press, 2013): 7.

28 Marisa Guthrie, "Tyler Perry Talks Race in Hollywood, Bill Cosby, and Creative Freedom: 'I Don't Get Notes'," *Hollywood Reporter*, May 15, 2017, www.hollywoodreporter.com/features/tyler-perry-talks-race-hollywood-bill-cosby-creative-freedom-i-dont-get-notes-1003287.

29 Buckley, "Tyler Perry Builds a New Kingdom."

30 Aymar Jean Christian and Khadijah Costley White, "The Decline of Black Creative Production in Post-Network Television" in *From Madea to Media Mogul: Theorizing Tyler Perry*, eds. TreaAndrea M. Russworm, Samantha N. Sheppard, and Karen M. Bowdre (Jackson: University Press of Mississippi, 2016): 148.

31 Robyn Mowatt, "Tyler Perry Responds To Highly Criticized Viral Video: 'Early On, I Had a Writer's Room And It Was a Nightmare For Me,'" *Okayplayer*, January 2020, www.okayplayer.com/news/tyler-perry-writers-room-video-response.html.

32 #blackAF, season 1, episode 5, "yo, between you and me... this is because of slavery," directed by Kenya Barris, written by Hale Rothstein, featuring Kenya Barris, Rashida Jones, and Tyler Perry. Aired April 17, 2020. www.netflix.com/watch/81093504?trackId=200257859.

33 Jackson, "Man of Action."

34 Nikki Finke, "Tyler Perry Fires 4 Writers for Union Activity; Atlanta Opening of Perry's New Studio Will Be Picketed; Invited Actors And Guests Being Asked Not To Attend," *Deadline*, October 2, 2008, https://deadline.com/2008/10/writers-at-tyler-perry-studio-to-take-strike-action-will-picket-grand-opening-and-ask-invited-guests-not-to-attend-7129/.

35 David Robb, "Actors Unions Boycott Tyler Perry's 'Madea On the Run'", August 10, 2015, *Deadline*, https://deadline.com/2015/08/tyler-perry-madea-on-the-run-sag-aftra-actors-equity-do-not-work-list-1201496778/.

36 Samantha N. Sheppard, "'Tyler Perry Presents': The Cultural Projects, Partnerships, and Politics of Perry's Media Platforms" in *From Madea to Media Mogul: Theorizing Tyler Perry*, eds. TreaAndrea M. Russworm, Samantha N. Sheppard, and Karen M. Bowdre (Jackson: University Press of Mississippi, 2016): 19.

37 Jenna Amatulli, "'Atlanta Angel' Tyler Perry Paid For Seniors' Groceries At More Than 70 Stores," *Huff Post*, April 13, 2020, www.huffpost.com/entry/tyler-perry-coronavirus-groceries_n_5e8dfd7fc5b670b4330a4264.

38 Kim Ford, "Inside Tyler Perry Studios' Grand Opening Gala With Oprah, Beyoncé and More Stars," *The Hollywood Reporter*, October 16, 2019, www.hollywoodreporter.com/news/inside-tyler-perry-studios-grand-opening-gala-1245752.

39 Morris, "The Year of Tyler Perry," 61.

40 Leah Aldridge, "Mythology and Affect: The Brands of Cinematic Blackness of Will Smith and Tyler Perry" *Spectator* 31, no. 1 (2011): 45–46.

41 Ava DuVernay (@ava), Twitter, October 10, 2019, https://twitter.com/ava/status/1182352731811405824.

7

STREAMING FOR BLACK LIVES

Adrien Sebro

The cord has been cut! In the 21st century, technological advances have redefined the term "media" on a yearly basis. The clear distinctions of film and television have all succumbed to convergence due to subscription video on demand services (SVOD) merging the mediums. Presently, the need for a cable connection for in-home viewing of media has largely been abandoned, to simply a need for an internet connection. With this trend of cord-cutting, major networks and studios have followed suit. After the dominance of subscription-based programming like Netflix, network and premium cable companies began to create digital platforms for streaming their media. In tune with these changing trends, this phenomenon has brought about new forms of Black cultural production and the means in which Black culture makers tell their stories to the masses, especially with the overwhelming majority of media platforms being white-owned and operated. In 2020, amidst the police brutality and murders of Breonna Taylor, George Floyd, and Ahmaud Arbery and other Black people across the nation, multi-media streaming companies such as Netflix, HBO Max, and BET+ have mobilized their platforms to respond to racial injustices through various strategic methods.[1] These responses, some more than others, have worked to reconstruct how their platforms exist as sites for telling Black stories, educating on racial injustice, and providing escapism in a time so fraught with violence and Black pain. It is of grave importance to address these different responses to Black injustices as they exhibit the power of communication mediums and what is at stake when such a political power is not exercised fully.

Consumption of media has rapidly taken new form. Changes in television technology, industry structure, and audience habits are dragging us into a post-television culture. Michael Strangelove's *Post TV: Piracy, Cord-Cutting, and the Future of Television* takes on the task of defining this new phenomenon in media culture. In the late 2000s, television was no longer referred to as an object to be watched;

DOI: 10.4324/9781003079682-8

it had transformed into content to be streamed, downloaded, and shared. Tens of millions of viewers have "cut the cord," so to speak, and have abandoned cable television. As an alternative, they have tuned into online services like Netflix, HBO Max, and BET+ and they watch pirated movies and programs at an unprecedented rate. The idea that the internet will devastate the traditional Hollywood film and television industry isn't so far-fetched. In 2012, around 3.4 billion movies were watched online through streaming services like Netflix. Indicative of the amazing speed at which the internet is changing audience habits, the number of online movies viewed doubled between 2011 and 2012.[2] Movie consumption is shifting from purchases of single physical disks to unlimited streaming services. Strangelove cites viewing on demand, distracted viewing, mobile access, and social viewing as viewing habits of this post-television generation that are causing upheaval throughout media industries.[3]

Streaming culture has found a way to infiltrate the daily lives of media consumers. Through sponsored ads in a simple social media scroll, I was introduced to the various ways that these SVOD services are now bundled into one monthly fee—with a Black focus. Through streaming apps like Xfinity, you can "take Black film and TV on-the-go." The simple act of saying "Black Film and TV" into one's Xfinity Voice remote enables them to experience the best in Black entertainment from any device and at any time. Whether HBCU sporting events, film festivals, or African TV shows, Xfinity offers viewers to "stream culture 24/7" through their bundling of various streaming services such as Netflix, Hulu, Prime Video, Brown Sugar, KweliTV, Urban Movie Channel, etc. This access to Black media culture at one's fingertips is a byproduct of not just the advanced technology of this 21st century moment, but a response to the heightening media coverage of Black Lives Matter moment (not to be confused with the Black Lives Matter activist movement, which will be discussed later). Through case studies of the SVOD services Netflix, HBO Max, and BET+, it is clear that each company deployed various social campaigns and creative strategies to promote Black artistry amidst a time so fraught with racial injustice while maintaining consumer loyalty.

It is difficult to keep up. No matter the speed at which one immerses themselves in binge culture, almost instantly a new show releases through one of the many streaming services available globally. Of course, there is a beauty in such a plethora of media at one's fingertips (for a modest monthly fee), but I cannot help but think about what these images are portraying and who they are speaking to. Whether they are the popular streaming services of Netflix, Hulu, Amazon Prime, HBO Max, Showtime, Starz, the more niche services such as Freeform, BET+, Disney+, or even YouTube, the Black image and access to Black stories *seems* to be easily attainable. Although streaming services offer a space for Black voices, reality and imaginary, the presence of Black media on these platforms is often coded as marketing schema, deliberately othering Black media from other forms of American entertainment. The algorithms that suggest to viewers "Others Like This" after watching a film or series with an all-Black cast, tend to rely on the focus being Blackness rather than genre. Some, often myself, may find this as a liberating feeling, to have the ability to binge and consume all the "Blackness" one desires click after click. Yet, it begs the question, are there damaging affects to this categorization that places Black media as the other and outside of an accepted and established American media canon? Indeed, like Safiya Noble states, "inevitably anything written about algorithms in the 21st century is out of date immediately upon printing due to the rapid changes of technology, so things may have changed upon your reading of this chapter."[4] But, in this moment of national unrest and fighting to make it extremely clear that Black lives *do* matter, we as consumers of media through streaming platforms must question what these subcategories and headings of Black imagery may actually be communicating.

With any SVOD service, a series of algorithms help determine what the service suggests for you to view. For instance, when it comes to Netflix, as a new viewer you must first express interest in Black media content through viewing or searching. Black film and television shows are somewhat hidden from the new viewer until the algorithm can track the Black. Algorithm writers assign descriptive tags to all content in the library and these tags (which often rely on identity-oriented descriptors, that is, African American, Black, LGBT, etc.) then determine the "more like this section" that appears after you view a selection. Activity of other users also works to inform one's algorithm based on similar viewing habits. If many viewers watch films by Black directors such as *Beyond the Lights* (Prince-Bythewood, 2014) and *Fruitvale Station* (Coogler, 2013), then the titles become associated with one another, no matter how dissimilar the films are.[5] Of course, there is some value in these categorizations by race, sexual orientation, or other identity markers. This method can help independent films and filmmakers to break through the Hollywood gatekeeping. A Black producer and director may even see this form of algorithmic pairing as beneficial because although "you may be pushed to a film because your media tastes are Black, but how would you find that film otherwise?" Without a varied enough selection of Black media content, popular streaming services often find themselves at a loss in terms of recommending new content after a selection is viewed. A drawback to this recommendation algorithm is knowledge of who is creating these identification tags, and what these descriptive tags are actually saying. Freelance algorithm writers assign descriptive tags to all content in these libraries, as these are all human beings with inherent biases, these descriptors can lead to a form of "algorithmic oppression."[6] There is always human decision making and human bias in these platforms and because they are better equipped to pare down choices rather than expand them, most of these media never get to viewers outside of the selected demographic.[7]

Writing this essay, I would be remiss to not address the present moment that the world is enduring, largely because this moment informs so much of the present culture of streaming Blackness. In the first quarter of 2020, under federal, state, and local order across America and beyond, the world as many knew it was drawn to a halt in order to slow the spread of the worldwide pandemic, Covid-19. The closing of schools, businesses, restaurants, and anything deemed non-essential to physical existence has pushed many to the brink. Those who are fortunate enough to work from home are in self-quarantine, while many others face the unfortunate reality of joblessness and precarious livelihoods. In addition to the fear of living amidst a global pandemic, 2020 also forced many to parcel through various media sources in order to not only understand the ways in which Black lives are facing systemic and state-sanctioned violence, but also to celebrate Blackness in all of its forms. The murders of Breonna Taylor, Tony McDade, Ahmaud Arbery, and George Floyd, to name the very few that have been receiving national attention, have caused worldwide uprisings and rebellions pleading for the humanity of Black Lives. In response to these atrocities, the Black Lives Matter movement, a political and social movement advocating for non-violent civil disobedience in protests against incidents of police brutality and all racially motivated violence against Black people, sparked demonstrations that were heard worldwide. Starting as a social media hashtag (#BlackLivesMatter) in 2013 after the murder of Trayvon Martin and subsequent acquittal of his murderer, the murders of Black people in 2020 reignited the movement to an even greater scale. The reignition of this movement also worked to create a Black Lives Matter moment, where many individuals, communities, and corporations claim their support of the slogan that "Black Lives Matter" but resist alignment with the Black Lives Matter movement, in efforts to not be politically aligned with an activist organization. In addition, the loss of these Black lives has led many to seek media literacy on the American racial condition to both educate themselves on the fact that these atrocities are embedded in this country's fabric, and to embrace the artistic brilliance of Black popular culture that is so often pushed away from the mainstream. The global desire for entertainment and escapism created a windfall for streaming services. These mandatory stay-at-home orders coupled with the search for Black livelihood resulted in an increase, anywhere from 20% to 50% depending on the channel, in consumer spending on streaming media.[8] Although this temporal moment led to an increase in the search of streamed Black media, efforts to create niche services, specifically for Black entertainment, have tried and unfortunately failed in the recent past.

Starting with just a Facebook page in 2014, a French startup joined the new media revolution. On the Facebook page of *Afrostream*, one could find Black movie trailers and teasing announcements for a streaming service.[9] Shortly after this idea was validated, the *Afrostream* team started building a service that would solely feature African diasporic films for English-speaking and French-speaking American, European, and African audiences. What was great is that a pre-existing library of the content already existed. *Afrostream*'s goal was to provide this streaming to an audience that didn't previously have any legal solution to access such content. Launched in September 2015, Afrostream was created to take advantage of the online video market. A former film producer and theater director, founder and CEO Tonjé Bakang launched the France-based company to cater to a niche African diasporic audience.

In an interview with *Ebony Magazine*, Bakang is much more personal about his passions in developing *Afrostream*. When asked, as a man who grew up in France, what enticed his drive to bring legal African American film and TV content to Europe and Africa, Bakang states:

> (These shows) showed me that we are connected as African Americans and Afro-Europeans and Africans. I believe that we are bound together. I believe from the bottom of my heart that we are all bound. We have this invisible connection because we share the same cultural heritage. Watching those shows, I realized we have the same sense of humor. The way we interact with our families is kind of the same. It was so different from the TV shows we see in France. For us it was a relief. We did not see ourselves on television in France. Not like this. This was positive. This was empowering.[10]

His passion comes from circulating images of people who look like him and have the same culture as him, an emotion he felt is shared with other individuals who cannot access this content on demand. Whether it be the 4 million Afro-French, the 10 million Afro-European, or the one billion Africans that feel a disconnect in media representations of themselves, Bakang aimed to have *Afrostream* serve as that link. Unfortunately, after garnering a subscriber base upon thousands, *Afrostream* closed its doors in 2017 due to lack of investors willing to finance the vision that Bakang set of telling Black stories globally. Two years after launch they stopped marketing of subscriptions. Almost overnight, thousands of subscribers lost their grasp of a once promising streaming service, solely meant for the consumption of Black media. The much larger white-owned and -operated streaming services have largely won the battle of streaming dominance and economy, so the search for Black culture has been relegated to these spaces.

On May 30, 2020, just five days after the murder of Black Minneapolis, Minnesota, resident George Floyd, Netflix took to Twitter to make a statement that shifted the ways in which media corporations were forced to contend with the reality of Black lives living in precarity. The tweet read: "To be silent is to be complicit. Black lives matter. We have a platform, and we have a duty to our Black members, employees, creators and talent to speak up." It was followed by the June 10, 2020, Twitter statement, which read:

> When we say 'Black Lives Matter,' we also mean "Black storytelling matters." With an understanding that our commitment to true, systemic change will take time—we're starting by highlighting powerful; and complex narratives about the Black experience. When you log onto Netflix today, you will see a carefully curated list of titles that only begin to tell the complex and layered stories about racial injustice and Blackness in America.

With these statements, Netflix was among the first media and entertainment companies to announce support for the Black Lives Matter moment after the Minneapolis police killing of George Floyd and the ensuing nationwide protests for equality and criminal justice reform. This action also put Netflix in

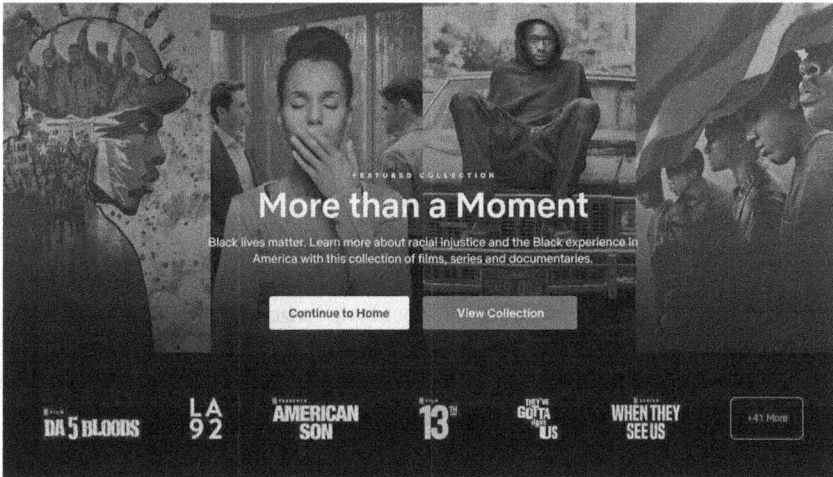

FIGURE 7.1 Still from Netflix. Screenshot by the author

alignment with other major corporations responding to the temporal moment with statements in support of Black lives, denouncing racism, and committing to diversity. Corporations have historically used social causes as a branding strategy. In efforts to practice corporate social responsibility, "corporations align themselves with social causes to bolster their representation as good citizens," this in turn earns consumer loyalty.[11] Consumers feel they are contributing to the greater good and they feel empowered in their business decisions—such as continuing subscription to a streaming service. Netflix wasn't alone in trying to elevate Black stories at this time—critical films taking on racial injustice like *Just Mercy* (Cretton, 2019) and *Selma* (DuVernay, 2014) became available to rent for free through various streaming platforms. Even music streaming services like Spotify also adjusted their playlists in support of Black artists in response to the national uprisings and protests.

In addition to the lip service given across Twitter and Instagram via Netflix's own account as well as Netflix's "Strong Black Lead" account, Netflix initiated multiple responses to the Black Lives Matter moment through their platform's marketing and media library.[12] Following their public statement, Netflix reframed their entire platform and promoted a collection specifically to all U.S. subscribers (although the collection was available worldwide) featuring over 45 titles about racial injustice and the experience of Black people in America and across the Diaspora. Upon logging into Netflix, the platform also featured a new home page meant to promote the visibility of Black stories present on the platform. "Netflix compiled the Black Lives Matter Collection after seeing an uptick in searches for the phrase across the internet."[13] This onscreen "road block" highlighted this new media list and the various subcategories on how an audience can engage directly with Black creators, stories, and entertainment.

With noticeable changes to the service layout and algorithm, Netflix's campaign to highlight Black stories took many different forms. Throughout this restructuring, Netflix targeted a niche audience of Black viewers by reverting to the nostalgia of cult Black television and films from the 1990s and 2000s. Marketing through their various social medias, Netflix announced the acquisitions to streaming rights for Black entertainment fare such as television's *Moesha* (UPN, 1996-2001), *Sister Sister* (ABC and The WB, 1994–1999), and *Girlfriends* (UPN and CW, 2000–2008) as well as films like *Set It Off* (Gray, 1996) and *Menace II Society* (The Hughes Brothers, 1993), to name a few. This strategy worked to retain their current Black audience base while attracting a new one. The largest change made by Netflix in response to the Black Lives Matter moment, however, is the creation of its new genre, "Black Stories." This particular subcategory under the list of Netflix's film and television genres establishes a space where Black media can directly be searched in relation to other shows or films that feature Black artists. The labeling of "Black Stories" may possibly work against some of these media's goals of being in conversation with a larger media canon that is often white. For instance, an American history and war drama like Spike Lee's *Da 5 Bloods* (2020) may otherwise not be brought into conversation with the greater discussed war epic like Steven Spielberg's *Saving Private Ryan* (1998). One may categorize *Da 5 Bloods* solely as a Black film as it exists in/within this "Black Stories" genre. To be clear, there is no fault to be seen as a "Black film," the potential issue is being seen as nothing more, relegating Black filmmaker's art into a box that often is not privy to the promotional reach and acclaim as their white counterparts.

Albeit, its potential negative impacts, the emergence of this new genre on Netflix offers a space on the platform in which a great majority of these medias may not have ever reached such a consumer base due to independent status or lack of advertising. The "Black Stories" genre consists of 12 categories blended together from a variety of different genres of film and television shows, what they all have in common—Blackness. I would be remiss if I did not mention the entirety of the subgenres in the collection: "Black Superheroes," "Black Comedy Icons," "Black Music Legends," "Black Stories for Families," "Black and Queer," "Stories from Africa," "Stories from the African Diaspora," "Black History Is American History," "Strong Black Lead," "Black Hidden Gems," "Black Behind the Camera," and of course "Black Lives Matter." The latter three speak the most to Netflix's new marketing for Black Stories mattering. Black Hidden Gems and Black Behind the Camera exist as important spaces where lower budget, independent films, and Black artists behind the camera are being acknowledged and pushed forward amidst the larger studio films that normally eclipse such media. While the Black Lives Matter subcategory, featuring Netflix's original programming, documentaries, and social justice media marks Netflix's attempt to make clear that Netflix has always felt that Black lives and stories matter. As stated earlier, Netflix may have enacted the most visible and publicized of streaming platform changes, and with these changes, other streaming services were also forced to contend with the political moment of radically addressing the precarity of Black lives and media's role in popular understandings and ideals regarding race. In competition with the powerhouse streaming service that Netflix is, the newly formed HBO Max also fell in line regarding the politics of their media's representation.

In 2019, the Turner Classic Movies Festival held a monumental event in which they contextualized, honored, and discussed the 80th anniversary of the classic Hollywood film, 1939's *Gone with the Wind* (Fleming). The event, "*Gone with the Wind*: A Complicated Legacy," featured prominent film historians Donald Bogle and Molly Haskell in conversation with film scholar Jacqueline Stewart and media producer Stephanie Allain. This cadre of dynamic individuals in their respective fields discussed the complicated history of the film. The roundtable discussion became the preface to a larger dialogue of race, history, film, and popular culture that HBO Max was forced to contend with upon their recent launch.

With the multi-platform claims of corporate responsibility in defense of Black livelihood made by Netflix, other media streaming services soon followed suit, such as the recently established HBO Max. Launched on May 27, 2020, through its parent company WarnerMedia and based on their Home Box Office (HBO) premium cable television service, HBO Max was introduced as an over-the-top streaming service featuring various content from its entertainment brands. With a substantial media library, HBO Max includes HBO's existing pay television rights and first-run original content as well as medias that are sourced from other studios including sister company Warner Bros. Pictures, Universal Pictures, and 20th Century Studios. In response to the widespread uprisings, HBO Max catered their platform to address and highlight Black stories in various ways. From curating a "Critically Adored Black-Led Films" genre in their film library, coupled with a "Culture-Defining Black TV" genre, HBO Max's most critical response to grappling with Black media imagery and histories of outdated content came with the recontextualization of arguably Hollywood's most beloved film, *Gone with the Wind*. A film that, according to film scholar Jacqueline Stewart, has undeniable cultural significance and is a major document of Hollywood's racial practices of the past that speaks directly to the racial inequalities that persist in media and society today.[14]

Reported through various trade journals in early June 2020, amidst the growing unrest and outrage in defense of Black lives, the newly formed "HBO Max has pulled from its library the classic film *Gone with the Wind* until it can give audiences context on the movie, on how it romanticizes slavery and the South during the Civil War."[15] The removal of this film with the aim to recontextualize its place in American history marks an important moment in the history of streaming media as it merges socially conscious education and critical media literacy to fictional entertainment. Many heralded pieces of early cinema, like *Gone with the Wind*, have cast Black characters in roles much less desirable than their white counterparts. Often, these films show Black characters sacrificing themselves at the behest of the storyline and white characters. Consequentially, these Black characters are not fully realized, leaving audiences to question: What are the Black character's goals? Values? Where does their agency lie? In a film that idolizes and romanticizes the

Antebellum South and denies the horrors of chattel slavery, these questions are all too apparent.

When *Gone with the Wind* finally returned to the HBO Max platform, it now existed alongside the TCM Festival Roundtable discussion of the film, a short biographical narrative of its Academy Award winning Black actress Hattie McDaniel, as well as a four-minute film introduction of *Gone with the Wind* by TCM host and film scholar Jacqueline Stewart. With these actions, HBO Max works to educate and hold a teach-in on why the highest grossing film of all time (adjusted for inflation), albeit its many shortcomings, should be viewed, contextualized, and discussed. In summary of her eloquent discussion of the film, Stewart states:

> Although watching *Gone with the Wind* can be uncomfortable or even painful, it is important that classic Hollywood films are available to us in their original form for viewing and discussion. They reflect the social context in which they were made, and invite viewers to reflect on their own values and beliefs when watching them now. These films indicate what images and stories Hollywood has deemed acceptable and what mainstream audiences found to be appealing and entertaining fare. Classic films have been and continue to be a major influence on popular views of history.[16]

Stewart helps to make clear to viewers that although we are in a large moment of racial injustices and uprisings, media history and its treatment of Black people and characters is even more valuable to investigate presently. Many, like the National Association for the Advancement of Colored People (NAACP) during *Gone with the Wind's* initial theater run, have called for the film to be boycotted and taken out of circulation. However, what we need is not a dismissal of this media, but rather a re-reading of it from a lens of understanding the trends, practices, and structure of Hollywood as a creator of popular culture. Since *Gone with the Wind* has shaped the way many generations of viewers worldwide have pictured slavery and the reconstruction period that followed, it is critical that this film is viewed with Stewart's newly added introduction in order to encourage viewers to approach the film with a recontextualization that promotes discussion of their own biases, beliefs, and (mis)education of a foundational moment in race relations and American history. With Netflix and HBO Max existing as two white-owned and operated streaming services, their reactions to the Black Lives Matter moment exist largely within the bounds of simply restructuring their media content. Without larger statements made in support of the Black Lives Matter activist movement, these companies are able to maneuver from making direct claims of political and social action surrounding Black lives. Claims that primarily Black media spaces refused to shy away from.

As a pay cable service built solely on Black media entertainment and targeting Black audiences, Black Entertainment Television (BET) and its SVOD service, BET+ practiced a much different response to the events of brutality against Black

lives and the Black Lives Matter movement.[17] In the wake of the murders of
Breonna Taylor, George Floyd, Ahmaud Arbery, and others, unlike the streaming
services of Netflix and HBO Max, BET+ did not have to realign the entirety of
their online media library to showcase that Black stories matter. Their support of
Black humanity and speaking on racial injustices was essentially already aligned
with their mission of streaming Black culture and Black content since BET was
formed in 1980 under the slogan "Yes to Black."

Although BET+ did not realign the entirety of their streaming platform, they
too used this moment to educate their subscribers on various systemic issues faced
in the Black community. Through the creation of the "Justice Now" category in
the film library, BET+ collected various films and documentary specials such as
Katrina: 10 Years Later, and *Rest in Power: The Trayvon Martin Story* to draw attention
to major events and people that tell stories of a history of racial injustice across
America and Black resilience. More critically, BET+ released a six-part documentary series special titled *Finding Justice*, which exposes inequality in Black
communities across America as this series follows the heroes, leaders, and activists
bringing change to the cities they call home. In episodes that respectively focus on
"Stand Your Ground," "Cash Bail," "Voter Suppression," "Criminalization of Kids,"
"Police Brutality," and "The Lead Paint Crisis," *Finding Justice* makes clear to its
viewers and BET+ subscribers that inequality and violence against Black bodies
takes many forms in the system of America. What is important to note here is the
alignment that the BET+ platform has with activists at the forefront of systematic
change. Differing from the parent companies or streaming services of Netflix or
HBO Max, BET and BET+ work to show support and alignment with the actual
Black Lives Matter Movement and not simply the Black Lives Matter moment
or slogan. As discussed earlier, many companies in the midst of corporate social
responsibility have made verbal claims, attempted to educate, have made social
media campaigns, and have shown media that expresses their belief that "Black
lives matter." BET and BET+ however, also pledged support to the Black Lives
Matter movement.

Tracking media companies and their social media responses to the global outrage, *TV Guide* even claimed that BET had been posting much more "forceful content" about the Black Lives Matter protests as they differed from their competitors
by highlighting the actual activist movement.[18] BET and BET+ continued to post
social media coverage in support of the protests on Twitter and Instagram, including
sharing activist Tamika Mallory's viral speech contextualizing looting as a form of
protest and calling for criminal charges against police that kill Black people.[19] On
Instagram, BET and BET+ took a step further and called on Minnesota Governor
Tim Waltz to assign state Attorney General Keith Ellison as special prosecutor on
the George Floyd case and shared donation links to organizations supporting on-
the-ground efforts in the fight for racial justice, petitions for legal action, a link to
register to vote, and resources to learn more about police violence and systemic
racism.[20] Robert Johnson, co-founder of BET, even suggested that Black Lives

Matter become a permanent part of American politics by transforming into a political party. Johnson went on to say that,

> 40 million African Americans who tend to vote as a block in one of the two parties limit their leverage in getting action from both parties…it's time that African Americans start an independent party, not be an appendage of one party or ignored by the other party, and using their leverage in a democracy to say we stand for things that are principally focused on the interest of the 40 million African Americans, and not have that diluted.[21]

Along with the additions to the media on the BET platforms, this so-called forceful content is what was necessary to push for reform such as defunding police forces and to promote the change and reconstruction of systems that reinforce racial inequality, systems in which Black people were seen as non-human in their establishment.

Through numerous social media campaigns, rewritten algorithms, and new media produced, it is clear that SVOD and streaming companies saw it dutiful to make their platforms exist as sites for telling Black stories, educating on racial injustice, and providing escapism in a time so fraught with violence and Black pain. The focus of this essay on the major streaming platforms of Netflix, HBO Max, and BET+ is deliberate in order to explain how the entertainment media plays a role in understanding, communicating, and teaching race relations. All of these platforms took very different approaches in response to histories of racial injustice that reignited in the present. With this political power of media as pedagogy, it is the responsibility of major platforms such as these to respond to global movements and how they impact historically disadvantaged people. As a niche platform founded by and for Black people, that is deliberately aligned with the fight for Black visibility and voice, it is clear where BET+ is aligned politically and socially. Concurrently, with the larger global reach of these platforms in homes across the world, white-owned and operated platforms, like Netflix and HBO Max, have the power and ability to match their words and pedagogy with more "forceful content," such as calling attention to legal systems that need realignment, and even more aggressively addressing their own internal executive leadership and hiring practices, if they truly believe that Black lives matter outside of and longer than the watershed moment in 2020.[22] The power of these platforms must move more radically and outside of the algorithmic space, to speak truth to their claims of Black lives mattering in perpetuity, not simply when they are being slain.

Notes

1 Breonna Taylor, a 26-year-old Black woman, was fatally shot in her Louisville, Kentucky, apartment, when a search warrant was executed by white police officers of the Louisville Metro Police Department. George Perry Floyd Jr., a Black man who was killed during an arrest in Minneapolis, Minnesota. A white police officer knelt on Floyd's neck for a period

initially reported to be 8 minutes and 46 seconds. Ahmaud Marquez Arbery, an unarmed 25-year-old Black man, was pursued and fatally shot while jogging near Brunswick in Glynn County, Georgia.

2 Strangelove, Michael *Post TV: Piracy, Cord-Cutting, and the Future of Television*, University of Toronto Press, 2015, p. 17.

3 Ibid.

4 Noble, Safiya. *Algorithms of Oppression*, NYU Press, 2018, p. 10.

5 Joyner, April. "'Blackfix' How Netflix's algorithm exposes tech's racial bias." February 29, 2016. www.marieclaire.com/culture/a18817/netflix-algorithms-black-movies/

6 Noble, Safiya. *Algorithms of Oppression*, p. 4.

7 Joyner, April. "Blackfix."

8 Martin Gontovnikas, "The (Surprisingly Complex) Impact of COVID-19 on Streaming Media." April 30, 2020. https://auth0.com/blog/the-impact-of-covid-19-on-streaming-media/

9 Romain Dillet, "Afrostream Is Netflix For African and African-American Movies," *TechCrunch* https://techcrunch.com/2015/07/17/afrostream-is-netflix-for-african-and-african-american-movies/

10 Suede, "Afrostream: The African Netflix," *Ebony Magazine* www.ebony.com/entertainment-culture/afrostream-the-african-netflix#axzz3yx4lf4GO.

11 Lily Kunda, "Ben and Jerry's, Black Lives Matter, and the Politics of Public Statements," in *FLOW Journal*, July 6, 2020.

12 Launched in 2018, Netflix's Strong Black Lead is a marketing (social media, podcasts, and video content) arm committed to amplify Black voices in Netflix's programming and their workplace.

13 Todd Spangler, "Netflix launches 'Black Lives Matter' Collection of Movies, TV shows, and Documentaries" in *Variety*, June 10, 2020.

14 Turner Classic Movies, *Gone with the Wind*, HBO Max, 2020.

15 "Entertainment Companies Express Solidarity with Black Lives Matter," in NPR, June 12, 2020.

16 Turner Classic Movies, *Gone with the Wind*, HBO Max, 2020.

17 Launching in 2019 BET+ features original BET films, television series, stage plays, and media from its parent company ViacomCBS.

18 Allison Picurro and Liam Matthews, "Netflix, HBO, BET, and More Companies Voice Support for Black Lives Matter amid Protests Over George Floyd's Death," *TV Guide*, June 19, 2020. www.tvguide.com/news/netflix-hbo-hulu-amazon-starz-black-lives-matter/.

19 Activist Tamika Mallory's viral speech, www.youtube.com/watch?v=7ecy0QLVES8.

20 Ibid. Picurro and Matthews, *TV Guide*.

21 Kelly Wynne, "BET Founder Urges Black Lives Matter to Form Independent Political Party," *Newsweek*, 6/23/20. www.newsweek.com/bet-founder-urges-black-lives-matter-form-independent-political-party-1512842.

22 Currently only 7% of Netflix's staff is Black/African American www.statista.com/statistics/1000578/netflix-employees-ethnicity/

8

OUT OF FORM INTO BEING

Black Women Filmmakers and Experiments in Expansive Cinema

Michele Prettyman

Dedicated to Michelle Materre

Black Women and Moving Images: A Metaphysical Approach

According to Barbara A. Holmes,

> it is nothing short of a miracle to be situated in a cosmos that keeps its secrets but reveals just enough to keep us intrigued. Each day that dawns is a celebration of the fact that we have been invited to consider how our lives are spent; how we embrace and recoil from the creative genesis of darkness, which is also light; and how we relate to others.[1]

Whereas Christina Sharpe reminds us "*we are constituted through and by continued vulnerability to this overwhelming force, we are not only known to ourselves and to each other by that force*" (emphasis in original).[2] Historically, a metaphysical impulse surfaces with some frequency across the archive of Black women's filmmaking practice beginning with the "first wave," Kathleen Collins, Julie Dash, Ayoka Chenzira, Barbara McCullough, Zeinabu Irene Davis, and Camille Billops, then through second wave figures like Cheryl Dunye and Kasi Lemmons. While some of my previous work explores the first and second waves, this essay identifies a third wave from roughly 2010 to the present, with two primary trajectories: the first, consisting largely of narrative/feature films and a second of short-form and experimental works viewed primarily at film festivals, museum spaces, and online platforms. In this essay I use a metaphysical framework to study contemporary film and moving image art focusing on a subset of works made by Black women makers. While the term "metaphysical" may feel vast and unwieldy, I do find "the metaphysical" everywhere—as an impulse that undulates in and through our conceptions of time and space, in sonic lineages, the photographic archive, religious and spiritual experiences, movement and performance, and in film and visual arts. I also embrace

DOI: 10.4324/9781003079682-9

a number of definitional variations of the term including "'meta'-physical," which connotes a move beyond the physical; and metaphysics, which refers to "a division of philosophy that is concerned with the fundamental nature of reality and being and that includes ontology, cosmology, and often epistemology."[3] This framework directs our attention to the relationship between being, which I define as the outcome of plumbing the depths of an interior-facing, yet not singular, consciousness and turning this awareness outward, and formal innovation: the tools, techniques, and technologies, which enable the out-picturing of this awareness. This mode of study is not interested solely in embodiment but rather in Blackness as a more expansive sphere connected to spiritual attributes like consciousness, ecstasy, intimacy, cosmic exploration, and transfiguration, tracing how creative and spiritual energies shape the conditions of production, exhibition, reception, and the interpretation of films and moving image art, and amplifying the ways we might experience them.

Many of the questions and arguments I raise and the metaphysical methodology itself is the result of my extended engagement with the work of Kathleen Collins who in many ways is the animating presence that shapes this project. In both her films *The Cruz Brothers and Miss Malloy* (1980) and the seminal *Losing Ground* (1982) Collins invites, gestures to, and literally captures the ethereal, formlessness of human *being* through the mechanism of cinema.[4] Her work is an exercise in the rendering of human consciousness, giving it form, yet relishing in its mysteries and its impermanence. Foregrounding Sarah, the protagonist in *Losing Ground*, and her pursuit of ecstatic experience, Collins lays bare how cinema is also grappling, both formally and metaphysically, with its own capacities and limitations. Years later Collins' influence surfaces in the work of Ja'Tovia Gary, specifically her short film *An Ecstatic Experience*, and both women's films and practice embody what I describe as an "expansive" paradigm. Gary reveals a vital part of her practice which makes a powerful connection between form and being in an online conversation with filmmakers Jason Fitzroy Jeffers, Loira Limbal, and Jon Sesrie-Goff. She describes pulling from her "archive" of 16 mm film and etching on top of the film, a process called "direct animation," which shows up in the film as white scratch marks, sometimes reverberating around the head of actress Ruby Dee delivering a powerful monologue.[5] Gary explains how the process of direct animation impacts her, saying:

> For me, the actual act of making it, can be, if I am doing it right, a kind of healing modality for myself, particularly the analog process of etching and painting on filmstrips. Whenever I'm doing any sort of meticulous and tedious work with my hands, there's a kind of meditation state that I slip into.[6]

I describe these and other practices as "metaphysical modes of encounter" to account for how the films often stage how we might *be with* them.[7] This includes the conditions under which we experience (and are moved by) them—how they invite us to contemplate astral, naturalistic, spiritual, and interior structures of feeling; how they touch our conceptions of human/otherworldly experience; how we might socialize our thinking together as we watch and discuss them.[8] A deeper exploration of these works and this mode of encounter has the capacity to enliven production, curation, and exhibition practices and modes of public discourse. And perhaps above all, this approach values life, Black life as life, Black life as creative power, creative power as being, and following Tina Campt, an investment in the generative powers of Black life in all its forms and refusals.[9]

The feature film trajectory of this impulse takes shape around the earliest work of Ava DuVernay, particularly her first two feature films *I Will Follow* (2011) and *Middle of Nowhere* (2012). DuVernay, with stellar cinematographers and personnel, envisages worlds where audiences are invited to be present with the desires, grief, even the banality of Black characters, with particular emphasis on the inner lives of Black women. She juxtaposes her characters internal everyday-ness against the forces of the outside world, the carceral state for instance, yet those external forces never supersede, never overtake the primacy of the internal power of Black life. Similarly, in her films *Pariah* (2011) and *Mudbound* (2017), filmmaker Dee Rees also invests in Black life as a space of often quiet, yet intense, transformation and discovery.

The second trajectory of Black women in this third wave includes the afore-mentioned Ja'Tovia Gary, recent work by Cauleen Smith, Madeline Hunt-Ehrlich, Nuotama Bodomo, Garrett Bradley, Jenn Nkiru, and Elissa Blount-Moorhead (these last two figures I discuss in more detail later). The works in this trajectory are fluid, defying categorization or sometimes embracing multiple frames—artistic and experimental, narrative and documentary, historical, personal/memoirist, immersive, music video—all embodying modes of technological world-building, not simply within, adjacent to, or at the behest of an industry. Central to understanding both trajectories is to locate them within an expansive ecosystem of art and mediated culture that is juxtaposed to a rich outpouring of public engagement, commentary, and scholarship. (See features of this era which have impacted Black film and media culture in Table 8.1.)[10]

In what follows, I construct a map, a way to read, feel, and, contextualize the work of Black film and moving image artists over the last 40 years, but with a pre-cise focus on Black women filmmakers and their expansive, collaborative modes of practice over the last ten years. Following this introduction to the metaphysical framework, the "meta"-narrative, if you will, I outline aspects of the Black media ecosystem which create the conditions for an expansive cinematic paradigm to emerge. Then I discuss *being* as an example of a metaphysical analytical paradigm, followed by a historiographical reading of the term "expanded cinema" and how it influenced my thinking about Black cinema as an expansive modality. Finally, to contemplate the impact of an expansive moving image/art practice I discuss the work of moving image artist/curator Elissa Blount-Moorhead who uses digital and immersive tools to render architectural and ethereal archives of Black life. A partner in the TNEG production collective with Arthur Jafa and Malik Sayeed, Blount-Moorhead works across many creative collectives building worlds that unearth the intimate histories of everyday Black life.

TABLE 8.1 The 21st Century Black Media Arts Ecosystem: How We Got Here

Just 20 years in, the 21st century has already been profoundly shaped by a series of expansive breakthroughs and technological ruptures impacting Black film and visual culture globally and our collective mediated futures. Some of these influences include:

—The explosion of Afrofuturism as a theoretical, pedagogical, cultural, and aesthetic formulation.

—Social media as an archive, a mode of dissemination, the public circuitry of the digital and as a conduit for discourse.

—The digitization and archiving of the films of the LA Rebellion, which included a national tour and the publication of the *LA Rebellion: Towards a New Black Cinema* anthology.[40]

—A wave of invaluable critical theory/Black studies and the interplay between artists and theorists.

—Deeper explorations into the Black photographic archive.

—The rediscovery and digitization of the work of the first wave of Black female filmmakers including Kathleen Collins, Jessie Maple, Julie Dash, Ayoka Chenzira, and Camille Billops.

—Two invaluable film series co-programmed by producer/professor Michelle Materre: first with Jake Perlin: "Tell It Like It Is: Black Independents in New York, 1968–1986" with the Film Society of Lincoln Center in 2015 and another program co-programmed with Nellie Killian and co-curated with BAMcinématek "One Way or Another: Black Women Filmmakers 1970–1991."

—The growth of Nollywood and other African national cinemas and the increased production and circulation of films by African and diasporic filmmakers.

—The growth of Black/African diasporic film festivals (American Black Film Festival, BlackStar, Pan African Film Festival, BronzeLens Film Festival) and an increasing Black presence in international, regional, and niche festivals.

—The emergence of the #BlackLivesMatter movement and political activism around police brutality and anti-Black violence and the leveraging of cell phone cameras to capture violence.

—The emergence of other social media advocacy movements, that is, #OscarsSoWhite.

—A reckoning around gendered forms of sexual violence, harassment, and discrimination against women led by activist Tarana Burke and the emergence of the #MeToo movement.

—The rise and monetization of user-generated content via YouTube and TikTok and the interplay between user-gen context and mainstream platforms (for example, Issa Rae's web series "Awkward Black Girl" is reimagined as HBO's *Insecure*).

—The growth of Black arts multi-media installations, exhibitions, and the cross-pollination between the visual arts, digital media, and filmmaking.

—The opening of the National Museum of African American History and Culture, specifically its curation around film and photography and exhibitions at countless other museum spaces.

—The increased visibility of queer filmmakers, artists, and discourse.

(*continued*)

TABLE 8.1 (Cont.)

—Vital second waves of work created by Black filmmakers from the 1980s and 90s: Spike Lee, Julie Dash, Ayoka Chenzira, Cheryl Dunye, and Kasi Lemmons.

—The emergence of Tyler Perry and his creation of a Black-owned studio in Atlanta.

—The emergence of Black filmmakers Ava DuVernay, Barry Jenkins, Dee Rees, Ryan Coogler, Jordan Peele, et.al. who move successfully between "independent" and commercial spheres.

—The emergence of Black American women feature film directors like Gina Prince-Bythewood, Nia DaCosta, Radha Blank, Melina Matsoukas, Channing Godfrey Peoples, and Regina King et.al.

—A proliferation of Afro-British filmmakers, artists, and actors whose work and presence permeates global screens including Steve McQueen, Amma Asante, Cynthia Erivo, Daniel Kaluuya, and David Oyelowo.

—The emergence of a number of vital collaboratives/collectives: ARRAY, TNEG, the Ummah Chroma, New Negress Film Society, Brown Girls Doc Mafia et al.

—The growth of Southern film and cultural influences from hip-hop and literary culture to Donald Glover's FX TV show *Atlanta* and OWN's *Queen Sugar*.

—The codification of the "Howard University Pedagogy Lab" of filmmakers/cinematographers including Arthur Jafa, Malik Sayeed, Bradford Young, and Jenn Nkiru.[41]

—The impact of popular music artists as moving image artists—Beyoncé, Jay-Z, Kanye West, Rihanna, Donald Glover, Common et al. collaborating with filmmakers like Kahlil Joseph, Arthur Jafa, Bradford Young, Jenn Nkiru, and Melina Matsoukas.

—The rise of Black TV writers/showrunners including Larry Wilmore, Shonda Rhimes, Kenya Barris, Mara Brock Akil, Ava DuVernay, Lee Daniels, Issa Rae, Terence Nance, Justin Simien, Lena Waithe, Donald Glover, Courtney Kemp, Michaela Coel, and Misha Green.

—The 2020 protests and the "racial reckoning" emerging in the wake of the murder of George Floyd, Breonna Taylor, and too many others.

These works claim the freedom to explore countless ways of seeing, knowing, and being, in fact, as Michael Gillespie (through Abbey Lincoln and Max Roach) might declare—*they insist*.[11] I am hopeful that this approach expands the tools for engaging this work and in subsequent sections hope that readers can *feel* the strokes of its impact and the nuances of its innovations. I position film history and this era of Black cultural life as the opening of countless doors to countless new worlds. Ultimately, I aim to excavate how we see and experience *being*, the interior qualities of a film, image, character or even the filmmaker's creative process, and how interiority *spills* (as Alexis Pauline Gumbs might suggest), or perhaps interfaces, with the cosmos.

Cosmologies of Being

I return to the opening passages that frame this essay to articulate ways of thinking about being. First, the words of Barbara Holmes, whose work lives at the intersection of race and theology. Holmes astutely reminds us to rethink the cosmological orientations of Black life, announcing that it is, "situated in a cosmos" not at some liminal edge, fringe, or underbelly, nor solely within national, sociopolitical, or cultural spheres. This is a vital reordering of things, but I would go so far as to say that we are *one with* the cosmos (life, world, universe and beyond) and co-creators of it, making it visible, decipherable, tangible, inhabitable. And if we are, what kinds of cosmological renderings are possible? Holmes provides an opening for thinking about macrocosmic structures and frameworks and our creation of them. Holmes' perspective aligns with the sentiments of Jheanelle Brown who in her essay "Rupture and Reparative Modes of Care from the Women of the LA Rebellion" provides another poignant take on the cosmos, Blackness, and the visual sphere:

> To be seen is to feel the cosmos in my bones. To be seen is to contemplate celestial bodies. To be seen is to grind and spit and gnaw and question until you reach the mountains and you know what you were looking for. To be seen is to touch the earth and know that you are home...When I am seen, I bloom within myself.[12]

To unpack the analytic of *being*, I (re)turn to Christina Sharpe's treatise *In the Wake: On Blackness and Being* (2016) and perhaps her seminal claim:

> And while the wake produces Black death and trauma—"violence ...preceded and exceeds Blacks" (Wilderson 2010, 76)—we, Black people everywhere and anywhere we are, still produce in, into, and through the wake an insistence on existing: we insist Black being into the wake.[13]

Sharpe later offers several powerful examples of how being surfaces in film and literature. For instance, she discusses Abderrahmane Sissako's film *Timbuktu* (2014), alongside writers Fatou Diome and Edwidge Danticat, saying: "I hear an echo of Danticat (1996) capturing the insistence with which Haitian women speak themselves into the present. Their greeting: "How are we today, sister? I am ugly, but I am *here*."[14] Being, then, is a contravening, primoradial force unto itself, a kind of "hereness"—the awareness of a full sense of selfhood within a complicated universe or a cosmological set of forces. Later Sharpe describes a metaphysical encounter she has with several Roy DeCarava photographs in which she is drawn to the image of little children explaining that "His look, like the look of the girl, reaches out to me across space and time."[15] These images and her description of them are reminiscent of those captured by cinematographer Bradford Young in his collaboration with Common in *Black America Again* (2017), specifically the wide-eyed, luminous little boy on whose face the camera is trained for some time. Sharpe's study, then, clarifies my investment in *being* emphasizing its "insistence on existing" and how we might see, know, and be with ourselves and with one another apart from those forces.

Garrett Bradley's film *Time* (2020) similarly draws us into the emotional being of a family separated by incarceration. Bradley reimagines the conventions of traditional documentary film form by using video and audio recordings of wife and mother Fox Rich and her sons as they document their lives for their incarcerated husband/father. The poignance of the family's voices, particularly those capturing the children's emotional growth, Rich's longing for her husband, and her frustrations with the carceral state, are meant to displace the need for a traditional narrator. They also intensify the family's presence, compelling the audience to reckon with their humanity rather than that of a disconnected vocal presence. Being is reiterated in Racquel Gates' eloquent take on the film as she writes:

> Fox's collection of tapes is a labor of love meant for Robert's eyes, yet the extensiveness of her archived life is underwritten with a sense of urgency: to document, to record, to say "I was here" in a world where Black families, and Black lives, must continue to insist on their right to live and love in a world openly hostile to their very existence.[16]

Thus, part of *being*'s power is its capacity to reach out to us, to touch us, move us, drawing us deeply to one another.

A final useful, yet complicated, example of being is found in Lee Daniels 2009 film *Precious: Based on the novel "Push" by Sapphire*. Consider the scene in which the titular Precious attends literacy classes in which she is expected to write in her journal each day. On one particular day the young women in the class are introducing themselves and, after initially declining to speak, new class member Precious decides to participate. Teacher Blu Rain asks her how it feels to speak in class for the first time. Precious responds, "I feel, here." This moment is punctuated, even amplified, by the naturalistic sound of chirping birds, who also seem to take notice of Precious's expanding sense of awareness. Not simply an abjection who has been raped, molested, and abused in multiple ways, as she speaks and writes Precious becomes one with the animating forces of life inside her and around her, one with the natural world evoked in the chirping birds and the world of form (language and writing).[17] She is a sentient, feeling, self-aware being and the opening for that being to become one with a universe of choices, language, relationships, and intimacies.[18] "Self" here designates a particular location of selfhood as a more expansive experience, as one who feels, who knows, who is; one who insists on existence, leaning into Fred Moten's "preference for the terms *life* and *optimism* over *death* and *pessimism*."[19] Thus the film, through Precious' inner habitus and her use of writing and language, provides a useful frame illuminating how we might theorize being as a central feature of a metaphysical mode of analysis. This study is aptly described then as "being-work" because of its investment in existence and in film/moving image art emerging out of the vitality of immanence rather than the ontologies of abjection and death.

From Expanded to Expansive Cinema

While American commercial filmmaking, and other mediated infrastructures, have largely functioned in a state of *contraction*, lacking narrative and artistic inspiration, recycling staid formulas, maintaining white male ideals and creative control, and divesting themselves of the fullness of human imagination, there have always been other universes, other spheres of influence enacting a more *expansive* relationship to moving image innovation.[20] Building on the phrase "expanded cinema," coined in the 1960s, I use the term "expansive cinema," to account for the proliferation of a set of moving image art practices, innovations, and formal experiments advanced by a set of contemporary Black moving image makers whose work reanimates form, while also interfaces with *being* not simply as an analytic, but as a recurring metaphysical presence in the work itself. The notion of "expanded cinema" and its origins intrigued me as I was becoming increasingly aware of the work of friends, colleagues, and other moving image artists who were working in immersive media and creating augmented and virtual reality projects, including film and animation pioneer Ayoka Chenzira, filmmaker/producer Jameelah Nuriddin, and filmmaker/producer Taura Musgrove.[21] The expansive paradigm lives beyond the borders of familiar categories like narrative, lived experiences, industry, even filmmaking. The term expanded cinema comes to life in the late 1960s, primarily through two texts, Sheldon Renan's *An Introduction to the Underground Film* published in 1967, in which he devotes a chapter to the concept and later Gene Youngblood's titular text *Expanded Cinema*, first published in 1970 and recently re-released as a 50th anniversary edition in 2020.[22] Products of 1960s countercultures, both writers envisioned media in provocative ways, but were positioned tangentially to media studies and the still-forming academic discipline of film studies. Their writing, particularly Youngblood's, aligned closely with voices like F. Buckminster Fuller, Marshall McLuhan and a community of largely West Coast thinkers, theorists, practitioners, and disaffected scientists and artists exploring media's speculative futures, yet each also uses strikingly metaphysical language to explore the relationship between film/moving images and human consciousness.

In the last chapter of his book, Renan argues that expanded cinema is a new area of "film and film-like art," which appears in the 1960s. But his most relevant definition follows: "Expanded cinema is not the name of a particular style of filmmaking. It is a name for a spirit of inquiry that is leading in many different directions."[23] He goes on to describe the broadened use of technological tools: "different projectors at once, computer-generated images, electronic manipulations of images on television. It is cinema expanded to the point at which the effect of film may be produced without the use of film at all."[24] Youngblood even more boldly advocates for a metaphysical reading of the moment, as he writes: "When we say expanded cinema we actually mean expanded consciousness. Expanded cinema does not mean computer films, video phosphors, atomic light, or spherical projections. Expanded cinema isn't a movie at all: like life it's a process of becoming, man's ongoing historical drive to manifest his consciousness outside of his mind in front of his eyes."[25] While Renan's phrasing in the 'spirit of inquiry' might be understood in a number of colloquial ways, I find that the literature on expanded cinema, particularly this first wave, is replete with both implicit and explicit metaphysical references, which were, not surprisingly, viewed with skepticism.[26] Some have dismissed the term and the approach of Youngblood, in particular, as less an academic study than a compilation of mystical ruminations, yet the term has enjoyed a significant resurgence over the last 15 years.[27]

Regardless of the criticisms, as both Renan and Youngblood lean into the intersection between media studies and esoterics, they touch a void in our conception of cinema's possibilities aligning with my investment in the metaphysical attributes of being and form. Thomas Beard emphasizes the metaphysical in his reading of Youngblood explaining that "the boundary to be broken for Youngblood was, ultimately, metaphysical" and that his investment was "the outward realization of an interior experience in all its evocative complexity—as well as their design: a continual metamorphosis characteristic of the 'universal unity' engendered by the global communications network."[28] Renan and Youngblood were upswept in the zeitgeist of media and philosophy and the work of filmmakers like Stan Brakhage, Stan VanDerBeek, Carolee Scheenman, Andy Warhol, even Stanley Kubrick, yet I argue that it would be generations of Black filmmakers, whose existence they could likely not imagine, who would become the fulfillment of their beleaguered vision. And while Renan and Youngblood's texts are also histories of experimental and underground filmmaking, but their work was not yet aware of the deeply underground nature of Black filmmaking practice of the time (experimental, documentary or otherwise), which existed, but would have still been in a nascent phase. This might include the work of Black filmmakers like Bill Greaves, Bill Gunn, Mike Henderson, and Edward Owens whose work was often experimental. Thus, expansive cinema is also the recognition of a void needing to be filled as we rewrite the histories of generations of Black filmmaking practice and complicate the narratives around experimental and underground cinemas. I outline some of the tenets of an expansive paradigm referring to frameworks, themes, and practices below (see Table 8.2).

The expansive sensibility is not the sole property of "experimental" or "underground" sensibilities, but circulates, imagining alternative spaces (above ground) and in the creation of other worlds. We are given some cues to unlocking the power of expansive cinema in Youngblood's discussion of a screenshot of the famous "Starchild Embryo" from Kubrick's *2001: A Space Odyssey*.[29] Describing this image Youngblood writes that, "The image of the Starchild, its umbilical feeding from no earthly womb, elegantly symbolizes a generation gap so sudden and so profound that few of us believed it possible." I find that the "Starchild Embryo" figuration and Youngblood's reading of this cosmic child not yet touched by the world also has profound resonance in the expansive work of contemporary Black filmmakers and moving image artists. I find a parallel to the "Starchild Embryo" in the figure of the "Black Starchild," a recurring cosmological symbol in films in the expansive paradigm. These figures embody a metaphysical reading of Blackness, which may feel some of the reverberations of racialized trauma, but which retains a powerful connection to the unpolluted freedom and beauty of being.

To explore this further, consider the work of British Nigerian director/filmmaker Jenn Nkiru, a dynamic exemplar of an expansive moving image practice. In her powerful montage film *Rebirth Is Necessary* (2015), Nkiru interweaves a stream of images and sound capturing Black diasporic life, faces, bodies and movement.[30]

TABLE 8.2 Black Filmmaking Practice as "Expansive Cinema"

—Moving image art that engages in and complicates "narrative" frameworks evoking Saidyia Hartman's notion of "critical fabulation" and personal/historical remembering.[42]

—Aspects of Afrofuturist and speculative discourses, particularly work and scholarship that engages the "Black Radical Imagination."[43]

—Investments in collaboration, the creation of film collectives, alternative modes of attribution, and directorial agency.

—Expanded modes of exhibition and ways of reaching audiences, sociality, and public engagement.

—Films that emphasize internal reflection.

—Films that are intermedial, emphasizing multiple modes of media and/or performance hip-hop, spoken word or theatrical/performance.

—Innovations in photography, animation or virtual and augmented realities.

—A rethinking of scale through innovations in spatial, temporal and architectural logics.— Films constructed using complex montagistic techniques.

—Films that engage deeply with the sonic archive and/or music video conventions.

—Films vested in life cycles: birth, death, regeneration/transfiguration.

—Works which consider alternative modes of encounter and engagement: we watch in our personal spaces, we move through an exhibit or installation, we sit on floors or stand.

—Depictions of stream of consciousness, and/or visual and oral poetics.

—Worked invested in technological innovation: installations, multiple screens, immersive technologies, or making use of projection.

—Works that may have been inspired by personal meditation or internal rumination, spiritual discovery.

—Work which foregrounds spaces of consciousness: flights of ecstasy, the mundane, stillness, transfiguration, or otherworldly imagination.

Describing her archival materials, Jenny Gunn cites Nkiru's usage of the term "cosmic archaeology" and categorizes her practice in strikingly "expansive" terms, saying, "Through montage, Nkiru's film touches on modes of embodiment, sexual and gender fluidities, spiritual and ritual practices, and theories of the Black experience from Afro-pessimism to Afrofuturism."[31] The film taps into the resplendent visual power of Afrofuturist imagery including images of Sun Ra and a range of Black astral figures as the film's opening onscreen text explains "WE HEREBY DECLARE OURSELVES TO BE ANOTHER ORDER OF BEINGS." A film deeply aware of the power of movement in performative and spiritual contexts, bodies move forwards and in reverse, as whirling dervishes in fits of ecstasy, possession, and dispossession. Images of children abound, often in closeups, pictured in their "church clothes," bathing in a river, dancing, sometimes juxtaposed to elders, family, and friends. Yet one particularly memorable image in the film powerfully evokes my description of the Black Starchild. The image (Figure 8.1) depicts a child of perhaps five or six, hovering above the ocean, arms and face covered in a powder blue substance. Nkiru's "Starchild" is not embryonic, but a more evolved figure who surfaces

FIGURE 8.1 Still from *Rebirth Is Necessary*. Screenshot by the author

sometimes with the hint of a smile, sometimes covering her eyes in distress, but here shrieking. This transcendent child is not contained by the womb-space, but his capacity to hover in mid-air suggests that he is, also, of "another order of beings."[32]

The otherworldly "Black Starchild" surfaces across many works within this expansive paradigm as a mediating force between the world of the mundane and a broader world of cosmological mysteries.

Consider "the Unborn child" in Julie Dash's seminal *Daughters of the Dust* (1991) who, as a child still in her mother's womb is visualized as a spectral presence guiding her parents through distress; young Eve Batiste in Kasi Lemmon's mystical *Eve Bayou* (1992), who has "the gift of sight;" and the young girl in Nuotama Bodomo's powerful short *Boneshaker*, whose family brings her to a religious healer, but who physically refuses the religious indoctrination. In other works, a child or young person moves or "performs" the connective tissue to otherworldly experience, like Storyboard P's dancing presence in Kahlil Joseph's collaboration with musician Flying Lotus, *Until the Quiet Comes* (2012) or the child singer in Arthur Jafa's video for Jay-Z's *4:44*, an "old soul" who conjures the power of Nina Simone as he sings "Feeling Good." Also consider the images of young women and girls who haunt the plantations of the Southern past in Beyoncé's *Lemonade* and the children who hover, fly, and burst through the air in the short film *As Told to G/D Thyself* based on the music of Kamasi Washington and helmed by members of the Ummah Chroma collective which includes Nkiru, Bradford Young, Marc Thomas, Terence Nance, and Washington. These figures offer a compelling window into the investments of these films/makers and the worlds they create. What is also significant is that many of the figures mentioned in this section have been consistent co-collaborators demonstrating the power of these circulating creative energies and collectives, another vital aspect of the expansive paradigm.

Elissa Blount-Moorhead's Expansive Experiments with Form and Being

In the fall of 2020, Elissa Blount-Moorhead discussed her recent moving image art project *As of a Now* virtually with the *Liquid Blackness* research group as the culmination of its 2019–2020 research project devoted to the study of her work. Blount-Moorhead's practice has been shaped by her curatorial work, which includes her co-curation of "Funk, God, Jazz and Medicine: Black Radical Brooklyn," and by her extensive list of creative partnerships including a collaboration with Bradford Young on the four-channel film and art installation called *Back and Song* (2019).[33]

Her work and practice are explored in her essay titled, "The Eight-Point Plan of Euphorically Utopic World-Making."[34] In it, she explains that her upbringing helped to shape her project of making worlds out of the generative "diasporic bounty" she found around her and in the "poetics of quotidian Black life."[35] Her *As of a Now* project is described as an "x-ray" film projection installation which is 3D mapped onto a vacant row house, using audiovisual narratives, augmented reality, and artifacts which reference its former Black denizens."[36] Blount-Moorhead's projects, particularly AOAN, are notable exemplars of the expansive framework and they are also guided by an awareness of a particular dimension of *being*. Her work embodies Campt's notion of Black visuality, as "still-moving-images: images that hover between still and moving images; animated still images, slowed or stilled images in motion or visual renderings that blur the distinctions between these multiple genres; images that require the labor of feeling with or through them."[37]

As of a Now (AOAN) literally *projects* life onto the façade and into the interior of a Baltimore rowhome first recognizable by its brick shell, then shifting to an image of a dollhouse-like interior view of eight rooms (Figure 8.2).

FIGURE 8.2 Still from *As of a Now*. Screenshot by the author

The installation unfolds as a series of moving images and the figures move in and out of rooms across the screen and across three moments in time: 1908, 1968, and 2008. Each time period unfolds with mother, father, and child and culturally specific décor/mise-en-scene appropriate to the time period—a Pele poster on the bedroom, a record player, a woman wearing an afro, wall hangings etc.—all markers of the 1968 era, for instance. At points later in the installation, the home's residents of different time periods occupy the space simultaneously, their histories, memories, and intimacies converging, coming and going, moving in and through space and time. The familial histories are temporally superimposed, entering and exiting, sometimes one on top of the other. Blount-Moorhead explains the vision for the project as:

> ... a cross-sectioned view projected onto a vacant building façade depicting vernacular life, movements, and the ways people conduct familiar rituals such as family care, gathering, grooming, mourning, conflict, and celebration. These voyeuristic vignettes are designed to humanize spaces that are otherwise considered blighted and void of life. The quotidian and meditative images inspire the public to re-imagine their meaning and give voice to the remaining communal memories that are familiar and sacred, and celebrate their evolution over time. These are stories of fugitivity and introspection, of familial exchange, and private withholdings. The film challenges the notion, in the face of gentrification, that urban buildings are neutral commodified spaces. It proposes, rather, that they are sites of memory which are imbued with cultural potency and residue. It poses the question, "How can stories that are attached to objects and now vacant buildings live beyond the loss of their material vessels?[38]

As an exculpatory project, this work does not tell a story, per se, but instead asks—what are the substances of the stories whose traces, memories, echoes, and fragments live in us, through us, and around us? Also central to this project is the figuration of a boy, whom Blount-Moorhead describes as:

> a boy/spirit who is unable to commit to any of his living families. In each story, the boy is a harbinger for disruption of the banality. An Abiku in Yoruba mythology refers to a child who dies and returns repeatedly. It means "predestined to death." His presence is a metaphor for the instability of Black urban life despite our constant quest for equilibrium.[39]

The boy emerges at the end of what might be considered a "climactic" moment in the film. The 1908 mother and father who are dancing intimately hear a doorbell, and receive some kind of document, one which, judging by the gestures of distress and ominous audio cues, brings some bad news (Figure 8.3).

Then slowly, animated sepia-colored documents and records spill from the woman's hands gradually bursting across the screen, followed by the superimposition

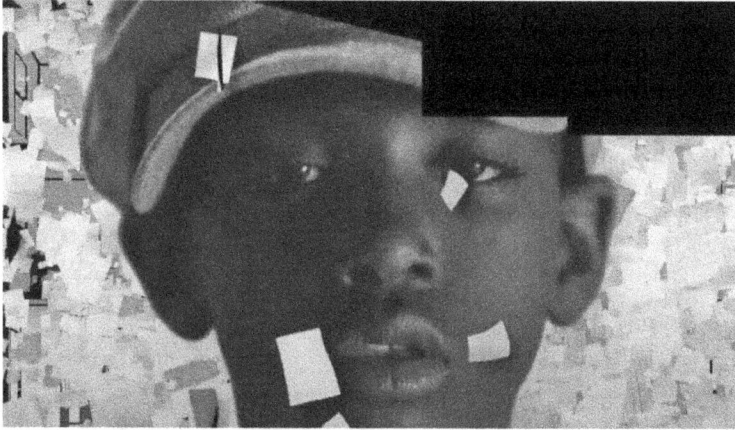

FIGURE 8.3 Still from *As of a Now.* Screenshot by the author

of a boy's face over the soft explosion of papers. This, the only closeup in the film, is of another "Black Starchild" whose innocent face is awash in the flood, or perhaps the wake, of what might be birth, marriage, and death certificates, bills of sale, deeds, mortgages and eviction notices, insurance policies, report cards, certificates, love letters, old telegrams, funeral programs, birthday cards—all of the printed matter than shapes the historical archive of the families who inhabited this space. The force of these experiences and memories is embodied in the life of a single child and through him to generations into the future. Blount-Moorhead's work and much of the work of this expansive era gives substance to the ethereal, galvanizing creative energies and the power of collectives and collaboration. These works attend to feeling, care, curiosity, and generative modes of awareness circulating in and through modes of production and engagement amplifying the insistence of being with Black life. Taken together these works and this mode of study emphasize the power of training our gaze toward the mysteries and powers in a subset of Black women's work, not as an isolated sphere, but as a circulation of energies or possibilities, making the case that these works indeed have something to say to us, if we are willing to be with them.

Notes

1 Barbara A. Holmes, *Race and the Cosmos: An Invitation to View the World Differently* (Harrisburg, PA: Continuum International Publishing Group, 2002) 172.
2 Christina Sharpe, *In the Wake: On Blackness and Being* (Durham, NC: Duke University Press, 2016) 174.
3 See www.merriam-webster.com/dictionary/metaphysics.
4 The term "capture" is vital here as it means to seize or contain the elusive nature of the ethereal. See also Michelle Materre's essay "Capture and Release: Curating and Exhibiting the East Coast Independent Black Film Movement, 1968–1992." *Black Camera*, Vol 10, no. 2 (Spring 2019): 149–158.

5 The conversation was part of Firelight Media's Beyond Resilience Series—"The Black Gaze" at: www.youtube.com/watch?v=Ym-GOoDSu7o&t=2830s.

6 "The Black Gaze" conversation cont'd.

7 Much of my thinking about the notion of "encounter" emerged from my dissertation work in early hip-hop visual culture, music video, and the study of how artist Jean-Michel Basquiat navigated the external landscape (the art world, whiteness, and urban space).

8 Alessandra Raengo uses the term "socializing our thinking" to account for how our ideas take shape and acquire clarity as we are in conversation and share space with each other. I also briefly note the proliferation of production collectives along with platforms, spaces, communities, and events both before and during the Covid-19 pandemic, which allow us to be with and share this work in compelling ways.

9 See Tina Campt's "Black Visuality and the Practices of Refusal," *Women & Performance: A Journal of Feminist Theory*, Vol. 29, No. 1 (2019): 79–87, https://doi.org/10.1080/07407 70X.2019.1573625.

10 Much of the first decade of the 20th century followed a largely commercial trajectory: a series of Tyler Perry films, Black family dramas, comedies, and biopics.

11 Michael Gillespie evokes Max Roach's "We Insist: Freedom Now Suite" with vocals by Abbey Lincoln in the introduction to *Filming Blackness: American Cinema and the Idea of Black Film* (Durham, NC: Duke University Press, 2016) 1.

12 Jheanelle Brown, "Rupture and Reparative Modes of Care from the Women of the LA Rebellion." *Seen* Iss. 1 (2020): 101–114.

13 Sharpe, *In the Wake* 11.

14 Sharpe, *In the Wake* 130, emphasis mine.

15 Sharpe, *In the Wake* 132.

16 Racquel Gates "An Archive of Love: A Review of Garrett Bradley's TIME." *Seen* Iss. 1 (2020): 89.

17 In Mia Mask's "The Precarious Politics of Precious: A Close Reading of a Cinematic Text" *Black Camera*, Vol. 4, No. 1 (Winter 2012): 105, she anticipates an expansive paradigm suggesting that surrealism, realism, and a range of modalities might co-exist in one film. I also share Mask's reading of Precious as being in "the process of becoming" rather than an "abjection" (112).

18 This evokes a connection to Yellow Mary's voiceover monologue in *Daughters of the Dust*:

> I am the first and the last. I am the honored one and the scorned one. I am the whore and the holy one. I am the wife and the virgin. I am the barren one and many are my daughters. I am the silence that you cannot understand. I am the utterance of my name.
>
> *(Daughters of the Dust, Julie Dash, 1991, Columbia TriStar)*

19 Fred Moten "Blackness and Nothingness (Mysticism in the Flesh)." *The South Atlantic Quarterly* 112:4 (Fall 2013): 738. doi 10.1215/00382876-2345261.

20 In a slightly different context, Alessandra Raengo discusses the "expansiveness of Blackness" in LA Rebellion films as "Blackness as a form of historical consciousness. . . Blackness as immersive experiences, forms of cultural memory" . . . and as "cosmic principle. . . life force and truly vibrant matter," 312. See her essay "Encountering the Rebellion: *Liquid Blackness* Reflects on the Expansive Possibilities of LA Rebellion Films" in *LA Rebellion: Creating a New Black Cinema*. Eds. Allyson Field, Jan-Christopher Horak and Jacqueline Stewart (Berkeley: University of California Press, 2015) 291–318.

21 See Ayoka Chenzira's interactive projects at https://ayomentary.com/interactive/. Find elements of Taura Musgrove's *Freedom Fighter: The Lillie May Carroll Jackson Technology Project* at https://hyparlink.com/jackson. Jameelah Nuriddin is a producer/editor of *See Me* (2019) described as a "womanist body-reclamation film" according to her website.

22 Gene Youngblood, *Expanded Cinema*, 50th Anniversary Edition (New York: Fordham University Press, 2020).

23 Sheldon Renan, *An Introduction to the Underground Film* (New York: E. P. Dutton & Co., Inc., 1967) 227.

24 Renan, *An Introduction to the Underground Film* 227.

25 Youngblood explains that the phrase "expanded cinema" was coined in 1966 by the American experimental filmmaker Stan VanDerBeek, famous for building his "movie drome" in upstate New York where he would stage his expanded cinema performances, 41.

26 Some recent criticism can be found in Thomas Beard's essay/review "Cosmic Consciousness: *Artforum International*, New York, Vol. 58, Iss. 7 (Mar 2020).

27 See Eds. Susan Lord and Janine Marchessault *Fluid Screens, Expanded Cinema* (Toronto: University of Toronto Press, 2015) (in which Youngblood contributes the coda.), Jonathan Walley, *Cinema Expanded: Avant-Garde Film in the Age of Intermedia* (New York and Oxford: Oxford University Press, 2020) and Andrew Uroskie, *Between the Black Box and the White Cube: Expanded Cinema and Postwar Art* (Chicago, IL: University of Chicago Press, 2014).

28 Beard, "Cosmic Consciousness" 1–2.

29 Youngblood, *Expanded Cinema* 89.

30 The title likely referencing Detroit musician/producer J. Dilla's song of the same name, emphasizing the influence of the sonic archive on many of these filmmakers.

31 Jenny Gunn, "Intergenerational Pedagogy in Jenn Nkiru's," *JCMS: Journal of Cinema and Media Studies* Vol 59, No. 2 (Winter 2020) 164.

32 See also Christina Knight's discussion of *Rebirth* in b.O.s.10.4 /*Rebirth is Necessary*/ Christina Knight (July 2020) http://asapjournal.com/b-o-s-10-4-rebirth-is-necessary-christina-knight/.

33 Blount-Moorhead's website describes the piece as "a meditative …kaleidoscope installation… which considers the labor and care provided by generations of Black healers…" www.elissablountmoorhead.com.

34 Elissa Blount-Moorhead, "The Eight-Point Plan of Euphorically Utopic World-Making" in *How We Fight White Supremacy: A Field Guide to Black Resistance* (New York: Bold Type Books, 2019) 248.

35 "Diasporic bounty" found on p. 248. Blount-Moorhead discusses the notion of quotidian experiences in Black life in a number of places including the *As of a Now* booklet p. 2.

36 *As of a Now booklet* 2.

37 Campt, "Black Visuality and the Practices of Refusal" 80.

38 *As of a Now* booklet 2.

39 *As of a Now* booklet 3.

40 Eds. Allyson Field, Jan-Christopher Horak, and Jacqueline Najuma Stewart. *LA Rebellion: Towards a New Black Cinema* (Oakland, CA: University of California Press, 2015).

41 Alessandra Raengo coins this term in conversation with filmmaker Bradford Young during the *Liquid Blackness* event titled "Bradford Young and the Visual Art of Black Care," Georgia State University, April 15, 2018. https://vimeo.com/291961328

42 Hartman describes "critical fabulation" in "Venus in Two Acts." *Small Axe* 26 (June 2008): 11.
43 "Black Radical Imagination" is a powerful screening tour curated by Erin Christovale and Amir George, which showcases the possibilities of Black 'new media, video art, and experimental narrative.' See https://blackradicalimagination.com.

9

STRANGERS IN THE VILLAGE

Black Independent Cinema in the 21st Century

Artel Great

The new millennium began in this country with a tsunami of mixed messages and emotions. There was a general feeling of exhilaration, coupled with a media-induced sense of dread. The impending doom reported in "Y2k" news coverage generated enough panic among the American populous that many citizens in December 1999 flooded local supermarkets to stock up on canned goods, toilet tissue, and bottled water—as if preparing for the direct impact of a category five-level hurricane. The emotional contagion of doomsday was upon us. And no one knew if the world's computer networks or the banking system, for that matter, would suffer a colossal micro-processing meltdown when the clock struck midnight on New Year's Day. At the same time, the ubiquitous rhythm of Prince Rogers Nelson's classic tune "1999" blared ad nauseum from sound systems and radio stations across the country. If this was, in fact, the end of the world, Americans intended to go out with a bang— *partying*, of course.

Yet, the world did not end on January 1, 2000, at least not in the way Americans were primed to imagine it might. "Y2k" did, however, mark a significant end—an end to the energy and promise of Hollywood's 1990s Black film boom. Throughout the 1990s, the film industry saw a considerable rise in the production and distribution of studio-financed motion pictures that showcased Black-oriented themes and Black talent. Not only that, most of these mainstream Black movies were helmed by, then, unknown Black directors, both women and men. This decade-long expansion of Black cinematic visibility ushered an influx of critically acclaimed and financially successful Black films into Hollywood. From the teen comedy *House Party* (1990) to the feminist drama *Waiting to Exhale* (1995) or the Black western *Posse* (1993), the sheer variety and volume of Black motion pictures released during this era was astounding.

However, one year into the new century, the United States found itself embroiled in what became dual 20-year geopolitical quagmires with dubious and, ultimately,

DOI: 10.4324/9781003079682-10

disastrous military engagements in Iraq and Afghanistan. Not long after active military conflict commenced, the momentum and abundance of 1990s Black cinema was halted in Hollywood and replaced by a sharp uptick in the production and distribution of a slate of white big-budget war films that were quickly churned out by the major studios. Films like *Blackhawk Down* (2001), *Pearl Harbor* (2001), *To End All Wars* (2001), *The Pianist* (2002), *Wind Talkers* (2002), *Hart's War* (2002), *Tears of the Sun* (2003), and *Alexander* (2004) are prime illustrations of Hollywood's post-9/11 war film cycle and the ideological register that dominated the industry in the early 2000s. Equally important to this decline in Hollywood's production of Black films was the material impact of the Clinton administration's Telecommunications Act of 1996, which paved the way for a series of high-profile corporate mergers on Wall Street. What followed was the formation of giant media conglomerates that rapidly swallowed up many of the mid-major studios in Hollywood. Several companies like New Line Cinema, which specialized in Black mid-budget comedies and dramas, were either significantly downsized or shuttered. And Black movies, for the most part, were largely abandoned in the commercial film industry's primary cinematic output. Black filmmakers since the turn of the 21st century have found themselves grappling with the decline of Hollywood's production and distribution of Black-oriented movies. And the same economic and ideological tensions that underpin long-running debates over *independent* versus *mainstream* production models for Black filmmakers remains intractable.

The idea of Black cinema has long been complicated and contested in America. However, when film projectors first became commercially available in 1896, well before the rise of the cultural and financial behemoth of Hollywood, Black entrepreneurs and religious leaders started promoting motion pictures as a tool to help "uplift" the race.[1] They believed movies possessed the power to forge a modern image of Black culture, to help advance collective racial progress, and to generate great economic opportunity for Black communities. Several Black social clubs held early film presentations that mesmerized audiences with their novelty. Soon, these early pioneers were using movie cameras to recreate short scenes from the Bible, so-called passion plays, which were screened at Black churches.[2]

By the early 1900s, motion pictures had become an alluring pastime in many Black communities. The city of Chicago emerged as the heart of the early Black cinema movement. Robert Motts, a colorful proprietor of popular gambling spots and taverns, launched one of the country's first Black-owned movie houses, the Pekin Theater, on Chicago's South Side in 1905. Noted feminist, activist, and journalist, Ida B. Wells hosted a successful charity event there, lending credibility to Motts' establishment. By 1914, under the vicious American apartheid regime, over 200 Black-owned theaters had opened across the United States, ranging from small storefront shops to resplendent marble movie palaces. These communal spaces became potent symbols of Black self-determination and economic independence, as well as sites for entertainment, resistance, and cultural celebration.[3]

During this period, William D. Foster rose as an early advocate of cinema's radical potential to champion Black lives. He recognized that movies could be used as a vehicle for Black America to recuperate its cultural image, which suffered from grotesque distortions in the national imagination throughout the 19th century. Racist caricatures in literature and white performances of blackface minstrelsy, on stage and in film, crystallized dangerous myths that denigrated and devalued Black life.

Foster insisted that cinema portray "the finer aspects and qualities" of Black life and "set the race right with the world."[4] He culled together capital, purchased a motion picture camera and film stock, and founded the Foster Photoplay Company in Chicago—two years before the establishment of Universal Pictures, the first Hollywood studio. His visionary efforts helped usher in the golden age of Black independent cinema during the silent era, which peaked in the 1920s. Many of these independent movies were financed largely with Black capital, filmed by Black directors, featured all-Black casts, and depicted the world from Black points of view for the enjoyment of avid Black moviegoers, who watched in the comfort of Black-owned theaters.[5]

It is one of the painful ironies of American history that despite the innovations and aesthetic contributions of Black people to the motion picture industry, from its very inception, Black cinema has been studiously devalued and suppressed by the white establishment. The ubiquity and dominance of studio films as the arbiters of cultural authority has long supported Hollywood's imperialism of consciousness in the United States and abroad. And yet in spite of advancements in the democratization of technology that have expanded the means of production, many Black filmmakers still find themselves clamoring and squirming for a seat at the Hollywood table. This fact remains constant, despite the industry's long history of repression, spiritual traps, and the psychic costs that tend to accompany that seat. Thus, the debate around the marginalization of Black independent filmmaking versus Black "dependence" on the financial and ideological instruments of the Hollywood studio system remains tenacious and fraught with tension.

As the story unfolds, the Black filmmaker, to borrow a poetic turn of phrase from James Baldwin, is forced to maneuver as a "stranger in the village" of the American film industry.[6] Yet, it is also true that Black independent cinema in the 21st century is not one-dimensional, nor does it solely revolve around economic factors. Black independent cinema, in a contemporary sense, is about voice. It is about control—creative control (i.e., who determines the aesthetic vision of the film and how Black stories are rendered on-screen), *and* it is also about narrative control (i.e., who decides what stories are told and from whose point of view). In the third decade of the new millennium, Black cinema, sadly, still wrestles with white-manufactured images from an over one-hundred-year history of regressive depictions of Black people. In fact, the industry actively banned Black directors from working in Hollywood from 1915 until the late 1960s when the major studios faced economic disaster. Gordon Parks was the first Black director to breach the exclusively white world of Hollywood studio filmmaking, directing *The Learning Tree* for Warner Brothers in 1969. Parks, a legendary photographer at *Life* magazine, spent decades producing award-winning images of Black life like "Emerging Man" and "American Gothic." However, it was not until the arrival of Melvin Van Peebles as the hip "French" auteur, whose third feature *Sweet Sweetback's Baadasssss Song* (1971), became the top-grossing independent film of the year, that the industry devised a plan to pull itself back from the brink of financial ruin. Hollywood studios set forth a new money-making formula by co-opting Van Peebles' low-budget, action-oriented Black film blueprint. Infuriated by *Sweetback's* radically independent success story, haughty studio executives ruthlessly froze Van Peebles out of Hollywood filmmaking. And the industry began producing cheaply made, Black-cast action flicks, later dubbed Blaxploitation—and raked in huge profits.[7]

Tyler, Ava, and Jordan

With the success of *Spider Man* (2002), formulaic superhero movies were announced as Hollywood's new money-making machine. Such films, one could argue, are an extension of the war film cycle introduced into the industry post-9/11. And seemingly overnight, given the sudden proliferation of superhero pictures and war films, the decade-long gains of 1990s Black cinema in Hollywood were halted. Rather than wait for permission from out-of-touch white studio executives, the multi-hyphenate mogul Tyler Perry built an entire film and media empire by focusing on self-financing and retaining ownership of his independently produced *Madea* movie franchise. He also signed lucrative television deals with networks like TBS, Oprah Winfrey Network (OWN), Black Entertainment Television (BET), and the streamer BET+ that aided in solidifying his media dominance. Perry has continued to find motion picture success, on his own terms, by targeting his remarkably loyal following within a faith-based segment of Black audience members. His independent production model, alongside Lionsgate as his distribution partner, led to Perry emerging as the dominant voice in Black cinema during the first decade of the 2000s.

However, the energetic arrival of filmmaker Ava DuVernay ultimately aided Black independent cinema in achieving a renewed social velocity. Her debut feature, *I Will Follow* (2010), is a modest drama about life after losing a loved one. DuVernay self-financed the film on a budget of $50,000—and later strategically "four-walled" the picture for a limited theatrical release. Undeterred by the industry's disinterest in the work of independent Black filmmakers, DuVernay launched her own social activist distribution company, initially dubbed AFFRM (African American Film Festival Releasing Movement), which she later expanded and rebranded under the name Array. The enterprise functions not only as a distribution company but also as a call to action to garner broad support for Black independent cinema.

Her second film, *Middle of Nowhere* (2012), announced DuVernay as a rising voice. The picture stars Emayatzy Corinealdi as a registered nurse and aspiring medical doctor in Compton who selflessly relinquishes her professional dreams after her husband is imprisoned on drug-trafficking charges. With this film, DuVernay crafts a nuanced examination of the interior lives of Black women left behind by the nightmares of mass incarceration. *Middle of Nowhere* also solidified

DuVernay's professional relationship with frequent collaborator, cinematographer Bradford Young.[8] The movie was produced on a budget of $200,000 and premiered at the Sundance Film Festival, where DuVernay won the U.S. Directing Award for Drama. Her third picture marked a massive leap in production budget and her visibility as a filmmaker. She was tapped to direct the Hollywood period piece, *Selma* (2014), depicting the role of Dr. Martin Luther King, Jr. in the events leading up to the historic Civil Rights–era march to Selma, Alabama, in 1965. The film was later nominated for two Academy Awards (Best Picture and Best Original Song).

When improv comedy actor Jordan Peele joined the cast of the Fox Network's sketch comedy series *Mad TV* in 2003, no one could have predicted the enormity of his future impact on Black cinema. Peele spent five years on *Mad TV* before he and fellow castmate Keegan Michael Key landed their own sketch series, *Key & Peele*, on the basic cable network Comedy Central. From 2012 until 2015, the program was successful among Comedy Central's predominately white demographic. Peele's breakout work, however, arrived not as a performer but rather as the writer/director of the now-classic social horror film *Get Out* (2017), which is widely recognized as a monumental achievement in Black independent cinema. Peele's genre-blending motion picture takes on the conventions of horror, drama, comedy, and suspense to create a cinematic tableau that unmasks America's love–hate relationship with Black bodies. The movie also cleverly denounces the fallacy of the United States as an enlightened post-racial society.[9] *Get Out* skyrocketed in popularity as, perhaps, the 21st century's first feature to implore Black-Americans to *stay woke*.

Produced independently on a $4.5 million budget, the movie brought in $255 million at the box-office. Such enormous financial returns distinguished Peele as the first Black director to gross over $100 million with their debut feature. The film now stands as the most profitable independent Black film in American history. *Get Out* managed to strike a profound chord with both Black and white audiences in a divided nation reeling from centuries-old racial injustices at the precise moment when Black social resistance gained momentum following an unseemly rise in state-sanctioned police killings of unarmed Black citizens. Not only was *Get Out* a huge commercial sensation, but the film also played well with critics, receiving four Academy Awards nominations: Best Picture, Best Director, Best Original Screenplay, and Best Actor. Peele won the Oscar for Best Original Screenplay, making him the first Black person to win in that category.

"The Black Cinerati"

The success of Tyler Perry, Ava DuVernay, and Jordan Peele are, indeed, incredible milestones in Black independent cinema during the first 20-plus years of the century. However, a new generation of underground Black filmmakers, trained at the nation's top film schools, are also working assiduously to recode Black images and reimagine Black cinema's potential with an energetic style and panache. I refer to this group of diverse and mainly independent filmmakers as *"the Black Cinerati"*—a loose coterie of writer/directors, cinematographers, artists, and producers who represent the third generation of Black film school-trained practitioners in the United States. This group of predominately Millennial filmmakers are the creators of an emergent and increasingly original body of work that explores visions of the Afrofuture and other varied, nuanced, and complex ways Black life is lived in this country.

The historical context that underpins the classification of the Black Cinerati filmmakers flows from the intentionally ironic sobriquet coined in 1925 by Zora Neale Hurston and Wallace Thurman, who dubbed their network of Black creatives the "Niggerati," during the Harlem Renaissance.[10]

The group included writers like Hurston and Thurman, Langston Hughes, Dorothy West, Countee Cullen, Helene Johnson, and artists Augusta Savage and Aaron Douglass. They aimed to collectively inject new voices into the Black cultural discourse—voices that elevated and honored working-class life and aesthetics, pushing back against the "New Negro" conceptions of older bourgeois Black intellectuals like Alain Locke and W.E.B. DuBois. Similarly, the Black Cinerati is composed of a diverse network of film artists who are deeply concerned with the cultural politics of cinema. These filmmakers are creating thought-provoking work driven by a renewed sense of social responsibility and a salient desire to transcode Black visual frequencies and aesthetic practices. The Black Cinerati filmmakers balance a similar cultural heritage and political experience, having come of age as artists in the immediate wake of highly publicized white vigilantism that triggered the death of young Black citizens like Trayvon Martin, Jordan Davis, and Ahmaud Arbery— events that exposed the untenable fragility of Black life in America and the tangled depravity of whiteness and institutional racism. These generation-defining moments have radicalized Black Cinerati filmmakers to varying degrees along the socio-political spectrum, aligning with the movement to support the dignity and humanity of Black lives.

It is important to note that the Black Cinerati are also avid students of film. They are, without question, deeply influenced by previous generations of Black film school–trained directors: The L.A. Rebellion and the 1990s Black directors. L.A. Rebellion filmmakers, a label conceived by film scholar Clyde Taylor, represent the first generation of Black film school graduates who studied at the University of California at Los Angeles (UCLA) predominately in the late 1960s through the 1980s. These filmmakers include Julie Dash (*Daughters of the Dust*, 1990), Charles Burnett (*Killer of Sheep*, 1979), Billy Woodberry (*Bless Their Little Hearts,* 1983), Haile Gerima (*Bush Mama*, 1979), Barbara McCullough (*Water Ritual #1*, 1979), Jamaa Fanaka (*Penitentiary*, 1979), Larry Clark, (*Passing Through*, 1977), Zeinabu irene Davis (Compensation, 1999), among others.[11] They used cinema as a weapon to resist Hollywood's cultural hegemony and the persistent racism that poisons American social transactions. Many of the pictures they created as graduate film students are now recognized as culturally significant masterpieces of Black independent cinema and are included among the white establishment's art film canon.

The second generation of Black film school graduates, or the 1990s Black directors, migrated frequently between independent and mainstream production models during the ephemeral progress created with the industry's decade-long Black movie fad. Filmmakers like Spike Lee, Ernest Dickerson, and Darnell Martin (at NYU Tisch), John Singleton (USC), Gina Prince-Bythewood and Cauleen Smith (UCLA), Carl Seaton (Columbia College), as well as Arthur Jafa and Malik Hassan Sayeed (Howard University) stand out among the most successful filmmakers of this generation.

The daring cultural productions made by the L.A. Rebellion and the 1990s Black directors inspired a new generation of young Black creatives to follow in their footsteps and seek admission into top film programs. Hence, most Black Cinerati filmmakers are graduates of four leading film schools: New York University (NYU), University of Southern California (USC), University of California at Los Angeles (UCLA), or Howard. First, there are the descendants of Spike Lee, Ernest Dickerson, and Darnell Martin at NYU: Black Cinerati filmmakers like Dee Rees (*Pariah*, 2014), Nia DaCosta (*Candyman,* 2021), Melina Matsoukas (*Queen & Slim,* 2019), Shaka King (*Judas and the Black Messiah*, 2020), Daniel Patterson (cinematographer of *Da Sweet Blood of Jesus*, 2014), Terence Nance (*An Oversimplification of Her Beauty,* 2012), Nikyatu Jusu (*Nanny*, 2022), Darius Clark Monroe (*Evolution of a Criminal,* 2014), Stefon Bristol (*See You Yesterday*, 2019), Reinaldo Marcus Green (*King Richard,* 2021), and television director Pete Chatmon. At USC, John Singleton's legacy as the youngest Academy Award nominee for Best Director has informed the career trajectory of cinematic offspring like Ryan Coogler (*Marvel's Black Panther*, 2018) and Steven Caple, Jr. (*Creed II*, 2018). While UCLA graduates Garrett Bradley (*Time,* 2020), Desha Dauchan (*Covered*, 2018), and Artel Great (*Love Walks In*, 2022) are among the directors who descend from the L.A. Rebellion filmmaking tree. The historically Black institution, Howard University, on the other hand, has produced noted cinematographers, Bradford Young (*Solo: A Star Wars Story*, 2018) and Hans Charles (*13th*, 2016), both of whom carry the torch ignited by famous Howard alums, Arthur Jafa and Malik Sayeed.

The term Black Cinerati also reflects the critical connections among this loose network of artists or cinematic "literati," if you will. Several figures in this generation, including Ja'Tovia Gary (*The Giverny Document*, 2019) and New Negress Film Society members like Chanelle Aponte Pearson and Stefani Saintonge, as well as Justin Simien (*Dear White People*, 2015), Kahlil Joseph, and others, exemplify the range and radical ambitions of the Black Cinerati as an assemblage of creative-imagemakers who emerged as film directors in the racially and politically charged cauldron of the 2010s. This period witnessed both the tumultuous rise and fall of the Occupy Wall Street movement and the viral spread of the movement for Black lives. Given this context, many Black Cinerati filmmakers are fiercely engaged with redefining Black cinema on their own terms. They consistently employ intrepid voices and a discernible preoccupation with Black radical thought as both students of film and film professors. The group's engagement with Black visual culture expresses a potent social depth and a commitment to experimentation with the formal and technical aspects of the filmmaking process. At the heart of their cultural practice lies an empowering vision for expanding the possibilities of a distinctly *Black* cinematic language.

Take the cinematographer Bradford Young, for instance, who has led the charge in developing a fresh and influential visual style of lensing Black films under the tutelage of his Howard film professor Haile Gerima and the close mentorship of Arthur Jafa. Young's multi-layered visual aesthetic embraces the depth of shadows on-screen, offering viewers a splendid use of color and lighting that accentuates Black skin tones with incredible richness and texture. Young's refined photographic eye has led to his emergence as the premier Black cinematographer in the film industry, inspiring the craftsmanship of rising Black directors of photography like Shawn Peters and Daniel Patterson.

Filmmakers like Kahlil Joseph, Ja'Tovia Gary, Bradford Young, Hans Charles, and Shawn Peters draw deep inspiration from their relationship and collaborations with the renowned artist, director, and cinematographer, Arthur Jafa—who has emerged as an unofficial ideological architect, filmic godfather, and esteemed avuncular figure to many Black Cinerati directors. Jafa's work as a cinematographer first gained attention in Julie Dash's landmark film *Daughters of the Dust* and Spike Lee's *Crooklyn* (1994). However, he ultimately left the commercial movie business, disenchanted with the warped politics of whiteness that overdetermines the capacity for rendering the Black world with the social and expressive depth that resides at the core of his filmmaking practice. Instead, Jafa sought a career as a visual artist before eventually walking away from the suffocating racist configurations that dominate the American art exchange. For several decades, he struggled to produce his creative vision while working, at times, as a film professor and freelancer. In 2016, an extensive collection of his over 200 three-ring-binders containing images juxtaposing Black visuality went on display as a part of the "Made in L.A." exhibition at the Hammer Museum.

During this exhibition, Jafa participated in a public conversation with the cultural critic Greg Tate, and publicly screened his short film *Apex*, which attempts to actualize Jafa's theory of "Black visual intonation."[12] This conversation with Tate and the "Made in L.A." exhibition, once again, generated interest in Jafa's work in the art community. Later that year, his seven-and-a-half-minute film *Love Is the Message and the Message Is Death* (2016) was acquired by a prominent art dealer Gavin Brown, which changed the trajectory of Jafa's career and broke new ground in the art world. *Love Is the Message*, conceptually, aims to activate Jafa's oft-stated ambition and mantra of developing a "Black cinema that possesses the power, beauty, and alienation of Black music."[13] Visually, the film oozes with social urgency, composed of a bedazzling combination of original video shot by Jafa himself and found footage mined from internet sources like YouTube. The images collide in rapid-fire succession, tracing the profundity of over 100-years of Black-American cultural expressivity—playing over Kanye West's brilliant maximalist, gospel-infused hip-hop record, "Ultralight Beam." *Love Is the Message* is a poignant and evocative visual feast, a masterpiece, at once tragic and triumphant.

The film exploded at a cultural moment in America when the nation, deeply divided by its racial demons, found itself collectively engrossed by the simultaneous destruction of, and advocation for, Black lives. Saidiaya Hartman describes the film as

> a series of iconic images that show the brilliant virtuosity of the Black thinkers, artists, and athletes that ordinary Black folk have given to the world, alongside some of the forces that have negated Black life. You don't have to know the exact reference for each image to feel the work's density and power.[14]

If *Love is the Message* does not fully achieve Jafa's theory of Black visual intonation, it, perhaps, comes exceedingly close. Jafa's subsequent work has included several major exhibitions and installations of his visual art at museums in the United States and Europe. He has also directed music videos for Black artists like Shawn "Jay-Z" Carter, Solange Knowles, and Kanye West. Jafa released a 20-minute follow-up to *Love Is the Message*, titled *The White Album* in 2018, which won the Golden Lion Award for Best Artist at the Venice Biennale. In addition to his museum exhibitions, Jafa spearheaded an independent film studio, TNEG, with collaborators Elissa Blount-Moorhead and Malik Sayeed.

The art world, museums, and gallery spaces have also been vital alternative sites of expressive activation for Black Cinerati filmmakers like Kahlil Joseph, Garrett Bradley, and Ja'Tovia Gary. Joseph's films, sometimes experimental in form, often convey the fractured nature of time with surreal, dream-like sequences that explore the imbrications of cinema and the aesthetic frequencies of Blackness. Joseph studied film at Loyola Marymount but did not graduate. Instead, he found work at a production company, gaining practical experience working on various mediamaking gigs, including shooting B-roll footage for filmmaker Terrence Malick. Joseph soon began directing music videos for hip-hop acts like Kendrick Lamar, Flying Lotus, and Shabazz Palaces before being tapped to direct segments of Beyoncè's, now iconic, visual album *Lemonade* (2017). Joseph's work has screened at galleries and museums worldwide, and his feature debut *BLKNWS®*, based on his video installation of the same name, is slated for production at the film company A24, with Bradford Young set as the cinematographer.

The experimental documentarian Ja'Tovia Gary has also carved a space for herself in the art world after helping establish the New Negress Film Society, a collective of Black women directors, in 2013 while she was still a graduate film student at the School of Visual Arts in Manhattan. Gary first garnered attention in the art world while exhibiting her six-minute film *An Ecstatic Experience* (2015), later acquired for the permanent collection by the Whitney Museum of American Art. Gary's opus, a 40-minute film, *The Giverny Document*, addresses issues of race, gender, and violence. Set in Harlem and the impressionist painter Claude Monet's verdant garden in France, the film poses a central question to everyday Black women that Gary encounters on the street: "Do you feel safe in your body?"—an inquiry that offers no simple answers. Gary uses archival and original video to craft an intense film mosaic that grapples with the tradition of Black radical thought and the perpetual state of rage experienced by many Black-Americans trapped within the inexhaustible systems of trauma endured while surviving the pernicious U.S. experiment.

The films of Baltimore-based Black Cinerati collaborators, director Terence Nance and cinematographer Shawn Peters, stand out among the collective as both poignant and visually arresting. Their enthralling collaborations include several short films and music videos and the genre-melding feature, *An Oversimplification of Her Beauty*, which announced their creative vision and voices as artists, premiering at the Sundance Festival in 2012. The film combines documentary and narrative elements with hand-drawn animation and Afrosurrealism in a mind-bending love story. Nance and Peters have also joined forces on the visually appealing, intellectually dense, and inventive late-night sketch series *Random Acts of Flyness* on HBO.[15] In a surprising commercial turn, Nance was hired by the Warner Brothers studio to direct the big-budget sequel *Space Jam 2* (2021), starring NBA superstar Lebron James. In 2019, after spending months in preproduction, writing the screenplay, and developing the film's visual world, Nance began production in Los Angeles with cinematographer Bradford Young. However, a month into principal photography, the on-set atmosphere was writhe with tension between Nance and executives at Warner Brothers. Soon it was announced that Nance was being removed as the film's director due to "creative differences," an all too familiar Hollywood cliché. When Malcolm D. Lee replaced Nance as director, the Black Cinerati's preeminent cinematographer, Bradford Young, exited the picture in solidarity with Nance.

After graduating from the film program at UCLA, director Garrett Bradley relocated to New Orleans and began developing her debut feature, *Below Dreams* (2014), a cinema verité style Millennial coming-of-age story. Her short documentaries *Alone* (2017) and *America* (2019) were well received at Sundance. The latter film repurposes archival footage from the unfinished and unreleased *Lime Kiln Club Field Day* (1914), the oldest surviving feature film with an all-Black cast, starring Bert Williams and Odessa Warren Grey. But it is Bradley's work on the feature-length documentary *Time* (2020) that garnered her an Oscar nomination for Best Documentary. The film depicts a heart-wrenching tale of survival and a deeply personal love story between Sibil Fox Richardson and her husband Rob Richardson, who was sentenced to 60 years in prison under the brutal conditions of the notorious Angola Penitentiary in Louisiana. Bradley adroitly utilizes personal video footage from the Richardson family archive shot by Sibil throughout her 18-year struggle to keep her children, husband, and family together through unimaginable hardships. *Time* captures the painful realities and widespread consequences of the carceral state and the racist mass incarceration of Black-Americans, not only on those it renders unfree, but the film also emphasizes the largely devastating impact imprisonment has on the lives of families of the unfree.

In the early 2020s, the internet, new media, and digital technologies have drastically altered how movies are produced, marketed, distributed, and consumed. The

Covid-19 pandemic transformed the way movies are made and how we think about the medium of cinema—in many ways, forcing the industry to collapse onto itself. In 2020, as the world struggled to cope with the rapid spread of coronavirus, American film festivals and streaming platforms scrambled to adapt their methods of operation and content offerings entirely on the fly. Black film festivals and streaming giants like Netflix, Hulu, and Amazon emerged as meaningful platforms for rising Black Cinerati filmmakers like Stefon Bristol. His teen sci-fi feature *See You Yesterday* (2019), produced by Spike Lee, screened at the American Black Film Festival before landing on Netflix. Bristol's debut taps into the socio-political agency at the heart of the philosophy of Afrofuturism. The narrative depicts two Black science prodigies who use their homemade time machine to go back and prevent the inventor's brother from being murdered by police. *See You Yesterday* thrives in the spirit of classic teen flicks like *The Goonies* (1985) and *Explorers* (1985) that relish in the thrill of childhood adventures. Yet, Bristol's film manages to accentuate the gravitas of its resistant Black themes and social justice impulses. The movie won a Film Independent Spirit Award for Best Original Screenplay. Bristol's sophomore effort, *Breathe*, is a post-apocalyptic sci-fi survival film, starring Oscar winner Jennifer Hudson.

On the other hand, my work as a multi-hyphenate filmmaker and cinema scholar has generated two features, *Love Like Winter* (2021) and *Love Walks In*, marking the initial installments of the film tetralogy "The Love Cycle," which draws conceptual influences from playwright August Wilson's legendary Pittsburgh Cycle. With this series of films, my aim is to recalibrate social discourses around Black lives by shifting the conversation away from the exploitative recycling of Black pain, trauma, and suffering that is far too often depicted on Hollywood screens. "The Love Cycle" films focus on the nuances and complexities of Black love in America. The movies, both self-financed, contribute a Black Millennial sensibility to the self-determined legacy of the L.A. Rebellion. Like my predecessors at UCLA, my cinema practice is preoccupied with amplifying the "everyday-ness" of the Black world in a manner that is poetic and political. The debut *Love Like Winter* is a quiet, understated slice-of-life picture that follows a star-crossed former couple, over the span of 12 hours, as they unexpectedly reconnect after ten years apart. Stylistically, the film embraces an Ozu-inspired ascetic minimalism as the cornerstone of its visual grammar. The movie was nominated for Best Director at the Pan African Film Festival and honored in a 30-year Retrospective celebrating the top films in the festival's history.

As of this writing, the most commercially successful Black Cinerati filmmakers are Barry Jenkins and Ryan Coogler. Jenkins studied film at Florida State University before relocating to San Francisco after graduation. There he wrote and directed his first feature, *Medicine for Melancholy* (2008), an artful, underappreciated yet influential film that quietly depicts the entangled interactions between two strangers attempting to establish a rapport the morning after their inebriated one-night stand. Set against a backdrop of San Francisco's epidemic of white gentrification, the film's would-be couple represent divergent cultural and political views on life and Blackness. With *Medicine for Melancholy*, the only movie Jenkins has directed from an original screenplay, he achieves, perhaps, his best work. He brilliantly captures a complicated and messy Millennial love story that reveals a refreshing, alternative world of "ordinary," bike-riding, Whole Foods–shopping, museum-going Black hipsters never portrayed on-screen. Jenkins depicts their encounters and conversations with a slow quietude and exquisite attention to detail rarely associated with Black movies in the Hollywood context.

After *Medicine for Melancholy* premiered at the South by Southwest Film Festival and screened at the Toronto Film Festival, Jenkins spent years struggling to make another feature. In 2016, he directed his breakthrough picture, *Moonlight*, eight years after the release of his first film. *Moonlight* became a landmark achievement in cinema, a heartbreakingly beautiful exploration of love, Black masculinity, queer identities, and belonging. Based on the unpublished play *In Moonlight Black Boys Look Blue* by Tarell Alvin McCraney, *Moonlight* tells the semiautobiographical story of a young Black male in Miami struggling to come to terms with his sexuality and find his place in the world. Jenkins' visual style pulls inspiration from the work of Bradford Young and Hong Kong director Wong Kar-Wai, meticulously using color, light, and sound design to produce an immersive feel and emotional reson-ance. *Moonlight* was produced on a budget of $1.5 million, minuscule according to Hollywood standards. Yet, the picture was a commercial hit, grossing $65 million at the box-office and winning three Oscars: Best Picture, Best Supporting Actor, and Best Adapted Screenplay. Jenkins' third film, an adaptation of the James Baldwin novel *If Beale Street Could Talk* (2018), also won a Best Supporting Actress Oscar for Hollywood veteran Regina King, who delivered a trademark powerful performance.

Likewise, Ryan Coogler served as the writer/director of his first feature *Fruitvale Station* (2013), based on a true story, chronicling the last days in the life of Oscar Grant, a 22-year-old Black father unjustly murdered by a white police officer in a Bay Area train station. The emotionally and politically charged film predates the contemporary Black resistance movement that engendered social uprisings in 2014 following the police killing of Michael Brown, an unarmed Black teenager in Ferguson, Missouri. *Fruitvale Station* won the Grand Jury Prize at Sundance and also cemented the collaborative relationship between Coogler and actor Michael B. Jordan who have, so far, completed four films together. Despite, or perhaps, because of its social justice themes, the film was a financial success, bringing in over $17 million at the box-office on a $900,000 production budget. In addition, the Coogler–Jordan combination breathed new life into the career of Sylvester Stallone and his *Rocky* franchise with two spin-offs, *Creed* (2015) and *Creed II* (2018), which combined to gross nearly $400 million at the box-office. However, the economic success of Coogler's first two films pale in comparison to the financial returns and cultural tidal wave brought on by his following picture, *Marvel's Black Panther*. The movie became a global phenomenon, triggering Harry Potter–level fandom and raking in a massive $1.3 billion at the box-office, becoming the highest-grossing film made by a Black director and spawning the sequel *Wakanda Forever* (2022).

By and large, the Black Cinerati filmmakers represent a generation of creative innovators, disruptors, and motion picture artists, grappling with urgent questions of survival, love, identity, and cultural fragmentation in the face of the nation's renewed foreclosure and deepening repression of Black voices and Black lives. In that sense, Black Cinerati filmmakers, to varying degrees, are engaged in cinema as resistance, challenging the nihilism and sinking social expectations of this twilight period in late America. To be certain, the Black Cinerati are the next important wave of filmmakers who are expanding cultural and social horizons, pulverizing Hollywood's catalog of nightmare images that inundate Black audiences with its perverse fascination with *slaves, maids, butlers, pimps, hoes, gangstas*, and *dope boys* that tend to enervate the Black social psyche. Instead, the Black Cinerati are defining a new brand of Black cinematic expressionism; though differing in subject matter and approach, they share a solid commitment to multi-layered visual storytelling. While the poetry of language and dialogue is essential to their practice, their filmmaking enunciates a dynamic visual frequency that expresses the interior worlds of Black-American life—worlds that exist beyond the limitations of words, constructing a cinematic vocabulary that sets them apart stylistically and politically. The Black Cinerati are auteurs who engage with film culture as a way of drawing attention to their unavoidable Blackness, with the intent of embodying the full weight and complexity of what it means to be a Black-American—creating motion pictures that offer new ways of perceiving American systems of reality and opening new technical, perceptual, and expressive possibilities for rendering the poetry and politics of the Black world.

Beautiful Dark-Twisted Fantasy; or Living (In)Visible Blackness

Another key distinguishing facet of independent Black cinema in the 21st century is its often-close proximity to the mainstream film apparatus itself, if not in a budgetary capacity, then in terms of on-screen talent acquisition. The ability to raise hundreds of thousands, if not millions, of dollars for production, coupled with the ability to cast well-known actors, exposes the fluid imprecision of the concept of independent filmmaking in a modern context. This begs the question: Is a film truly "independent" if it boasts a big movie star in the cast? And then the long-running debate over what constitutes a "Black film" comes into play. In other words, if a film has a Black cast but a non-Black director or writer, is that film considered "Black?" The answer, quite simply, pivots on the axis of the film's ideological register and the prevailing cultural specificities and multi-dimensionality of the film's stories, themes, and characters. As Michael T. Martin rightly puts it, "American film exists within a system of knowledge that is shaped by ideologies of race and cannot be understood outside of its visual grammar."[16] Thus, it is conceivable for a non-Black director to create a film that aligns with Black cultural politics; case and point, *Nothing But a Man* (1964). The reverse is also true: it is altogether possible for a Black director to make an anti-Black movie. So, contemporary independent Black cinema should not merely refer to parochial notions relating to race and economics, but rather to a more complex worldview concerning ideological registers, alongside creative and authorial voice and vision. Although an independent filmmaker may have access to capital and commercial talent, their filmmaking can still be aimed at transforming the status quo with "nuanced interpretations of Black life against the co-opting, homogenizing pressures of the commercial cinema system."[17] Contemporary independent Black cinema is guided by the ability to engage with radical conceptual, aesthetic, and narratological approaches demonstrated toward representing the Black lifeworld.

Culturally specific Black films that possess narrative depth and social urgency, although they may represent precisely what Black audiences crave, such films are still actively suppressed in the dominant cinema industry. And every once and a while, a movie like *Blindspotting* (2018) leaks into the independent film scene and generates positive buzz. Directed by Mexican filmmaker Carlos Lòpez Estrada, this interracial buddy film starring Daveed Diggs—a Tony Award–winning actor from the hit Broadway musical *Hamilton* and Rafael Casal—is a flick under-recognized for its significance in delivering a cultural history of the city of Oakland and for its brilliant incorporation of hip-hop lyrics as a clever narrative device. *Blindspotting* reinvigorates worn-out formulas found in interracial buddy films like *Cop Out* (2010) and *Get Hard* (2015), by adeptly using hip-hop culture, drama, and comedy to confront pressing social issues such as race and the carceral state, class struggle, gentrification, and unbridled police violence against Black bodies, and the debilitating challenges one faces upon being reinserted into society after years of incarceration. Through Diggs' character, a recently released Black felon, *Blindspotting* articulates an unpleasant reality that despite one's best intentions, systemic racism so permeates the social fabric of our nation that it has, inevitably, created the conditions for many Black-Americans where certain acts of violence cannot help but erupt. In that sense, the film visualizes for audiences the often-surreal absurdity and social precarity of Black life in this country—akin to the brilliance Donald Glover skillfully achieves in his acclaimed FX television series *Atlanta.*

The persistent difficulty faced by Black independent filmmakers does, however, remain bound up in the lack of widespread circulation for Black films that seek to offer audiences something more the typical one-dimensional Hollywood fare. The demands of the movie business as a commodity-driven system, unfortunately, have impeded the dissemination and visibility of at least three recent critically important Black independent features, *Luce* (2019), *Waves* (2019), and *UnCorked* (2020). In writer/director Julius Onah's *Luce,* we find a promising psychological-racial thriller that speaks to the complexities and unspoken anxieties that have come to define "post post-racial America." Adapted from a play by J.C. Lee, the film tells a story of identity, power, and race through its protagonist Luce, a Black all-star student-athlete and soon-to-be valedictorian at a predominately white high school. This character is brought to life intriguingly on-screen by newcomer Kelvin Harrison, Jr. As a seven-year-old, Luce was adopted by Peter (Tim Roth) and Amy (Naomi Watts), a well-to-do white couple who brought him to America from a war-torn Eretria, where he was forced to witness and participate in unimaginable horrors as a child soldier. After years of therapy and adapting to the spoils of his new (white) American life, Luce grows into a well-adjusted and exceptional young man. Until a devoted history teacher, Ms. Wilson (marvelously portrayed by Oscar winner Octavia Spencer), becomes concerned when Luce writes a paper in the voice of Franz Fanon, advocating for the use of violence as a political tool for achieving global decolonization. Although this was, in fact, what the assignment called for, Ms. Wilson is alarmed, given the tragedy of Luce's traumatic past. After Ms. Wilson brings the paper to the attention of his white adopted parents, the couple begin to question Luce's exemplary reputation.

The audience also questions: How well do we know Luce? Is he a "good guy" or merely performing the role everyone has come to expect him to play? Activating the genre conventions of the psychological thriller while also engaging elements of mystery and suspense, the film calls out the deterministic forces of America's racial neurosis. Throughout the picture, Luce carries out manipulative acts, playing on racial expectations, which keep him one step ahead. He turns his parents against Ms. Wilson and creates scenarios where she seems unhinged. He appears suspiciously in Ms. Wilson's classroom, at her grocery store, and at her home, posing veiled threats. Within this context, the director, Onah, cleverly invokes the 19th-century poem by Paul Laurence Dunbar, "We Wear the Mask," which is made hauntingly relevant in the film as an indictment of the illusions of a post-racial America and the performative masks Black-Americans are often forced to adopt in order to survive and advance in a white-dominated system. Kelvin Harrison Jr.'s performance is complexly drawn, seemingly innocuous yet possessing the qualities of a dubious trickster. Luce's masking techniques and crafty self-fragmentation exploit white guilt and the vulgar expectations of America's imagined Black male enemy, playing both sides against one another, manipulating weaknesses to divide and conquer.

The most powerful undercurrent of *Luce* lies in the film's capacity to engage with the subtleties of Black epistemology, exposing the instability of this nation's racial contract juxtaposed with the multitudinous ways of seeing and being Black

FIGURE 9.1 Octavia Spencer, Kelvin Harrison, Jr., and Naomi Watts in *Luce*. Screenshot by the author

that Richard Wright once described as the Black "gift of double vision."[18] In effect, the film reveals a Black-American funambulism, a critical superpower—the ability to discern the perplexing and bitter realities inherent in both the white *and* Black worlds. Onah's film shatters the hypocrisies of white privilege and neoliberalism, exposing the barely repressed prejudices of Luce's white adopted parents, who are forced to reconcile their idealized image of their Black son. At the same time, the film demonstrates the hazardous fallacies of Black tokenism, questioning the social conditions that allow Luce only to be viewed as either a "saint or a monster." This condition is especially pronounced in the contrast produced by the characters Luce and DeShaun (Brian Bradley). Both young men are students and budding track stars, but DeShaun is expelled from the team after Ms. Wilson discovers cannabis in his locker. As a result of the expulsion, Deshaun loses his track scholarship and heads on a downward spiral, even though the illegal substance likely belonged to Luce. However, DeShaun is an easy target, and Luce is insulated by his clean-cut image and the powerful presence of his white parents. Through the relationship between these two students, *Luce* reveals a social dichotomy of Blackness: DeShaun is perceived as "Black-Black"—always expendable, a clear and present danger, while Luce is regarded as "less Black," considered safe and worthy of white acceptance and support. The film delights in its ambiguities and lays bare virulent truths regarding the social ambivalence of Black men, constantly forced to maneuver under the rubric of suspicion in America. As the movie ends, the camera pulls back to reveal Luce's face as he jogs along a tree-lined street, and the audience must come to terms with his slick and complicated double consciousness. Luce is a riddle wrapped in an enigma, mirroring the ambivalent and unresolved fictions of a "post post-racial society" and the toxicity attached to delusions of the American dream/nightmare.

Another stellar performance by Kelvin Harrison Jr. anchors the film *Waves* directed by Trey Edward Shultz. Here, Harrison Jr. shines in a Black bildungsroman, portraying a troubled high-school wrestler in a heartrending and penetrating family drama. The camera movement in this feature takes its cues from the film's title; it moves with a fluid, swirling, restless energy that ebbs and flows through scenes like waves of the ocean. The adrenaline-charged cinematography, vivid lighting, and lush color design grab the viewer's eye, pulling them into a fast-paced world bubbling with a dark intensity. The film is episodic in structure, divided into two sections that differ in style and content, though each focuses on the love and travails of an upper-middle-class Black family and its children of privilege. Harrison Jr. plays Tyler, a high school wrestler on the verge of obtaining a full scholarship to college. All he needs is a successful season, which we quickly learn is in dire jeopardy when an MRI (magnetic resonance image scan) reveals a high-grade tear in his labrum that threatens to derail his entire athletic future. Tyler hides the severity of his injury from his demanding and agathokakological father, Ronald, a role brilliantly performed by Sterling K. Brown. Ronald is responsible for Tyler's weight training and constantly pushes him to go harder and achieve more. Ronald is well-meaning yet domineering and intense, ostensibly disinterested in his son's emotions or personal feelings. Instead, he challenges Tyler physically and mentally, striving to prepare his son for the cruel and foreboding actualities that lie ahead in a country that far too often views Black boys as "the problem" and Black men as having little to no value, or as the authors of a white-imagined danger that must be extinguished.

The first section of *Waves* brings into view issues of Black masculinity through its depictions of the relationship between Ronald and his son. Tyler must confront the pressures of excelling as a student and an athlete in a nation where college and professional sports represent multi-billion-dollar industries and player health and safety are, at best, an afterthought. Tyler elects to hide his severe shoulder injury to avoid disappointing his family and coaches, who expect so much from him. In response to his increasing physical pain and social anxiety, Tyler becomes addicted to Oxycodone pills that he pilfers from his father. Tyler's issues are further compounded when his Latina girlfriend, Alexis (Alexa Demie), learns she is pregnant with his child. The couple agrees to terminate the pregnancy. However, Alexis cannot go through with the procedure once inside the clinic. When Tyler learns of her decision to keep the child, he explodes, and the young couple unleash a flurry of anger and insults. Days later, Tyler contacts Alexis via text message, hoping to ameliorate the situation. But she informs him that after speaking with her parents, she remains intent on keeping the child. Tyler reacts negatively, sending a series of aggressive texts that force Alexis to block him from contacting her. Tyler snaps and resorts to drinking and drugs to numb the pain of cascading crises. The couple's break up via text message and the subsequent social media cyberstalking that Tyler embarks upon reveals the complicated and fragile nature of modern romantic relations and twisted notions of intimacy troubling new generations now living a large portion of their lives impersonally or entirely online in the digital world. Tyler is suffused with jealousy when he sees Alexis partying with another guy as he watches in real-time via Facebook and Instagram live. With Kanye West's high-octane tune "I Am a God" blaring on the soundtrack, Tyler spirals out of control. In a drunken fury, he curses his stepmother, gets into a physical altercation

FIGURE 9.2 Still from *Waves.* Screenshot by the author

with his father, steals the family car, and drives to the party to confront his now ex-girlfriend.

The director, Shultz, builds the film's tension to a fever pitch as Tyler arrives at the party. The audience is swept away by ear-pounding music and surging waves of kinetic energy generated from the film's free-flowing and immersive cinematography. Inside the party, Tyler's encounter with Alexis takes a catastrophic turn that leaves her lifeless body lying in an ever-expanding pool of blood. In an instant, Tyler's life is ruined. He tries to run from the police. But he is ultimately arrested, tried, found guilty, and sentenced to 30 years in prison—succumbing to the exact fate his father, Ronald, had groomed him to avoid. The enormity of the film's tragedy sends *Waves* pivoting into its second section, a slow-burning character study that focuses on the family's attempts to cope with the aftermath of Tyler's actions and the waves of resentment and grief surging over them. Special attention is given to Tyler's sister Emily (portrayed with delicate nuance by Taylor Russell), who becomes the centerpiece of the film's final chapter. Emily's interior and exterior life collapses under the weight of her brother's sins, rendering her a pariah among her schoolmates who now regard Tyler as an anathema.

The stylistic vigor and pirouetting cinematography that Shultz employs throughout the film serves as an interesting counterpoint to the anguish and tragedy experienced by what was once a seemingly picture-perfect suburban Black family. The film thrives in the tradition of fervid and penetrating family dramas like *Ordinary People* (1980), *Cider House Rules* (1999), and *In the Bedroom* (2001). *Waves'* thematic strength rests in its ability to summon the myriad ways the pollution of American violence can seep into and destroy Black life, despite one's proximity to, or distance from, the trappings of the urban inner city. In that sense, *Waves* stands out as an unruly surprise of a film—the antithesis of stereotypical Black dramas in the way it accentuates momentum and tension, Black subjectivity, interiority, and multi-dimensionality—within the framework of its artful and stylish aesthetics, intricate conflicts, and unique narrative construction.

The shifting strains and contradictions of Black family life is also one of the primary thematic strands woven into Prentice Penny's vividly realized debut feature *Uncorked*. On the surface, the film bears the markings of a conventional father-son drama; however, the movie pushes past stale formulas to achieve a fresh take that exudes emotional complexity and social depth. *Uncorked* tackles the paradox of identity and the perils of essentializing Blackness in America—with a measure of honesty, nuance, and dramatic force that defies Hollywood's assumptions of what a "Black film" can be. The narrative depicts the life of Elijah (Mauritanian-born actor Mamoudu Athie), whose intense passion for wine sends him down the arduous path to becoming a master sommelier, a designation reserved for the world's most elite class of wine connoisseurs. This description alone distinguishes the film from standard Black productions as well as from white Hollywood "wine films" like *Sideways* (2004) or *A Good Year* (2006).

Set in Memphis, the deep South, Prentice Penny (showrunner for HBO's *Insecure*) draws the audience into an undeniably Black and familiar world. Yet, he manages to contemporaneously reveal an aspect of Black experience never portrayed in cinema. Traditionally, wine culture is associated with the exclusive world of privileged and haughty white snobs—a world seemingly light-years removed from Black neighborhoods like Orange Mound Memphis. In that respect, Penny crafts an entirely new on-screen character in Elijah, a 30-something Black oenophile. Elijah's passion for wine runs deep. However, his interest is derided by his stern father, Louis (excellently played by Courtney B. Vance), a second-generation Black entrepreneur who owns and operates a popular Memphis barbecue restaurant founded by his father before him. Louis is more interested in teaching Elijah how to run the ever-expanding family business. Elijah is industrious, working at a wine shop: tasting and pouring velvety vino and working at the family restaurant: chopping juicy rib-tips and handling the cash register. But when he decides to enroll in an intensive wine course to prepare him for the dauntingly formidable master sommelier exam, it requires him to quit the family business—much to his father's chagrin. Elijah announces his decision to pursue a full-time career in wine at Sunday dinner, which leaves his family members confounded. The scene produces several moments of well-acted hilarious banter. A sommelier? What is that?

> *"An African?"*
> *"Oh, like one of them pirates."*
> *"So, you wanna go to Africa?"*
> *"No, not a Somalian… a sommelier."*
> *"What's the difference?"*

The only supportive party is Elijah's mother, Sylvia (Niecy Nash), who encourages him to follow his dream and offers to help raise the money he needs to travel to Paris to study wine theory and tasting.

Throughout the film, the director offers exciting contrasts, defying essentializing notions of Blackness with ironic juxtapositions like the heavy basslines of southern hip-hop music playing over luxurious images of wine culture or hilariously describing Pinot Grigio as the "Kanye West" of white wines. Penny has an emotional affinity for Black communities that aligns with non-monolithic Black Millennial sensibilities. *Uncorked* delights in displaying a plethora of multi-layered Black experiences. The film showcases a quirky yet appealing Black cultural awareness while highlighting the conditions of socio-economic diversity few filmmakers attain. As Elijah seeks a broader social horizon, his journey into wine culture serves as the symbolic vehicle transporting him to parts of the world unattainable to his family, community, or others in the same social class structure. After Sylvia's sudden passing, Elijah returns home from Paris to help his father with the business, forsaking his wine career for the greater good of the family. This decision ultimately creates a shift in the relationship dynamic between Louis and his son. The two men slowly begin to understand their commonalities, which leads to mutual respect and Louis finally supporting Elijah's ambition to become a master sommelier.

FIGURE 9.3 Mamoudu Athie as "Elijah" in *Uncorked*. Screenshot by the author

The energy and power of *Uncorked* resides in its ability to elude the filmic pitfalls of Afro-pessimism and Hollywood's perverse enthrallment with Black pathology and pain and the rigidity of racial tropes. Instead, the film creates a communal space for multiple modes of Black experience to thrive—each honest, non-stereotypical, and worthy of serious treatment on-screen. The Black characters we encounter are good-natured, working, and middle-class folks. They are not suffering and struggling, scratching, and surviving, or paralyzed by the inextinguishable fear of police violence and Black death that awaits them at every turn. For these reasons, the film pushes the cinematic conversation forward by exhibiting the fascinating and unique possibilities available for Black culture and Black masculinity that are ripe for motion picture exploration. *Uncorked* is not defined by Afro-pessimism, nor does it ignore Black-American social realities. Instead, the film operates as a showcase for finding extraordinary elements within ordinary Black life. *Uncorked* is not a film about the nightmares and pathologies that have come to define white expectations for Black movies, but rather it is a film about Black dreams and aspirations that escapes the traps and chains of cinematic Afro-pessimism that flatly condense Blackness as the bane of American life.

The range and variety of aesthetic and social visions of the Black world represented in films like *Uncorked*, *Waves*, and *Luce* succeed in further evolving the developmental trajectory of Black independent cinema in the 21st century. These films deliver to audiences a more nuanced understanding of Black vulnerability and interior worlds against the cultural and economic demands of the Hollywood system. It is also interesting how these movies offer new ways of seeing Black families and the possibilities of Black romance within twisted scenarios of what now qualifies as intimacy in the high-tech world of the metaverse, cryptocurrencies, and non-fungible tokens (NFTs). An intriguing and reemerging theme of contemporary Black independent cinema seems to be an exhausting sense of malaise and hypnotic loneliness conjured by an era dominated with the false sense of closeness one encounters through constant interactions via social media, dating apps, the metaverse, and other digital ephemera. In that sense, these motion pictures offer a stark reality check for a modern society that comments on the social and cultural implications of living one's life increasingly online. When the three films described above are considered alongside the work of the Black Cinerati filmmakers, a discernible strategic continuum is revealed—a strategy that embraces the act of radically recoding Black images, not for the pleasure and acceptance of the proverbial white viewer, but from a position of strength and power generated within what Tina Campt describes as a "Black gaze."[19] For Campt, a Black gaze

> is a structure of visual engagement that implicitly and explicitly understands Blackness as neither singular nor a singularity. It is a critical framework, a reading apparatus, a term that describes an artist's practice, and a spectatorial mediation that demands particularly active modes of watching, listening, and witnessing.[20]

Within this fresh perspective, contemporary Black independent cinema appeals to the social psyche of Black America by cultivating intimate portraits of Black life that function culturally and politically as cinematic acts of resistance.

Operating from and creating cinema within, a distinctly Black gaze is, undeniably, an act of love. Such filmmakers produce disruptively innovative work with the courage to resuscitate, reimagine, and reevaluate the myriad ways one might be and live Black in this country. The overriding insights drawn from contemporary independent Black cinema are primarily concerned with the social diagnosis of a dawning realization that the power of Black cultural vision, that is, embracing and asserting one's identity without compromise, is fundamental to advancing the future of film itself. And Black independent filmmakers are, once again, the vanguard of rewriting the standards of cinematic language with an unapologetically *Black* film grammar. Moreover, the fundamental power of cinema lies in its ability to allow viewers to occupy the subject position of another person, if only for a brief moment. If cinema is to fulfill its potential, its subject positions must extend far beyond that of white men. We cannot disguise or deny the fact that Black-Americans remain largely absent from dominant screens, and when they are portrayed in the Hollywood system, their roles are too frequently frozen in bizarre racial tropes manufactured in the white social imagination more than one hundred years ago. The cultural tactics of Black independent cinema, in that sense, must destabilize Hollywood "norms" with vibrant interpretations of Blackness that go against the homogenizing pressures of the industry.

The future success of Black independent filmmaking, quite simply, rests on its capacity to harness direct-to-consumer technologies and creative strategies for distribution while continuing to amplify a Black gaze with narrative and stylistic innovations, pushing for deeper social and political engagement—moving toward a true decolonization of cinema. Perhaps creating a sustainable distribution model for Black independent filmmakers requires looking back (Sankofa) at the cultural moves of independent pioneers like Oscar Micheaux or taking cues from indie rock bands. Considering the modern digital onslaught of corporate media's semiological warfare in popular culture, reaching wider Black communities with independent cinema requires a strategic process of social re-programming and educating communities in film and media literacy. Public scholarship and digital education campaigns are essential to cultivating new audiences and empowering Black communities with the critical consciousness to abjure Hollywood's ill-informed and laughably inaccurate renditions of Black life. This recalibration of the motion picture palate, in turn, will stimulate viewers to acquire new cultural tastes that value and appreciate the artistic and social significance of new Black cinematic expressions. After all, there remains a vast and untapped Black audience, a market segment with high earning potential, thirsting for alternative Black films that speak to their lived experiences and espouse the radical politics and poetics of a Black gaze—in all of its oppositional and aesthetic glory.

Notes

1 For expanded discussions see Jacqueline Najuma Stewart's *Migrating to the Movies: Cinema and Black Urban Modernity* (Berkeley: University of California Press, 2005) and Allyson Nadia Field's *Uplift Cinema: The Emergence of African American Film and the Possibility of Black Modernity* (Durham: Duke University Press, 2015).

2 See also Cara Cadoo's *Envisioning Freedom: Cinema and the Building of Black Modern Life* (Cambridge: Harvard University Press, 2014).

3 Artel Great. "Black Cinema Matters," *The New Republic*, September 11, 2020, https://newrepublic.com/article/159336/black-cinema-matters/ Accessed July 17, 2022.

4 Ibid.

5 Ibid.

6 James Baldwin. "Strangers in the Village," *Baldwin: Collected Essays* (New York: Literary Classics, 1998), p. 117.

7 Great, 2020.

8 Ibid.

9 Ibid.

10 See also Mako Fitts Ward's "Queen Bey and the New Niggerati: Ethics of Individualism in the Appropriation of Black Radicalism," *Black Camera*, vol. 9, number 1, Fall 2017.

11 For expanded discussions see Field, Horak, and Stewart's collection *L.A. Rebellion: Creating a New Black Cinema* (Oakland: University of California Press, 2015).

12 See Arthur Jafa's essay, "69" in *Black Popular Culture: A Project by Michelle Wallace*, ed. Gina Dent (Seattle, WA: Bay Press, 1992).

13 Calvin Tomkins, "Arthur Jafa's Radical Alienation," *The New Yorker*, December 14, 2020, www.newyorker.com/magazine/2020/12/21/arthur-jafas-radical-alienation/ Assessed July 17, 2022.

14 Ibid.

15 For a more detailed analysis of *Random Acts of Flyness*, see my essay "Too Hot for TV: Black Sketch Comedy and the Politics of Crossing-Over" in *Black Camera* vol. 13, Number 2, Spring 2022.

16 David C. Wall and Michael T. Martin. *The Politics and Poetics of Black Film: Nothing But a Man* (Bloomington: University of Indiana Press, 2015), p. 4.

17 Ed Guerrero, *Framing Blackness: The African American Image in Film* (Philadelphia, PA: Temple University Press, 1993), p.169.

18 See Richard Wright's *The Outsider* (New York: HarperCollins, 1953), p. 47.

19 Tina Campt. *A Black Gaze* (Cambridge, MA: MIT Press, 2021).

20 Ibid, p. 21.

10

PRISON NOTES

Cinematic Tales from the Black Gulag

Ed Guerrero

I jot these notes from the perspective and authority of a *brother*, that magical five percent of the country's demographic comprised of Black-American men, who by not so mysterious social and political circumstances make up 50 percent of our prison population living in or held captive by the forces of state economics, violence, and incarceration. Accordingly, for the record, I must say here that I am not a "criminal," but, rather, like all *brothers* I've been *criminalized* under the optic of surveillance capitalism. However, I am also a film critic, writer, professor…etc. So, I wish to explore the expression of Black gulag tales, located in the genre of prison movies. Consequently, my remarks come from several different angles that intersect: the ontological, the systemic, and the personal. Looking at origins (ontology), we must recall that Black people entered this historical horror movie several centuries ago (1619) as captives, prisoners, (enslaved). And as of this writing, many of these conditions transformed, reimagined, and rewritten are still today, painfully relevant. As for the term describing the penal system as the "Gulag," literary credit must go to Alexander Solzhenitsyn for his stark and brilliant non-fiction account of the Stalinist penal system, *The Gulag Archipelago,* and now to Ruthie Gilmore for *The Golden Gulag,* for further exploring, localizing, and popularizing the term in her equally brilliant sociological exploration of the prison industrial complex in "the Golden State," California. Though interpreting different historical and political moments, both works deploying the term, engage the phenomenon, with both works focusing on sweeping waves of "mass incarceration."

But also, many more have labored in the real, the discursive, and the literary vineyards of the American penal system, striving to produce the hard-earned grapes, be they of justice, or wrath. To name a few, these writers, inmates, and works include the compelling breakthrough interventions of Michelle Alexander's *The New Jim Crow: Mass Incarceration in the Age of Colorblindness*, Nicole R. Fleetwood's *Marking Time: Art in the Age of Mass Incarceration*, as well as the works of H. Bruce Franklin,

DOI: 10.4324/9781003079682-11

Chester Himes, Angela Davis, Etheridge Knight, Malcolm X, Malcolm Braly, George Jackson, Barbara Harlow, Nathan McCall, Fyodor Dostoyevsky, Wilbert Rideau, Antonio Gramsci, and Donald Goines. The list is long and as of this writing it's an ongoing and perhaps an endless project. Tellingly however, in the here and now in mass mediated, post-industrial consumer-debt slave America wobbling on the edge of planetary collapse, we must return to the metrics of pain that in so many ways define the boundaries of "the Black world." The numbers add up with oppressive certainty: fully one-third of Black men will experience the gulag in their lifetimes and in large urban areas more than half of Black male youth are under some form of state correction or supervision, meaning prison, parole, or proba-tion.[1] Yet, even this number isn't a fair estimate of the nonwhite penal population, for we must factor in all brown men, plus the population of Black, brown women incarcerated in various modalities of "the system."

In the broader frame, the mainstream Hollywood prison flick mediates a series of cinematic protocols: prison rules, "gang" hierarchies and cultures, dilemmas, ironies, and dialectical challenges, all of which are also intensely relevant to the construc-tion and maintenance of the carceral state. Perhaps foremost, from the perspective of the dominant white, middle-class consumer audience, the prison flick weaves a cinematic tale of innocence and/or guilt; confinement/freedom; escape/redemp-tion, or some combination or variation of these themes. However, for its Black/brown inmates, the gulag and its tales are determinedly more complex. In this case, the color of one's skin, and one's racial, economic, and sociological circumstances, along with the fluid ambivalence of constitutional law in matters of color and class, come together with brutal material and psychic force in the confined spaces of the yard, the cell, and in solitary, in "the house of many slams." For the dominant audience constitutional law means essentially that you are "innocent until proven guilty." However, for the Black/brown subaltern, already doubly conscious, socially ambivalent, and chewed up in the cogs and gears of the system, you are "guilty until proven guilty." Or, as Richard Wright so eloquently argues with ontological cer-tainty through so many of his characters, "you were born guilty."[2]

Consider the contrasting outlooks of the white versus the Black/brown prisoner as "new fish" thrown into the penal tank. Generally, the middle-class, hetero-white American male caught up in the system reasons that: *he has fucked up*, failed the society and system that produces, interpolates, and most importantly, protects and privileges him. Conversely, the Black/brown prisoner reasons the inverse—that the same system has failed him and that society has *fucked him up*. A deep social ambiva-lence comes as a consequence of this view, for the convict/ex-convict feels he owes little to nothing, to a class-dominated, culturally white hegemonic world that works relentlessly to keep him in his inferior socioeconomic "place."

So, upon entering the gulag the demolition of the white male, middle class, protected ego comes as a complete cultural, dialectical shock as the new white "fish" realizes that the carceral is a world turned upside down, a world of social, racial and class inversions. With nonwhites from guards to prisoners, making the unwritten but most consequential "rules," and with two-thirds of the prisoners being Black or brown, at best whites form a large but weak minority in a triangulated racial power game in a fluid, dangerous environment. White inmates do not represent the omniscient structuring white influence behind all social transactions and power relations, endemic in all systems "on the outside." But most importantly, it is the prisoners, their counsels, committees, religions, gangs, rackets, and honorific codes that run the penitentiary, not the guards, bureaucrats, or politicians focused on containment, schedules, mechanics, and materials, or getting re-elected. Without the resistant, begrudging cooperation of the convicts in all aspects of the prison world, regulated and subversive, "the joint" would literally be an unmanageable space. Additionally, when looking at the sum of the metrics, the vast majority of the prison population range from the "check to check" working class, to the underclass poor. Regardless of intersections of *difference,* we can pose perhaps the most important question overdetermining to the fate of all prisoners in the criminal justice system: *just how much justice can you afford?*

While desire/pleasure or innocence/guilt cannot be reduced to simple binaries, or demographic/economic metrics, for most audiences, middle-class whites, nonwhites, the underclasses, the prison flick largely works as a cautionary, disciplinary tale. Yet simultaneously, cinematic tales of the gulag work as an adventure and subversive pleasure, with all of these motivations accounting for prison flicks' stunning popularity. We can start with the cinematic prohibitions of the Hays Code, explicitly stating that *crime* in no way was to be shown as alluring or rewarding, and running through to the code's liberal revision with the Motion Picture Association's film rating system (1968). With falling box office profits and the rising sentiments of the late 1960s, this liberal revision and cultural turn allowed many outlaw protagonists to be now recast as rebels, anti-heroes, or those who have found redemption in rejecting and dropping out of the system. Consider box office hits like *Bonnie and Clyde* (1967), *Butch Cassidy and the Sundance Kid* (1969), and *Easy Rider* (1969) as mediations of the great cultural rebellion known as "the 60s," with *crime* now being rewritten more as a subversive challenge to a decaying, twilight culture.

With Hollywood's numerous explorations of "the joint," several prison tales evince a long percolating colorization of the prison demographic, and optic. For example, the Great Depression era gangster/prison hybrid *White Heat* (1934), starring James Cagney as the criminal psychotic Cody Jarrett, who does a turn in the joint, manages a violent escape, only to blow himself up on top of a gas storage facility, thus fulfilling the titillating promise and double entendre of the film's title: *crime* is punished, yet it can be an insubordinate pleasure. Notably, Cody Jarrett's incarceration is a totally white affair. Regardless of the right/left, neoliberal or liberated politics of Hollywood's prison flicks, there's been hardly any change in the almost "white on white" optic, the Hollywood screen fantasy of a dominant white majority prison population, until the early 1970s rise of Blaxploitation, and the implementation of the Rockefeller drug laws, with its following waves of mass incarceration targeting Black and brown populations. Note these examples of the optically white prison scenario, *The Birdman of Alcatraz* (1962), starring Burt

Lancaster, *Escape from Alcatraz* (1979), starring Clint Eastwood, and *The Shawshank Redemption* (1994), starring Tim Robins and Morgan Freeman.

However, *The Shawshank Redemption* presents us with a slight variation on the leitmotif of the lockup and its vicissitudes by adding the extra twist of the Hollywood "bi-racial buddy," a formula that has made *The Shawshank Redemption* at this writing the most accessed and viewed movie on IMDb, ever. *The Shawshank Redemption* turns out to be a gulag tale spun by the African-American, "Red" (Morgan Freeman). Yet underscoring the white hegemonic setting, Freeman narrates a laudatory tale of a convicted but *innocent*, privileged white banker, "Andy Dufresne," played by Tim Robbins, from the view an African-American, *guilty* incarcerated and negotiating a white script and cinematic prison world. Additionally, consider the overarching theme of "redemption," which informs all three movies. The Alcatraz movies make the point of bad men that either have gone good, as the Burt Lancaster character "the Birdman" does; or stayed bad, individualist, enterprising rebels outsmarting and entirely escaping the system, as Clint Eastwood playing another "true story" character, Frank Morris, does in *Escape from Alcatraz*.

Besides presenting us with the standard narrative themes of white reclamation of innocence and freedom, to rebellion, escape and redemption, *The Shawshank Redemption* is additionally overlaid with the further complications of bi-racial buddies and their conflicting/converging aspirations and agendas across many genres and hybrids. Certainly, the bi-racial buddy combo has been in the "big house" before: lucratively in *Stir Crazy* (1980), with Richard Pryor and Gene Wilder and its money-making, formulaic echo *Get Hard* (2015), starring Kevin Hart and Will Farrell. But these tales have been remanded to solitary confinement, in the genre of comedy. Accordingly, compare *Shawshank*'s resolution to the ending Hollywood's last big investment in the big star, dramatic, bi-racial buddy prison flick, *The Defiant Ones* (1958), starring Sidney Poitier and Tony Curtis. In the film's ideological resolution, the final scene, Sidney Poitier sacrifices his shot at escape, jumping off of the "freedom train" to stay with his white buddy, Tony Curtis on a chain gang. Here, Poitier evokes the "noble Negro" stereotype that so provoked Black ire and critical scrutiny, à la James Baldwin and others, at a time of a rising, angry Black audience in the opening gambits of the Civil Rights Movement.[3]

Decades later, in the resolution to *The Shawshank Redemption,* we discern different, unequal outcomes for these two prison buddies. Andy redeems his innocence and freedom through an ingenious rigorous escape, crawling through a sewer line in a storm, as Red's voiceover puts it, "through a mile of shit," to a well-deserved, "retirement" on the West Coast of Mexico. Andy Dufresne is, after all, an ex-banker, relatively young, and from the educated classes when he literally busts out of the joint. Moreover, Andy's redemption adds the extra element of revenge to the tale that keeps the fragile, dominant white sense of justice in place, when he flips the script on the corrupt Shawshank warden who, upon exposure, commits suicide in his besieged office. As for Ellis "Red" Redding, the Morgan Freeman character and omniscient third-person narrator spinning this yarn, "redemption" remains at best, a studied ambivalence. Freeman portrays a Black inmate, convicted and guilty, arguably, at birth or by interpolation, or through social circumstance, or because of the misfortunes and bad decisions of a misled youth. However, the specificity of Red's crime remains a mystery, thus spicing the tale with suspenseful, dark matters: the mystery of *Black guilt* in contrast to *white innocence* and redemption. Red is released in his 70s, his life wasted, used up by the gulag's cruelest punishment, as the "thief of time." This metaphor becomes especially poignant when we consider the promotional slogan for the movie: "get busy living or get busy dying." And as I have argued elsewhere, Red is remanded into the "protective custody" of Andy Dufresne, a dénouement in which Red comes no way near being "redeemed."[4] The big takeaway for the audience, Black, brown or white, dominant or subaltern, is that while a "guilty pleasure," the joint is not a place to be somebody, or to "hope" as Red puts it. By keeping the con/ex-con permanently locked out of mainstream economics, status, and society, prison is the ultimate punishment of a consumer-driven late capitalist society squeezing the last resources and profits out of an exhausted, dying world, while keeping its swelling colored and underclass populations contained within the parameters of the carceral state, the prison industrial complex, and its end point gulag.

At the turn of this century/millennium in search of a Black cinematic point of view of the carceral state, we can start with the decline of the wildly popular and insurgent Blaxploitation wave and the rise of what has come to be known as the L.A. Rebellion in UCLA's film school and the confluence of these two lines of Black cultural production and politics in the mid to late 1970s with two unique, quite different but remarkable films: *Welcome Home Brother Charles* (1975) by Jamaa Fanaka and *Bush Mama* (1979) by Haile Gerima. While covering the same subject, set in the same terrain, Watts/Compton area of L.A., and sharing much of the same point of view, these two films differ intellectually and stylistically. *Brother Charles* spins a tale of Charles, a *brother* and a small-time drug dealer who is framed by the local cops and D.A.s, and winds up doing a stretch in the joint. *Brother Charles* is rare among prison films, Black or white, in that it explores the psyche, the deep to barely repressed feelings, payback fantasies, as well as the subversive adventures of a Black unrepentant ex-con *brother,* out on the streets. The only other film we can compare it to in the same time frame is the mainstream Dustin Hoffman tale *Straight Time* (1978). Both films explore life "on the outside," after prison, and both deal with the ex-con's Id, his unreformed, pent-up rage as he strikes out against society and the penal system that has taken such a painful bite out of his life.

In the case of Brother Charles, upon his return to the streets he inflicts revenge in the most horrific, surrealistic way on all of those white professional men in the criminal justice system, who locked him up, which says much about the brilliant cinematic imagination of director-writer Jamaa Fanaka. The film depicts prison as a series of long dark, empty corridors receding into a dark, funky infinity, underpinned by a painfully monotonous saxophone riff, playing nonstop. We see the metaphor, "thief of time" horrifically literalized as a dark *psychic* space receding to the vanishing point of endless boredom, punctuated with random violence, torture, and screams. The film also infers that Brother Charles has been the subject of prison experimentation, this revealed by the fact that upon release he has a 12-foot-long penis, which he uses to great effect to seduce the wives of the white men that sent him up. The wives, under the seductive spell of Brother's anaconda scale penis, betray and set their husbands up, so that Brother can strangle each of them in a slow gruesome constrictor manner, resulting in, arguably, the most surreal-Freudian, campy, prison-revenge, Blaxploitation mash-up ever. The film ends on the liberating note of revenge, with Brother Charles exacting genital justice on his oppressors with the fetishized essence of the Black male stereotype, with sex and violence, with as Fanaka puts it, with one of the film's aliases, *Soul Vengeance*. Fanaka went on to pursue the prison genre with his money-making, post-Blaxploitation hit *Penitentiary* (1979), and the sequel *Penitentiary II* (1982).

Gerima's *Bush Mama* (1979) turns the prison movie inside-out, shifts the perspective, and expresses a point of view rarely seen in the mainstream Hollywood prison flick. By spinning the tale from the view of Dorothy (Barbara O), a welfare mom with a baby girl, one on the way and her man in the joint, *Bush Mama* locates this gulag tale in what the inmates consider the bigger carceral of social and economic confinement on the outside; by focusing on those women, children, families marooned outside the walls and wire, held hostage in the cheap rentals, motels, ghettos, and crummy little "prison towns" that house them. Shot in neo-realist, grainy black, and white filmstock, much of it on the streets of South Central L.A., the film follows and documents Dorothy's struggles with poverty, the welfare system, corrupt, depraved police, as well as the false political consciousness of many of her surrounding friends and associates. In those short scenes where prison is depicted, it's theatrical, with Dorothy's husband, didactically, poetically, ruminating, on stage with bars, about family separation, injustice, prison life, etc. This, direct frank political address, stage setting, while literal and on political point, contrasts with the horrific nightmare prison depicted in the surreal dark places, the vengeful recesses of Brother Charles' mind. It is because each film's take on prison is so different and yet complementary, that at least a couple of possible narrative, thematic threads, tropes, or points of view are uniquely opened up, elaborated in these Black tales from the gulag.

Besides its inspired and utilitarian adaptation of the Italian neo-realist style to the gritty streets and improvised settings of South Central L.A., one of the notable contributions of *Bush Mama* to the genre has to do with flipping the focus to the much fantasized free and simultaneously dreaded "outside;" and flipping gender to those left behind or wasted by "the thief of time," the families, mainly women and children, with all the dreams and possibilities that could have been, that reside beyond the walls and wire, out there. Two films by Black directors, *Middle of Nowhere* (2012) by Ava DuVernay, and *If Beale Street Could Talk* (2018) adapted from the James Baldwin novel and directed by Barry Jenkins, are rare, somewhat mainstream exceptions, in that they take up a woman's point of view, looking at confinement from the "outside looking in." Yet these African-American women live with the sanguine knowledge that in reality, there is no "outside" to confinement for the inside-out Black world where all with not-white skin suffer to some degree under the rubric of suspicion in the carceral state.

In terms of reversed female point of view, as protagonists, Dorothy of *Bush Mama* and Ruby, played by Emayatzy Corinealdi in *Middle of Nowhere*, are related, in that Ava DuVernay renders a contemporary, beautifully filmed in color, granular exploration of a womanist look at Black male incarceration first suggested by *Bush Mama*. Ruby, like Dorothy, has a husband in the joint and is living a singular and single life, with her point of view tracking the many challenges and travails on the economic and social margins of the prison industrial complex, on the "outside" that sustains the "inside" of the gulag. In contrast to Dorothy, however, Ruby is educated, a professional, and her tale of the gulag starts with the choice to turn down her place in medical school to work as a registered nurse, remaining committed to her husband, while he serves a five-to-eight-year stretch.

Middle of Nowhere masquerades as a woman's drama, exploring feelings and emotional interiors, but unmasked, the film is really a prison movie seen from the perspective of a woman on the outside, emotionally shackled to her man on the inside. *Middle of Nowhere* has the dreamy, reflective surface and interiority of what the Hollywood system defines as a "woman's movie," and yet, Ruby's reflections and dreams are ironic, for they're all about the "good life" before her husband got popped in a drug-running scheme and drew down a five-to-eight-year bid. Then for Ruby, life changes, and Ruby and Dorothy's fates merge as they suffer what Amari Baraka and Fred Moten so poetically refer to as the great ontological and persistent crime overshadowing all of the African-American experience, the crime of stolen life. *Middle of Nowhere* starts in the gloom of a prison visiting room with the couple arguing and Derek (Omari Hardwick) telling Ruby that quitting med school to be near him while he does time is, at best, a romantic fantasy, and that she should get on with her life and dream of being a medical doctor. Conversely this gulag tale wraps up in the same dismal waiting room four-and-a-half years later, with Ruby, in a reflective poetic scene, breaking up with Derek, walking through the wire and into the sunlight, free. Yet for Ruby, now single and "free," this ending has a melancholy refrain, but it is also "open," as she has unexplored career and romantic possibilities on the horizon.

If Beale Street Could Talk, inspired by a James Baldwin tale, and adapted and directed by Barry Jenkins, takes up the same woman-centric, "on the outside" perspective of those wives, women, families, friends, on the other side of the walls, but never really outside of the system, its discriminations, cultural hegemony, and punishments. Fonny (Stephen James) and Trish (Kiki Layne) fall in love, and already expecting, confront the optimistic possibilities of raising a family in 1950s Harlem. Things go bad when Fonny gets set up by a racist cop on a bogus rape charge and winds up in the NYC "tombs" for an indeterminate stay while the details of his case worm their way through the system. Director Barry Jenkins manages to sustain Baldwin's novelistic, melancholy tone, which gives the film a slow, dejected atmosphere that mimics the tortured pace of justice for the vast undercaste caught up in the tangles and snares of the system.

The film's ending is agnostic and agonizingly unresolved as Fonny's case drags on for years and now we see him with Trish and his son, about four years old, framed in the iconic mise-en-scene of the prison film, the dreary visiting room. This ending tableau presents us with a brushstroke of double *bildungsroman*, that is, coming of age, as Fonny matures into a man in prison, and his son grows up in the gulag's visiting rooms, in the shadow of his father's circumstances and example. In this final visiting room scene, we see the family resigned to their oppressive, indeterminate collective sentence, dusted with a small note of resistance and adaptation. We can discern an undercurrent of surrender, of resignation to America's definition of Black, brown, and poor people as subaltern, surplus populations to be contained and controlled by the prison industrial complex. Yet also in the film, we see notes of resistance, comedy, and a bit of smuggled in *joy*. As said, the film's resolution is profoundly agnostic, for when it comes to Black people's civil rights, the old constitutional bamboozle applies: Fonny was born guilty and under the rubric of suspicion and guilt, until otherwise proven guilty.

Perhaps the mainstream Hollywood production that best explores, evokes, or alludes to almost every metaphor or trope of the slave narrative and Black male captivity from chattel slavery, to Jim Crow chain gangs, to contemporary waves of mass incarceration, to reform movements for prison literacy, legal aid, education, etc., is *The Hurricane* (1999) starring Denzel Washington as Rubin Carter. As inspired by and adapted from Carter's autobiography, the film tells the tale of the top-ranked boxer framed by corrupt New Jersey cops and D.A.s for a triple murder and sent up for life. Drawn from *The 16th Round,* written and published by Carter while in prison, the film sketches Carter's rough beginnings in Patterson, New Jersey, a stretch in "juvie," to his success as a champion boxer, to his frame-up and life sentence and his 20-year prison struggle to emancipation. Following the example of Frederick Douglass, Malcolm X, Martin Luther King, Jr., Nelson Mandela, and so many other "inmates" in history's ever shifting gulags and waves of mass incarceration, literacy, self-disciplined study, and writing are the keys to, as *The Hurricane* puts it, "transcending the place that holds you." Consequently, as the Hollywood tale is spun, Carter's story inspires the adopted family and legal team that organize the political and judicial push for his freedom on the outside, literally saving him from a terminal stay in the gulag.

Yet, almost all mainstream prison tales, as well as tales of successful singular Blacks in white professional scenarios, turn out to be about "exceptionalism," the exceptional individual in some combination of character, plot, and will. So, among "the fish," the vast subaltern prison population, Hurricane Carter stands out, the exception, celebrating the rugged American individual, having advantages over almost all inmates, including the notoriety of his case, celebrity status, and the self-discipline of a martial artist and self-educated intellectual in an environment where nonwhites are the majority, and so on. Notably, while acknowledging the iron cages of Rubin Carter's unjust social circumstances growing up in Patterson, New Jersey, and the lifelong prison struggles that shaped his will and character, *The Hurricane* shares philosophies with *The Shawshank Redemption,* in that the protagonists of both films articulate and celebrate the great culturally hegemonic American value of heroic, rugged individualism. Notably and importantly for mainstream approval at the box office, in the framing of the adopted white Canadian family that relentlessly pursues Carter's case to his release, the film argues for, and confirms, a foundational white belief in and expression of innocence and freedom. All of this presents us with a kind of "feel good," yet jumbled and subtly paradoxical ending. For as the film points out, these white people are "good" individuals organized into a legal team challenging injustice of a system that supports their privilege, if not their outlook, while keeping the "Hurricane" locked up. Yet simultaneously, "freedom" under the cold optic of surveillance capitalism and the prison industrial complex make the film's ending for Hurricane Carter a bit more agnostic, more problematic than strictly "feel good," heroic and resolvable for both Black and white. These tensions and ironies are inferred when the Hurricane votes with his feet and upon release from the carceral state, promptly exits "the land of the free" to advocate for justice, just across the border at a distance, in Canada with his adopted family where the parameters of justice might afford him a bit of breathing room.

I should also mention a few more films that underscore a couple of salient points I've tried to explore here. With *Short Eyes* (1977), *American Me* (1992), and *O.G.* (2018) we are given deep interior looks at the workings of Black and brown cultures and the honorific inmate codes that rule the gulag, from jail to penitentiary. *Short Eyes* was written for stage and adapted for screen in a writer's workshop by Miguel Piñero, while doing a stretch for armed robbery at Sing-Sing. Filmed in the staged setting of a jailhouse rec-room and surrounding cells somewhere in the depths of the NYC "tombs," *Short Eyes* concerns the predicament of the despised bottom of the prison hierarchy: a middle-class white male, alleged or convicted, pedophile, that is, in jailhouse parlance, a "short eyes." In this instance, given the Black/brown majority in this cell block and a general animus toward such offenders of all inmates and guards, the marker of "short eyes" proves fatal, resulting in a murder made to look like suicide. Besides its "slice of life" look at the close communal and tense plural existence among the undercaste, *Short Eyes* ends, perhaps ironically, automatically, or inadvertently, with the same ideological conclusion as the dominant prison flick: with a declaration, a constitutional guarantee of white innocence. After the white, middle class hetero-"short eyes" is set up, poisoned, and murdered, the captain of the guard announces in a concluding eulogy to an indifferent, cynical inmate audience that the so-called short eyes was falsely accused, "innocent." This again underscores one of the conspicuous binaries of the mainstream, Hollywood prison movie, that of *white innocence*, in this case, in stark contrast to *Black guilt*.

To the extent that the "inmates" run the prison system from the inside is made chillingly clear in *American Me*, starring Edward James Olmos as the legendary Mexican-American founding mafia leader Santana, who "called the shots" while spending the vast majority of his life in the tank. *American Me* takes a granular look at prison life through the lens of the inmate organization, strict codes of conduct, and an honorific system that make "the yard" a world of inverted social rules and power relations. The film makes the further point of the permanence of systemic

Black and brown guilt with the trajectory of Santana's "guilty for life" biography. His final transformation, and perhaps "redemption," comes with his rejection of the honorific, do or die, prison codes that fashioned his veridic American, gangsta, self, as the title suggests, *American Me*. This also is America.

As for the waves of mass incarceration and the industrial scale gulags of the *Afrofuture* and their cinematic depiction, several films are suggestive, such as *Escape from New York* (1981), set in the, then, far off future of 1997, with Isaac Hayes, an African-American, portraying the controlling "O.G." lord of Manhattan, now a maximum-security prison island. Or consider, *Demolition Man* (1993) starring Sylvester Stallone and Wesley Snipes, when as binary, cop/criminal, bi-racial buddy adversaries do battle in a future dystopia, 2032, where criminals are literally put on ice, cryogenically incarcerated, frozen. Or, for instance take *Alien III* (1992) with Sigourney Weaver and Charles Dutton, where incarceration has been expanded and displaced to a decaying max security prison planet, with Dutton, Black, playing the head prison monk among inmate monks.

Finally, *O.G.*, starring the always diligent and brilliant Jeffrey Wright, is, perhaps, the film that best underscores some of the insights and arguments I have pursued in these "notes." *O.G.* is a gulag tale that, in part, depicts the interiority of an "O.G." (Original Gangsta) Black prisoner "Louis," played by Jeffrey Wright, who's been in the system for 24 years on a murder beef, with parole and release pending. Much like Red in *The Shawshank Redemption*, Louis is guilty and much of his life has been usurped by the "thief of time," the carceral state. Conversely, "O.G." Louis is much younger than Red, and incarcerated in a mostly Black, homosocial world. Moreover, the details of his guilt are not a mystery, as revealed in one of the film's most intense scenes where a therapy session with the murder victim's sister goes sour, ending in anger and recrimination. The burden of a crime that Louis committed as a brazen youth and even now can't shake or explain, mixed with a deep fear of being released into a world that left him behind decades ago, haunt him with a reflective interiority, different from *Brother Charles* and more resonant with the bigger interiority of the women and families in all of these films, left on the outside. Much of this is due to a mix of the talent of Jeffrey Wright but also the complex portrayals of the other inmates, most of whom actually were "inmates." After guiding a young, new fish through the perils of the yard, and disrupting a gang plot without becoming a snitch, Louis is released, matured, transformed with deep feelings of ambivalence, anxious about walking into that new world on the outside.

Considering the political mire of the contemporary moment and the murky dystopian horizon of what increasingly looks like a twilight civilization, there is a fleeting and surreal moment in *O.G.*, where Louis expresses his ambivalence and fear of "the outside," the bigger amorphous gulag awaiting him after 24 years in the tank.[5] His fears bear much reality. For on the outside, Louis joins *all brothers,* who to some degree, are serving one big collective, indeterminate sentence under the gaze of the carceral state. As Louis walks along the inner wall of the yard, he drags his fingers over its surface. Suddenly his fingers, hand, and arm push through the thick concrete wall and feel, imagine the "outside" which has been a dream for 24 years.

Despite his fears, Louis' dream projects a deep curiosity and longing to see "what's out there." It's certainly not the world that he left in the fading 1990s. But O.G. Louis has matured in the system, used his "time" well to become broadly self-educated, wisely literate, and he has developed a reflective, artistic temperament. With deep unease, I can only imagine the challenges he'll face on "the outside." I wish him well in this neurotically accelerated, digital, knowledge worker, consumer-debt peonage world. In the very near future, three quarters of the gulag population will be nonwhite. So, for the sake of its box-office, perhaps, future mainstream prison flicks will grudgingly shift toward a more representational "colored" spectrum when spinning these yarns…if we should continue to invest in spinning these tales at all. On this last point, ex-political prisoner, writer, and activist Angela Y. Davis has much to say as she speculates about the American gulag and its role in manipulating the *Afrofuture*:

> I emphasize the need to disarticulate notions of punishment from crime because I want to argue for a serious consideration of abolitionist strategies to dismantle the prison system in its present role as an institution which preserves existing structures of racism as well as creates more complicated modes of racism in U.S. society. This strategy, I argue, is no more outlandish than is the fact that race and economic status play more prominent roles in shaping the practices of social punishment than does crime, which is always assumed to be the basis for punishment in this society.[6]

Conversely, since America's prison industrial complex, being a multifarious layered bureaucratic institution focused, like all institutions, on survival and expansion, is quite incapable of dismantling itself without the urge of determined social intervention and redefinition. Under these conditions, we can suspect that more prison movies, dominant industry, or from different subaltern social formations, intersecting or not, loom on the tempestuous cinematic horizon of the near Afrofuture.

Notes

1 Michelle Alexander, *The New Jim Crow: Mass Incarceration in the Age of Colorblindness*, (New York: The New Press, 2012), pp. 6–7.
2 Elie Mystal, *Allow Me to Retort: A Black Guy's Guide to the Constitution* (New York: The New Press, 2022). A great discussion the "ol Constitutional Bamboozle," used by old white men determined to return *all* nonwhites, the poor along with all *intersectional others*, to the slavery or indenture of the 19th century.
3 James Baldwin, *The Price of the Ticket: Collected Nonfiction 1948–1985* (New York: St. Marten's/Marek, 1985) "The Devil Finds Work" p. 596. Baldwin sums up Black anger succinctly:

> Liberal white audiences applauded, when Sidney, at the end of the film jumped off the train in order not to abandon his white buddy. The Harlem audience was outraged and yelled, "Get back on the train, you fool!"

4 Ed Guerrero, "The Black Image in Protective Custody: Hollywood's Bi-racial Buddy Formula in the Films of the '80s." Manthia Diawara ed., *Black American Cinema*. (New Jersey: Routledge, 1993), pp. 237–246.

5 James Baldwin and Cornell West both make this point. See "Black Strivings in a Twilight Civilization," (pp. 87–118). Cornell West, *The Cornell West Reader* (New York: Basic Civitas Books, 1999). "The Fire Next Time" (pp. 356–357). James Baldwin, *The Price of the Ticket: Collected Nonfiction 1948–1985* (New York: St. Martin's/Marek, 1985). But also see Morris Berman, *Dark Ages America: The Final Phase of Empire* (London: W.W. Norton & Co., 2006); Jane Jacobs, *Dark Age Ahead* (New York: Random House, 2004).

6 Angela Y. Davis, "Racialized Punishment and Prison Abolition," *The Angela Y. Davis Reader,* ed. Joy James (New York: Blackwell Publishing, 1998), p. 105.

11
FUTURE RHYTHMS IN AFROFUTURIST FILMS

Ytasha L. Womack

What Is Afrofuturism?

Afrofuturism is a way of looking at future and alternate realities through Black cultural lenses. It intersects Black cultures, the imagination, technology, liberation, and mysticism. Afrofuturism is an aesthetic, method, and practice all in one. All cultures have a relationship to space/time. African/African Diasporic cultures are no different. However, in some cases, those ideas are so embedded in cultural production, fine-tuned over decades or centuries that those who embody it may not think of it as a philosophical statement on one's relationship to the cosmos.

Afrofuturism, as I speak about it, articulates where Black cultures meet in their explorations of space/time. Afrofuturism differs from other future studies and science fiction generally because it pulls from Black cultures, views time as non-linear, values the divine feminine, values the realm of intuition, values nature, values community, and values African wisdom systems or wisdom systems generally as a way of knowing. To that end, time can run in all directions, not simply forward and one can connect with people, ancestors, or ideas across time. In short, Afrofuturism is a lens on space/time, navigating space in time, and identity as told from African/African Diasporic spaces. Who am I on Earth? Who am I in the universe? What is my responsibility to community, to ancestors, to the future? Afrofuturism is one lens cultivated by the experiences and histories of people of the African Diaspora and Continent on how do we, as humans, engage in space and time. As a practice, it often reclaims space and time in Western spaces that have created a hierarchy of values that don't engage African/African Diasporic wisdom. It serves as a reminder of Black peoples' contributions to science, philosophy, and creativity.

Afrofuturism exists in all corners around the world, from Bahia to Chicago to Copenhagen to Dakar. Black creators are thinking on lineages of interdimensionality and liberation, which stretch across times. As a genre, Afrofuturism, Afrosurrealism,

DOI: 10.4324/9781003079682-12

Africanfuturism, the EthnoGothic, Black Horror and its nonlinear, magical realism counterparts fall under the category of "Black Speculative Fiction." Scholar/artist John Jennings and scholar Reynaldo Anderson created this banner term to frame such works, arguing that we are having a Black Speculative Arts Movement on par with the Black Arts Movement of the 1960s and 1970s. Those familiar with my work in Afrofuturism know that I often emphasize the value of the imagination, creativity, and vision as resilience tools. For many, creativity and the imaginary realms were lifelines in tough circumstances. While Afrofuturism is a long-running history in literature, music, and the visual arts, its evolution in film is more sporadic.

In 2017, I decided to direct a short Afrofuturist film. I penned my book *Afrofuturism: The World of Black Sci Fi & Fantasy Culture*, several years prior, had directed and written romantic comedies in the past, and I wanted to explore a directorial vantage point that reflected my new lens. I yearned to capture my relationship to Afrofuturism as experienced in Chicago, a place where heightened realities, magic, and Diasporic threads of wisdom often abide in seemingly ordinary spaces. I found interest in Afrofuturism being nestled at the intersection of not so random folk in community.

My experience of Afrofuturism was often found in ordinary moments, hiding in plain sight. Although Atlanta, with its HBCU protopias and New Hollywood vibes, or New Orleans with its Mardi Gras and Africanist aesthetics are a bit more obvious in its Afrofuturist leanings, Chicago's Afrofuturism is a bit more matter of fact. A somewhat covert Midwestern temperament, where Afrofuturism as altered reality surfaces like a fog rolling off Lake Michigan. In some cases, the unfolding Afrofuturism space opens and closes like a sliding door, ignited by people, human lightning rods, who bring time with them. The interdimensionality of space as I experience it in Chicago is a byproduct of the people in the space and their universalist intentions and circling quests for truths. Where some onlookers unfamiliar with African Diasporic lenses, processed all they saw as blight or understated living, such spaces had shapeshifting powers, where real-time transformation and the fantastic is always at play. Annoyed at the recasting of Chicago's Southside as a space of violence by strangers who seemed to look at me as if I was making things up when I spoke of the beauty of community and the proliferation of metaphysical dialogue, I chose to make a film that went out of its way to give nods to Black communities.

Fascinated by the experience of what I came to know as the liminal space, I aimed to shoot a film where the magic sprung from serendipity. My grand idea was to shoot two lovers, one, a pilot from Andromeda in the so-called future, the other a goddess/pharaoh from Ancient Kemet of the so-called past. The two lovebirds crossed times to go on a date in otherworldly Chicago where they'd see pop-up performances in unlikely places and would visit a museum with artifacts. The two lovers would symbolize two times, two locations welded by a shared culture and love. They couldn't be with one another in their chosen spaces, but they could abide "out of time" in our present, dazzled by human performance. In this sense, I hoped to establish Chicago neighborhoods as a site and desired location for the otherworldly. However, nothing about my approach to this story was working.

I couldn't get the two main actors' schedules to sync and the primary location I wanted to use was unavailable. Time was slipping and the energy of pulling it all together just fell off. The only people available were the dancers in the project.

I was assembling this production a few months after I'd returned from my first visit or two to Cuba where I took salsa and rumba classes assembled by Erica Olivares Bowen, an African-American dancer devoted to introducing people to Cuban dance. I thought I was a decent salsa dancer until I went to Havana and studied with dancers who deeply understood that dance was life. Without sending you down the rhythm wormhole, I'll simply say that the default eight count I'd learned with lifelong training in modern dance had no relevance in Cuba's African-born music. My stronger relationships to the rhythms were tied more to my training in tap performed over complex jazz. Nevertheless, Cuban improvisation in salsa and samba was embedded in a structure more specific than it appears, with contained movements designed to enhance specific energy centers or orishas. The experience was life-changing. I had an epiphany about dance, cultural memory. I found new language to explain what I knew all along, that Black dance artforms are a testament to ideas about time and space. Dance is a language.

So, amid my frustration with the narrative short film I intended to shoot, I realized that this closing door was providing another opportunity for storytelling. I tossed the whole lovers date idea out the window and decided to direct an experimental dance film. It's easier to frame Cuban salsa and rumba with its specific African rhythms and movements to an African origin. Could I center house music dance culture in the same lineage? Could I present the improvisational freestyle of Chicago's dance scene as having both an African lineage and Afrofuturist in the way I'd experienced it dancing in that scene for eons? Could I create the sense of timelessness that dancing to house music for hours evokes?

The story and plot of the film changed. Dance would be this film's language. The locations and costumes would be as much a character as the dancers. I have to thank my experience in Cuba and my experience watching some highly experimental works I saw at the Sonic Acts festival in Amsterdam for freeing me from my narrative construction.

The film became a 14-minute experience in dance. It begins with Kenneth "Djedi" Russell's tap dance solo, a profiled pan from his MF Doom mask and all-black ensemble, to a single shot on his Jordan sneakers enhanced with taps. He performs in a bare stairwell, all eyes on his feet as they finesse a mix of deejay scratches, Morse code, and high-hat drumbeats. The sonics were reminiscent of Kodwo Eshun's breakdown of digital music as alien music. Djedi's solo was a statement of rhythm as the through line for the African Diaspora. The internalized drum as both foundation, technology, and the griot speaking. I did not think of opening with this scene until after his performance. While filming, I was giving Djedi directions, and in post we took my voice, layered it, and played it backward over his taps. The slight distortion enhanced the otherworldliness. Djedi's solo kicked off the Samba house fusion song "Viva a Vida Como Se Nao Hauveese Amanha (Batucanda Samba Mix)" by Shannon Harris. The film juxtaposes an array of dancers, most dressed in Black, some masked with unique styles performing freestyled solos in unseemly locations.

The film takes place in six movements nearly akin to kundalini snake or moving through chakra points. The drum, the onset, the distortion, deep funk space, the ironic, the reorientation, and the integration. I think of the film as being a portal, where a dimension opens, reveals itself as a funkateer carnival, and harmonizes and integrates into the viewers new normal. Perhaps it's a metaphor for expansion or soul evolution. The idea sprouted fully formed, much like Athena springing from Zeus' head ready for battle or the Ancient Egyptian god Ptah, the lone creator from Memphis, who gave birth to himself. The ideas were flowing and I was just trying to catch up with this new narrative racing to be born on screen.

The dancers' styles are characters. Joshua Ishmon is a modern/African contemporary dancer, Khari "Discopoet" B is a disco-leaning house dancer with James Brown flair, Yahkirah Beard is an African contemporary dancer with Caribbean aesthetic leanings, Daniel Talbert II is a footwork dancer, and Harold Dennis depicts a cyborg with latent pop lock skills. The only dancer in white was Gira Dahnee, a singer who appears as a spirit adorning an all-white ballroom gown and tribal-inspired face paint. On occasion, I pop up doing a shoulder stand in a red miniskirt, moving my legs bicycle style like an 1980s workout queen. Each dancer appears in a narrow apartment complex hallway that resembles the dreary halls in Stephen King's *The Shining*. The halls' narrow design and the dancers' movements is a mantra for creativity in confined spaces. The dancers also freestyle in bare stairwells on a single step, concrete basements, a worn art deco foyer, and beside an Egyptian obelisk in Marquette Park, the site of Martin Luther King's Chicago protests. The performers bring these understated spaces to life. Each shot juxtaposes the dancers performing and posing as they become interchangeable figures in the hallway. The film gives the effect of enticing one down a hallway, a soul journey to transformation.

The scene switches tone when Dahnee, who depicts an African spirit, teaches Dennis, a cyborg pop locker how to waltz. Sean Wallace composed the song, a piano solo with romantic notions. Inside a worn, dainty foyer, Dahnee playfully infuses our cyborg with a hint of humanness, albeit tenderness to soften his hardened edge. She twirls about, much like a pixie, walking him through the options until the piano's chords go off key. The characters sneer and morph into tricksters at play. We are tossed back into the disorienting world of dancers in the hallway, a world where our protagonists are now climbing walls, swinging capes, twirling whips, and vibing in caged elevators. Just as the viewer is getting a grasp on the disorientation of movements in a narrowing hallway, the scene cuts to four cyberfunk aliens in fur coats and fishnets walking up Pilsen's 18th street to see their leader, George Clinton, in concert. Metaphorically, the mothership lands to the heavy bass sounds of Ras G's "Been Cosmic." The foursome, including myself, are reminiscent of early 1980s village-era decadence and grit. They strut down the street and descend upon the concert venue. The scenes inside the venue were shot in a VIP balcony on a cell phone in a black-and-white sequence. The decadence heightens. Just as the funk gets deeper, the plug is cut and we're back in *The Shining*-like hallway, now our place of normal, with intersecting cuts of dancers in less foreboding acrobatic motions. Talbert, the footwork dancer, performs in a boiler room. Harris' ecstatic samba song returns and the obvious links between the Chicago dance and its Brazilian carnival counterpart could not be clearer. Beard leads us with smiles and joy in her Nefertiti bliss, dancing up the same hallway, now awash in pink. The uneasiness in the hallway dissipates, and one wonders was it ever as disconcerting as it first appeared. We end with a pronouncement of the Chicago, Gary, and Milwaukee communities that the participants hail from, neighborhoods that many don't equate with the majesty we've just witnessed. The participants represent *Bar Star City,* a fictional world of my own creation, the galaxy Andromeda, and Ancient Kemet, respectfully. The film ends with an embrace between our two lovers, from two different worlds hugging in a viaduct that hovers in the ethereal. I titled the film *A Love Letter to the Ancestors from Chicago.*

The Rise of Bast

Marvel's Black Panther (2018) is the shining beacon of Afrofuturist films. The film shattered box-office records and squarely placed Afrofuturist ideas in mainstream film. T'Challa, portrayed by Chadwick Boseman, is an African king in Marvel lore who struggled with his legacy as king and takes on the legend of Black Panther, as his father and royal lineage did before him. It stands as Marvel's greatest film or at the least, its deepest and boldest. Killmonger (Michael B. Jordan), the picture's vengeful nemesis, embodies issues of loss in the African Diaspora sometimes experienced as cultural trauma and memory, a fall out of colonization and enslavement.

At heart, *Marvel's Black Panther* is a family story of royal infighting and dueling philosophies on the responsibilities of a Kingdom. Father kills brother. Cousin kills cousin. Ultimately, the path of isolationism, one which preserved the advanced technology and wisdom in Wakanda is abandoned in favor of sharing the wisdom with the world to benefit humanity. The storied Wakanda provided a vision of a future, one that embraced traditional African ways and new technologies for audiences. The film addressed the longing and demand for a Black superhero and depicted an African protopia with utopian ideals. The picture hits all the points on the Afrofuturist pinwheel. African mysticism is expressed in the ancestral realm, which T'Challa visits; the Dora Milaje, Wakanda's all-woman army, are a futuristic version of the ancient Dahomey warriors; both the wisdom system and the innovations by T'Challa's sister and scientist Shuri (Letitia Wright) are integrated and viewed equally; women in the film are equally weighted with T'Challa himself. While Wakanda feels like the future, its design integrated traditional, ancient, and contemporary ways of being, feels like a remix of times that create a new story in the present. Because most of the world had not seen Africa depicted as futuristic in mainstream film, the entire aesthetic inspired by traditional fashion designed by award-winning designer Ruth Carter was mindblowing. In the traveling exhibition "Marvel: Universe of Superheroes," the film's aesthetics were described as Afrofuturist. Yet, even in this epic creation, T'Challa questions space, place, and identity. For all Wakanda's evolutions, it is in one sense out of time, its trajectory not lining up neatly with how the world views itself. It too hid in plain sight, much like the Chicago Afrofuturist experience I sought to depict, to preserve its heritage and future. The question of how one supports liberation is the story's cornerstone.

Space Games

Afrofuturist films create space for an engagement of futures, place, and African Diasporic cultures to integrate. They are the liminal space made visible, the crossroads of the visible and invisible world made through the African Diasporic/African Continental lens. I think it's interesting that Wakanda was hidden for so long, just as the liminal spaces which I explore appear to be hidden as well.

The arc of the multi-pronged conversation across times, a juxtaposition of times and realities, is a larger statement about community and humanity in Afrofuturist works. The success of *Marvel's Black Panther* has opened doors for other Afrofuturist films and TV shows to take center stage, most notably HBO's series the award-winning *Watchman* (2019), *Lovecraft Country* (2020), and Marvel Studios' *The Falcon and the Winter Soldier* (from writer Malcolm Spellman). Each series recovers a lost history. Both *Watchman* and *Lovecraft Country* revisit the Tulsa Massacre. And both *Watchman* and *The Falcon and the Winter Soldier* address the story of the Black hero whose story was lost to history and the tensions in recovering it.

Lovecraft Country posits a battle between magical lineages among two cousins, one Black and one white, bound by miscegenation of the Antebellum South and stolen magic. The narrative, based on a book of the same name, takes place in the turbulent 1950s, mixing historical moments, ancestral memory, body swapping, mysticism traditions, ethno-gothic horror, and Afrofuturism. Told through the lens of executive producer/showrunner Misha Green, the series broke new ground in possibility with characters that face the dueling horrors of battling racism and a persistent warlock/witch, all while recovering life for a brighter future. In what is described as *Lovecraft Country*'s Afrofuturist episode (episode 7), the character Hippolyta is drawn through a portal in a time machine. She lands in a futuristic space station with a looming woman of the future and must define herself. She proclaims that she wants to dance with Josephine Baker and lands in early 20th-century France, jettisons to being in an ancient African army fighting would-be conquerors, and winds up on jazz artist Sun Ra's Saturn as a curious astronaut in a scene that replicates his classic film, *Space is the Place* (1974). Hippolyta's idealized freedom is found in these spaces throughout time in a way she couldn't express as a married woman of the 1950s. Her astral travel freed her to be her true self. Hippolyta uses time travel to explore altered realities that ultimately inform her identity. Time travel frees her. She is not locked in space/time and the prejudices of the era but transcends them through connecting with empowered moments for

Black women across history. Hippolyta is not alone. Each of the heroes in this story must reassess identity and purpose, navigating time and space, recovering missing parts of themselves and new futures, to be their highest self.

Although *Marvel's Black Panther, Lovecraft Country, The Falcon and the Winter Soldier*, and *Watchman* are the most popular contemporary references of Afrofuturist works, they are not the first and clearly not the last. Several film curators have dedicated themselves to showcasing Afrofuturist films long before *Black Panther's* legendary rise. The Black Radical Imagination series curated by Erin Kristovall and Amir George, Black World Cinema and Black Future Month by Floyd Webb, and more recently The Criterion Channel's Afrofuturism series by Ashley Clark, are among the curated showcases at theaters and streaming devoted to highlighting Afrofuturist shorts and independent features around the world. The films in the canon are growing. For starters I point to *The Cry of Jazz* (Edward Bland, 1959), *Space Is the Place* (John Coney, 1974) *The Last Angel of History* (John Akomfrah, 1996), *Sankofa* (Haile Gerima, 1983), *Daughters of the Dust* (Julie Dash, 1991), *Les Saignantes* (Jean Pierre Bekolo, 2005), *Pumzi* (Wanuri Kahiu, 2009), and *An Oversimplification of Her Beauty* (Terence Nance, 2012).

These films, each possessing an independent spirit, transform the nature of identity, space, and place. Edward Bland boldly announces that jazz is dead in *The Cry of Jazz*, making parallels between the artform's structure and improvisation as a metaphor of creativity necessary for Black people to survive and thrive in segregated America. As the barriers, symbolized by form changes, so will the music. Once that shifts, it's no longer jazz. Sun Ra provides the film's soundtrack and Bland, who also stars in the film, positions jazz's evolution as one of innovation in how music sounds with limited freedoms, therefore, articulating a relationship to space and time that denotes liberation. In *Space is the Place*, Sun Ra (born Herman Blount) descends from Saturn and proclaims to a group of teenagers that they are not real, but rather myths, because they are asking for equal rights. "I don't come to you as a reality, I come to you as a myth," he says. The film is a lush visual representation of Sun Ra's philosophies on life and music.

The Last Angel of History uses the metaphor of a data thief of the future, a stark sunglass-wearing anthropologist of sorts, coming to the past to find artifacts of Afrofuturism. Again, the concept of recovering ancestral memory is highlighted. He finds works by Sun Ra, George Clinton, and authors Octavia Butler, Samuel R. Delany, and Ishmael Reed, among others. The first documentary to explore Afrofuturism, the film highlights the genre's pillars. While *Sankofa* uses a time travel story to hurl its carefree protagonist, Mona, a model posing before one of Ghana's harrowing slave castles. The film opens with a drummer asking the ancestors to rise, and as Mona dips into the castles themselves for her photoshoot, she is hurled back in time to experience the life of Shola, where she goes through the harrowing journey of the Transatlantic Slave Trade to work on a plantation in the American South. She suffers abuse of all kinds and rediscovers herself when the Yoruba god Shango gives her a Sankofa bird. Sankofa is the Akan symbol for reclaiming the best of the past to move forward, a common theme in Afrofuturist works. Thematically, the film aligns with Octavia Butler's book *Kindred*, forcing people to rethink their connections and resolutions around existence in the wake of enslavement histories.

Julie Dash's *Daughters of the Dust*, a film that follows a Gullah Geechee family preparing to move from their South Carolina, Island homestead at the turn of the 20th century. The film is narrated by an unborn child who anticipates the future. The question of how the culture will be preserved when the family moves away from the matriarch is questioned. How does identity shift when location changes? Curator Webb, who was also an associate producer on the film, says that Dash originally wrote the film as an Afrofuturist trilogy. Several scenes from the film were recreated in Beyonce's Afrofuturist/Afrosurrealist ode and visual album, *Lemonade* (2016).

On the other hand, *Les Saignantes* confronts corruption in Cameroon with a cohort of ignored Black women who channel ancestral and goddess energy through dance and sexuality to challenge power. A sexy, unconventional ode of magic and empowerment, the film is interjected with text and social commentary between these dancing usurpers of masculinized notions of power. Wanuri Kahiu's protagonist in *Pumzi* escapes a place where dream suppression and water shortages are a norm in search of nature beyond her techtopian world. Water is a luxury and her quest to find new life takes her to the arid world of sands where she eventually finds a tree. Life is born in the desert. *Pumzi* captured hearts and minds with its depiction of a futuristic, technologically advanced Africa, only underscoring how infrequently Africa was depicted in the future. Lastly, in *An Oversimplification of Her Beauty*, Nance questions the nature of connection and love through memory and dream. A mix of live action and animation, Nance, who also stars in the film, thinks on the constructs of a moment, creating a film with a dreamscape field of realities.

Art Installations in the Stars

Many Afrofuturist filmmakers are finding welcoming audiences in the art world. Among my favorites is Cauleen Smith, a longtime Afrofuturist. In the spring of 2012, Cauleen Smith debuted her art installation, *A Star Is a Seed* at the Museum of Contemporary Art in Chicago. Named after the Stevie Wonder album, the exhibition included an installation of short films. Viewers walked through a maze called The Infinity Vortex where they were led to the film projections. The film followed Nicolai and Regina, humanoids who descended from the Bird of Paradise flower. They navigate Chicago and are ushered through a world of music led by Chicago's Association for the Advancement of Creative Musicians (AACM). The film included stellar, otherworldly performances by Douglas Ewart and viola player/composer Renee Baker. Smith's exhibit was an outgrowth of her work studying Sun Ra's metamorphosis in Chicago. The AACM, formed in the 1960s, continued to play in the tradition of Sun Ra. Their motto, "Ancient to the Future" underscoring their Sankofic intentions.

The world of space–time contemplations from Black filmmakers are in full bloom. While music has a head start in articulating the wonderment of the interdimensional, the world of film is shifting culture. The Black Speculative Fiction Movement is upon us.

INDEX

For Product Safety Concerns and Information please contact our EU
representative GPSR@taylorandfrancis.com
Taylor & Francis Verlag GmbH, Kaufingerstraße 24, 80331 München, Germany

www.ingramcontent.com/pod-product-compliance
Lightning Source LLC
Chambersburg PA
CBHW070341270326
41926CB00017B/3939

9 780367 528751